Studying Fraud as White Collar Crime

Studying Fraud as White Collar Crime

Edited by

Geoffrey Smith
University of Portsmouth, UK

Mark Button
University of Portsmouth, UK

Les Johnston
University of Portsmouth, UK

and

Kwabena Frimpong
Nottingham Trent University, UK

First published 2011 by
PALGRAVE MACMILLAN

Palgrave Macmillan in the UK is an imprint of Macmillan Publishers Limited, registered in England, company number 785998, of Houndmills, Basingstoke, Hampshire RG21 6XS.

Palgrave Macmillan in the US is a division of St Martin's Press LLC, 175 Fifth Avenue, New York, NY 10010.

Palgrave Macmillan is the global academic imprint of the above companies and has companies and representatives throughout the world.

Palgrave® and Macmillan® are registered trademarks in the United States, the United Kingdom, Europe and other countries.

ISBN-13: 978–0–230–54248–8 hardback
ISBN-13: 978–0–230–54249–5 paperback

This book is printed on paper suitable for recycling and made from fully managed and sustained forest sources. Logging, pulping and manufacturing processes are expected to conform to the environmental regulations of the country of origin.

A catalogue record for this book is available from the British Library.

A catalog record for this book is available from the Library of Congress.

10   9   8   7   6   5   4   3   2   1
20   19   18   17   16   15   14   13   12   11

Printed in China

Contents

List of Figures

List of Tables

Acronyms

ABI	Association of British Insurers
ACFS	Accredited Counter Fraud Specialist
ACPO	Association of Chief Police Officers
APACS	Association for Payment Clearing Services
ARA	Assets Recovery Agency
BCS	British Crime Survey
CB	Child Benefit
CFE	Certified Fraud Examiner
CFPAB	Counter Fraud Professional Accreditation Board
CIB	Companies Investigation Branch
CIFAS	Credit Industry Fraud Avoidance System
CIPFA	Chartered Institute of Public Finance and Accountancy
CPS	Crown Prosecution Service
DEFRA	Department for Environment, Food and Rural Affairs
DLA	Disability Living Allowance
DoH	Department of Health
DTI	Department of Trade and Industry
DWA	Disability Working Allowance
DWP	Department for Work and Pensions
FSA	Financial Services Authority
HB	Housing Benefit
HMRC	Her Majesty's Revenue and Customs
IFB	Insurance Fraud Bureau
IFIG	Insurance Fraud Investigators Group
IS	Income Support
JSA	Job Seeker's Allowance
NAO	National Audit Office
NIC	National Insurance Credit
NFA	National Fraud Authority
NFI	National Fraud Initiative

NFSA	National Fraud Strategic Authority
NHS CFSMS	National Health Service Counter Fraud and Security Management Service
NRC	National Reporting Centre
OFT	Office of Fair Trading
PC	Pension Credit
RCPO	Revenue and Customs Prosecution Office
SFO	Serious Fraud Office
TSO	The Stationery Office
VAT	Value Added Tax

CHAPTER 1

Introduction: The Study of Fraud

Overview

The aims of this chapter are to

- compare fraud and its treatment with response to other volume crimes
- provide an overview of the study of fraud and where it fits into criminology, particularly with respect to white collar crime
- outline the organization and structure of the book

At the beginning of a new decade one can reflect on several historic exposes of fraud which occurred at the end of the 'noughties' which demonstrate how diverse, serious and devastating this crime can be, as well as why it is so important to study. In March 2009 Bernard Madoff pleaded guilty to perpetrating the world's largest ever Ponzi scheme (investment fraud), which involved thousands of investors and some $65 billion, for which he was sentenced to 150 years' jail (Department of Justice, 2009; BBC News, 2009a). The British Houses of Parliament were engulfed in an expenses scandal which showed systematic abuse of a chaotic system, which, if not legally fraudulent, was certainly perceived by the public to be so and, at the time of writing (March 2010), three MPs and one Peer had been charged with fraud-related offences resulting from the expenses scandal (BBC News, 2009b; CPS, 2010). However, these dwarf the cost of the Global Financial Crisis of 2008–09, which, in the summer of 2009, was estimated at $11.9 trillion by the International Monetary Fund (IMF), or, in plain terms, one-fifth of annual global world output (*Daily Telegraph*, 2009a). A significant contributing factor to this financial crisis was the sub-prime mortgage market in the USA where systematic failings encouraged applicants and providers of credit to be dishonest in the capacity of many to repay their debts. These sub-prime debts were then camouflaged by being wrapped up with other debts and then sold on in Collateralized Debt Obligations (CDOs) and the credit agencies generally give AAA status to sub-prime debts (Gee, 2009). As many of the mortgage holders then began to default, the seeds of the crisis were sown, the financial bubble burst and was exposed as being built upon systematic greed and, ultimately, fraud. These examples of what many criminologists would regard as white collar crimes illustrate three key themes which will be developed throughout this book:

- the significant damage this crime can and does reap on society,
- the blurred nature of fraud means it is often hidden, neglected or even not treated as a crime,
- the perpetration of frauds is often by the most powerful in society, the so-called 'white collar criminals', and not 'common criminals'.

The examples above would for most suggest substantial interest in the academic community in fraud, simply because of the costs and the involvement of the powerful. Indeed, in the UK, losses from fraud are estimated to amount to over £30 billion per annum (National Fraud Authority, 2010), and in the USA the Association of Certified Fraud Examiners (ACFE) estimates that employee fraud alone could amount to $652 billion (Levi et al., 2007; ACFE, 2007a). In the UK, 48 per cent of the population own up to have been targeted by a scammer, with 8 per cent admitting falling for it, and in the USA 58 per cent of the population have been estimated as targeted or falling for a scam (Shichor et al., 2001; OFT, 2006). Fraud has a far greater reach on society than any other crime has. However, by comparison with many other acts of deviance, fraud has received relatively little attention (Doig, 2006). Murder, domestic violence, hate crime, sex crime, drugs, burglary and anti-social behaviour have all been researched extensively. Fraud, by contrast, has been somewhat under-researched, often being subsumed under the broader subject of white collar crime, itself described as a 'minority interest' among criminologists (Newburn, 2007: 372). In the last decade policy-makers began to recognize the need to do something about this lack of attention to fraud. The result has been new initiatives, some of which have led to greater research and the provision of vocational and academic courses around the term 'fraud studies' in its own right or as part of white collar crime, criminological and even accounting and financial management courses. Before we examine this issue further, however, it would be useful to address the question of why we need to study fraud in its own right.

Fraud is different from other volume crimes

To some, the mere size of the problem of fraud would warrant its greater investigation, particularly with a view to identifying strategies for its reduction. There are, however, other compelling reasons for studying it. One of the most significant concerns the disparity between society's treatment of fraud and its attitude to what may be termed 'volume crimes'. This issue is best illustrated by showing what happens to most 'volume crimes' in the criminal justice system in England and Wales as set out in Figure 1.1.

A description of the above applied to a 'typical' crime would be as follows. A crime such as a burglary occurs. This is reported to the police by the victim. The police investigate, identify and arrest a suspect (although many such crimes are not investigated and the great majority of perpetrators are not caught!). The suspect is then charged and the file handed to the Crown Prosecution Service (CPS). The CPS will then decide whether to proceed with the charge. If the CPS chooses to proceed, the case goes to the magistrates' court or the Crown Court (depending on its severity). If found guilty, the offender faces a range of sanctions from imprisonment to a fine.

If a comparable diagram was to be created for fraud, it would be much more complicated than the above. Indeed, the production of a single diagram would probably be impossible. The reason for this is that although many frauds do find their way

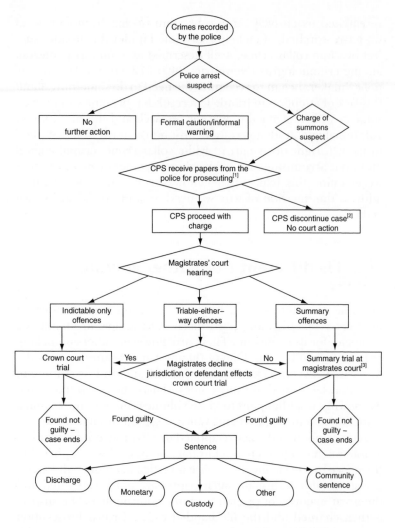

Figure 1.1 The prosecution process for typical crimes [adapted from Home Office (2000: 4)].

through the criminal justice system as above, others follow very different routes. There are a number of reasons for this:

- Many frauds are dealt with beyond the criminal justice system either through informal ways within organizations and private systems of justice or through the civil courts.

- There are many private and public bodies other than the police which investigate fraud.
- There are a number of bodies, other than the CPS, which prosecute fraud offences.
- A wider range of sanctions may be applied to fraudsters than is commonplace in the conventional criminal justice system.

Of course, fraud is not the only offence to deviate from the conventional prosecutorial process followed by 'typical' crimes. Much the same can be said for health and safety crimes and environmental crimes (Hutter, 1988, 1997; Tombs and Whyte, 2007). Fraud, however, constitutes the largest group of offences to follow such a different path, something which gives further justification for its greater research and study.

Fraud, criminology and white collar crime

Criminology forms the spine of fraud studies, largely through the concept of white collar crime. Though there is considerable debate both about what constitutes criminology and about how we define white collar crime, it is not our intention to explore these debates here (Garland, 2002; Newburn, 2007). Suffice it to say that the essence of criminology lies in the study of crime. What actions are defined as crimes and why? What causes crimes? How are crimes dealt with? What can be done to prevent them? Criminology is an inter-disciplinary subject drawing upon the more established disciplines of sociology, psychology, law, geography, political science and biology among others. What is perhaps most striking about criminology is its remarkable growth in popularity during the last 20 years, in the UK and elsewhere. From a situation when there were only a handful of courses and academic departments in the UK during 1980s, there are now dozens of departments staffed by academics running hundreds of courses for thousands of students.

However, despite the grounding of fraud studies in the discipline of criminology, there is a paradox between the two. The popularity of an academic subject is evidenced by the number of text books devoted to its study. Yet, until the publication of Doig's (2006) recent work, there was not one single British text book on the subject of fraud. Added to that, research monographs on the subject are few and far between (Levi 1981, 1987;

Cook, 1989). Indeed, most books on fraud are practical 'how to' books (e.g. Comer, 1985; Benson and Cullen, 1998; Jones, 2004). Compare this state of affairs with literature on the subject of hate crime, a topic where interest has expanded over the last decade and where, already, there are many texts and monographs (e.g. Perry, 2001, 2003; Hall, 2005; Winters, 2007; and Chakraborti and Garland, 2009). That is not to say that hate crime is unworthy of the academic interest devoted to it. It is merely to pose the question of why the study of fraud has not provoked significant criminological interest?

Fraud as a subject is usually located within a sub-division of criminology called white collar crime and sometimes to other designations such as 'corporate crime', 'occupational crime' or 'crimes of the powerful' (Newburn, 2007). While fraud undoubtedly forms part of each of these fields of study, such is the breadth of fraud as an offence that it invariably goes beyond them. White collar crime has become the most prominent field of study to encompass fraud (Doig, 2006). There has been much academic debate on what constitutes white collar crime (Newburn, 2007). The dispute that defines white collar crime has been characterized as 'the war of criminologists', with opinions split between those who see it as a very specific and precise concept and those who would purposely introduce elements of ambiguity in order to expand and extend its remit.

The term 'white collar crime' came into being with the work of Edwin Sutherland whose 1939 article, 'White Collar Crime', was followed by a book of the same title a decade later. In this book Sutherland defined white collar crime as 'approximately a crime committed by a person of respectability and high social status in the course of his occupation' (Sutherland, 1949: 9). This definition was intended to do two things: to highlight the fact that crime was not confined to the 'lower class', and to stress that criminological theory needed to be concerned with, and to collect data on, those in powerful positions in society, such as businessmen. This focus was intended to rectify what Sutherland considered to be the faulty premise of traditional criminological explanation. It was also an attempt to point out what he perceived to be bias in the criminal justice system in favour of the powerful.

However, his definition was attacked from the outset and it is now generally recognized to be deficient both for what it included and for what it excluded. Firstly, the notion of high social status was, in Sutherland's definition, associated with diverse crimes such as insider trading, 'long firm' fraud and embezzlement. Yet, such offences can be committed by a range of people across the status hierarchy (Geis, 1992). As Slapper and Tombs (1999: 7) concluded, 'Sutherland's usage of the terms seeks to cover a quite heterogeneous range of actions, with different kinds of offenders, offences and victims.'

Additionally and ironically, Sutherland's definition excluded employee crime – including fraud – at all levels within an organization. As Weisburd et al. (1991: 184) concluded in their study of white collar criminals, 'contrary to the portrait generally presented we find a world of offending and offenders that is very close to the everyday lives of typical Americans.'

Sutherland's definition also failed to make the distinction between those crimes committed by employees and those crimes committed by corporations. The importance of this distinction was emphasized by Pearce (1976), who pointed to the difference in treatment between the two, such as when white collar crimes involving employees are prosecuted, while those involving corporations are subject to regulation:

> Not all white-collar crimes are equally immune to prosecution. If for example, embezzlement was left unprosecuted and there was a large increase in such activity, capitalism may well collapse...on the other hand, violations of anti-trust laws do not pose a threat to the social structure of American capitalism, and can, therefore, be tolerated.
>
> (Pearce, 1976: 81)

Subsequently, there have been many attempts to define white collar crime (see Croall, 1992, 2001; Slapper and Tombs, 1999; Newburn, 2007, chapter 18). Without getting into the intricacies of these, many cover most, but not all, aspects of fraud (social security and credit card fraud are often excluded, for example). Fraud studies is thus entrenched in 'white collar crime', but also goes beyond it. Like criminology and white collar crime, it is also influenced by a range of other disciplines such as law, sociology, politics, management studies and psychology. As such, it is an inter-disciplinary subject focused upon a deviant behaviour called fraud.

As this book will show, fraud is probably the most costly crime to society in financial terms. It is undertaken by a wide range of people and, despite inflicting severe societal damage, is of only limited interest to the police. To make matters worse, it is almost certainly a growing problem. For these and other reasons fraud deserves more attention from researchers and students alike. This book will seek to raise the profile of fraud as a subject worthy of greater interest and as a discrete topic: that is, both as a specialist option within broader courses and as a course in its own right.

Organization of the book

This book has been written by four authors and it is important to remember this when considering the following chapters, as each author comes with their own ideas and perspectives which, in the blurred subject of fraud, often prove difficult to accommodate. The remainder of the book is divided into three parts. Part I, which is called 'Fraud in Context', contains four chapters. The first of these, Chapter 2, examines some of the academic and legal definitions of fraud before illustrating various forms of fraud including employee fraud, external fraud and corporate fraud. Chapter 3 addresses a different, but no less challenging, problem: how to estimate the extent of fraud in society. Chapter 4 examines evidence on why people commit fraud. Finally, Chapter 5 explores the politics of fraud, focusing on two particular issues: the wide range of organizations that have an interest in fraud and why fraud, generally, has such a low political priority.

Part II, 'Tackling Fraud', addresses the issue of how society deals with fraud. Chapter 6 looks at fraud prevention and at some of the strategies used to reduce fraud risk. Chapter 7 focuses on the investigation of fraud, considering the main investigative bodies and some of the strategies they use. Finally, Chapter 8 examines the prosecution and sanctioning of fraud. A strong theme in tackling fraud is the relatively marginal role of the criminal justice system, and in both Chapter 7 and Chapter 8, we illustrate the many non-criminal justice alternatives to prosecuting fraud.

Each of the chapters in Part III is devoted to the detailed consideration of a particular case study. Chapter 9 looks at insurance fraud. This is a major area of fraudulent activity, regularly perpetrated by otherwise law-abiding citizens, but which has been the subject of very limited research. By contrast, social security fraud, the subject of Chapter 10, receives substantial public attention and has been the subject of significant academic research. Chapter 11 shifts our attention from the domestic to the international arena by exploring the growing problem of transnational fraud. In the final chapter, Chapter 12, we reflect further on some key themes raised in the book by considering a recent example in which fraudulent or near-fraudulent behaviour has occurred.

Finally, it is worth saying something about the book's organization. At the beginning of each chapter, the reader will find a text box, providing a short overview of the chapter's key aims. Throughout the book, similar boxes provide case studies of specific frauds, some of which are cross-referenced to in other chapters. Each chapter ends with a brief recommendation of further reading and provides links to appropriate websites in order to facilitate follow-up research. Though the book is primarily focused on evidence from the UK, examples are also drawn from across the world, so as to make the book relevant to a wider readership.

Further reading

- For access to extensive resources on fraud and corruption, go to the fraud and corruption hub, http://www.port.ac.uk/ccfs.
- Australian Institute of Criminology. AIC publications on fraud and corporate crime. Available from http://www.aic.gov.au/crime_types/economic/fraud.aspx.
- Croall, H. (1992) *White Collar Crime*. Buckingham: Open University Press.
- Croall, H. (2001) *Understanding White Collar Crime*. Buckingham: Open University Press.
- Doig, A. (2006) *Fraud*. Cullompton: Willan.
- Levi, M. (1987) *Regulating Fraud*. New York: Tavistock Publications.

PART I

Fraud in Context

CHAPTER 2

Defining Fraud

Overview

The aims of this chapter are to

- outline what constitutes fraud
- examine some academic and legal definitions of fraud
- review the emergence of the Fraud Act 2006 which attempts to codify the offence of fraud in England and Wales
- outline some examples of the wide range of deviant acts regarded as fraud

Introduction

In this chapter we explore what is meant by fraud. Until the passage of the Fraud Act in 2006 there was no single codified offence of fraud. Deviant behaviour regarded as fraud was dealt with under various pieces of legislation such as the Theft Acts and specialist social security and taxation legislation, as well as the common law and civil law. Indeed, fraud is unusual among crimes in that it is regularly pursued in the civil courts (the complexity of civil law precludes this matter from being discussed here). This myriad of legal definitions makes fraud distinctive from other crimes in that the various behaviours defined as fraudulent by the public, the media, policing bodies, the courts and other organizations are often prosecuted under legislation that is not specifically concerned with fraud. The passage of the Fraud Act means there is now a clearly defined offence (although many of the 'specialist' fraud offences in social security, taxation and so on still also exist).

This chapter begins by exploring what constitutes fraud, before moving on to consider the Fraud Act 2006. It will then illustrate a wide range of different behaviours that are generally regarded as fraud under their distinct sub-categories to demonstrate the diversity of the offence.

What is fraud?

Numerous definitions have been offered as to what constitutes fraud, both from legal commentators and from those involved in investigating and prosecuting it. However, the one common element to most of them is the notion of deception in order to make some form of gain. In legal terms, until recently, Stephen's *History of the Criminal Law of England* has been regarded as an authoritative definition on fraud and fraud-related offences in the English Legal System. Thus,

> ...whenever the words 'fraud' and 'intent to defraud', or 'fraudu-lently' occur in the definition of a crime two elements at least are essential to the commission of the crime: namely first, deceit or an intention to deceive or in some cases mere secrecy; and secondly, either actual injury or possible injury or an intent to expose some person either to actual injury or to risk of possible injury by means of that deceit or secrecy.
>
> (Stephen, 1973: 121)

Academics, professional investigators and accountants have added to such legal definitions and opinions. Arlidge et al. (1996: 5) define fraud as containing the element of the neces-sity for there to be deceit, or intention to deceive, or secrecy, and secondly, for actual, or potential, injury to a second party. Aca-demics and professional accountants have added to these legal definitions and opinions. Wells (1997: 2) sees fraud as 'any crime which uses deception as its principal modus operandi', while from an accountant's viewpoint, Davies (2000: 3) sees it as

> all those activities involving dishonesty and deception that can drain value from a business, directly or indirectly, whether or not there is personal benefit to the fraudster.

What these definitions suggest is that fraud is based upon some form of intention of deception and/or dishonesty alongside the achievement of some kind of gain. Clearly this still leaves a wide range of potential behaviours that could be regarded as fraud. For example, politicians frequently promise the electorate things they know they cannot provide for the purpose of achieving a gain (election) and yet most would not consider this a fraud for which they should be prosecuted. Thus it is perhaps better to distinguish between two things: fraud as a theoretical concept, which might include a very wide rage of potential behaviours, some difficult to define legally as fraud; and fraud as a legal concept, providing a narrower and more specific definition regarding the actions which can be prosecuted as frauds.

Towards the Fraud Act 2006

Following the implementation of the Fraud Act in January 2007 there is now a codified piece of legislation covering the general offence of fraud in the English Legal System. Before this, provisions for the defining and prosecution of fraud lay under the common law offence of conspiracy to defraud and by the remit of the 'deception' acts as included in the Theft Acts 1968, 1978 and 1996. However, over a period of years, there was a growing recognition that the 'deception acts' had introduced unwanted degrees of complexity that made convictions difficult to secure, and enabled defendants to be acquitted. The Acts had also failed to keep up to date with technological developments and the way business was conducted (e.g. the increasing use of computers, see below).

These problems culminated in The Law Commission publishing a report on fraud in 2002. This identified a number of drawbacks with the deception offences: principally revolving around them being overly prescriptive and technical in their nature and left them open to legal objections that made for complicated and long trials that often bewildered juries.

More pertinently, as far as defining fraud was concerned, the deception acts omitted or missed offences that could well be characterized as fraud, leaving no alternative but to attempt to use conspiracy to defraud (see below). The Law Commission cited 16 examples of fraud and fraudulent behaviour including abuse of position and trust, where the narrowness of the sections on deception militated against prosecution under them. These included the misuse of credit cards where it could be contended that, in a retail outlet, staff tended not to consider themselves deceived about a fact which was of no direct interest to them (Law Commission, 2002: 3.33).

Similarly they also pointed to the role of computers and other machines in the pursuance of fraud. As it stood, the argument went that because computers had no mind they could not be deceived. So anyone gaining dishonestly by the use of a computer could not be charged with a deception offence. If a 'property' was obtained during the course of events, this could be covered by a charge of theft; but if it was a service, the picture was less clear and there might be no offence at all. This became an increasingly important issue because of the growth of services capable of being paid for via a machine. For example, one would usually pay an Internet service provider by entering one's credit card details on its website. Using card details to pay for such a service without the authority of the owner would not, at the time, have constituted an offence (Law Commission, 2002: 3.35).

The Law Commission also pointed to the ambiguity surrounding non-disclosure of information and abuse of position in committing a fraud. Thus while it was possible to defraud someone without making false statements, a deception offence may not always have been appropriate, or available. Alternatively, when someone providing some form of service is not told anything by the fraudster, it is difficult, if not impossible, to describe someone as being deceived. In these cases the offender abusing his/her position of trust achieved the benefit without having to deceive anybody.

Behind the offences of deception in the Theft Acts was the common law offence of conspiracy to defraud. This was often used to avoid the technical arguments that can arise from using the deception offences. Doig (2006: 35) defines it as concerning

> ... an agreement by two or more persons to dishonestly deprive someone of something which belongs to that person or in which they have rights, as well as a dishonest agreement between two or more persons to 'defraud' another by deceiving them into acting in a way contrary to his or her duty.

The offence can be illustrated by the case of *Scott v. the Metropolitan Police Commissioner* [1975] AC 819 at 1039 (Smith, 1995: 51). In this case Scott and some employees of a cinema borrowed some of the films to copy (returning them after) to sell on the black market. It was held they had committed conspiracy to defraud, although no theft had actually taken place.

The response to the Law Commission Report was a recognition that the deception acts needed to be abolished and replaced with more general fraud offences that would make it easier for prosecutors to successfully prosecute suspected fraudsters, by broadening the law on fraud. As such it should be seen in the context of other measures designed to make it easier and less expensive to try and convict fraudsters.

Thus when the Fraud Act 2006 was passed, it did abolish the 'deception' offences as outlined above and replaced them with three main categories recommended by the Law Commission Report. Specifically, the Act made it an offence to commit

- Fraud by false representation (Section 2)
- Fraud by failing to disclose information (Section 3)
- Fraud by abuse of position (Section 4)

Additionally, the Act replaced the offence of dishonestly obtaining services by deception (as contained in Section 1 of the 1968 Theft Act) to obtaining services dishonestly (Section 11 Fraud Act 2006). Also Section 6 of the Act made it an offence to be in possession, or under the control, of any article for use in the course of or in connection with any fraud, and Section 7 made it an offence if 'he makes, adapts, supplies or offers to supply any article knowing that it is designed ... for use in the course of a fraud.' Section 9 extended the offence of fraudulent trading from companies to any person (individual or sole trader) who carries on any 'business' fraudulently or with intent to defraud creditors (Farrell et al., 2007: 1).

It must also be noted that some of the very special areas of fraud where there is specific legislation have been left on the statute books. These include the following:

- Social security fraud
- Tax fraud
- Insider trading
- Forgery and counterfeiting offences
- False accounting
- Misleading market practices

The Fraud Act 2006 also retained the common law offence of conspiracy to defraud on the basis that it provided flexibility in dealing with a wide variety of fraud. Summers argued that the new Act was welcomed by prosecuting authorities as it was making the process of investigating and prosecuting fraud easier and quicker (and by extension, cheaper), leading to a 40 per cent increase in fraud-related offences being tried in Magistrates' court (2008: 12). However, Ormerod (2007) criticized the Act for defining fraud too broadly and for shifting the emphasis to a defendant's intention to be dishonest, rather than results of his/her actions. Thus where the deception acts made it necessary for there to be proof that the actions of person 'A' caused person(s) 'B' to do whatever was being charged (e.g. to transfer property), now it is sufficient to prove that person 'A' intended to make a gain or cause a loss by his/her actions. According to Ormerod, this represented a significant widening of the scope of fraud as an offence, such that, for example, it could be said that Section 2 of the Act criminalized lying (2007: 2). Ormerod was also particularly scathing of the implications of Section 6 (possession of article) as potentially applying to a wide range of everyday objects likely to be owned by almost everyone (2007: 12).

Overall, he concluded that while the new Act simplified the process of investigating and prosecuting fraud, it was 'overbroad' in its coverage. Also, because of its reliance on the concept of dishonesty, it potentially breaches Article 7 of the European Court of Human Rights (ECHR) (2007: 16–17).

The diversity of fraud

This section will now explore the wide diversity of behaviours that are regarded as fraud. The section is not exhaustive, but it will show some of the most common types of fraud.

Employee fraud

The Summer 2008 Fraud Track produced by BDO Stoy Hayward highlighted that the biggest threat to organizations was not from external criminals, but from internal management, accounting for 46 per cent of fraud cases and costing businesses £541 million. This constituted 77 per cent of the costs of fraud (BDO Stoy Hayward, 2008). In a profile of the typical fraudster, KPMG

(2007a) published research based upon 360 cases of fraud from 700 investigations in their European, Middle Eastern and African regions. Their profile of a typical fraudster was of a male (85 per cent), who was middle-aged (between 36 and 55) (70 per cent), who committed a fraud against his own employer (89 per cent), who acted alone (68 per cent) and who had worked for the employer for at least 6 years (over 50 per cent). These two studies illustrate the threat of employee fraud.

The phenomenon of fraudulent or dishonest employees is by no means a new one. Whoever the primary victim may be, the costs of the offence are borne by both the organization and the client. The archetypal form of staff fraud is one where the employee defrauds his/her company acting alone. However, sometimes there are cases of collusion between employees and outside firms. Also, there are occasions when employers know of 'fiddles' conducted by their staff against customers and ignore, condone or even encourage such activity. Ditton (1977), for example, researching a bakery company, discovered that it paid low wages and imposed penalties on its delivery staff for lateness, knowing that the employees would compensate themselves by fiddling the customers. The same has been discovered among bar staff (Gill et al., 1994).

Frauds committed against organizations by external individuals and organizations

Organizations' suppliers, clients and customers can perpetrate external fraud. Among these are credit card and cheque frauds. Credit card and plastic fraud first became an issue in the 1980s, with an estimated loss of £50 million being recorded in 1985. This declined as a proportion of total retail loss in the late 1980s even though the absolute figure in 1991 was reportedly in excess of £150 million. However, subsequent growth in the 1990s made it an issue again. Thus in 1997 the Credit Industry Fraud Avoidance System (CIFAS) reported that 31,107 frauds were either perpetrated or attempted against banks, with 28,221 frauds against the retail sector (Levi, 1998). Another example of fraud against companies is long-firm fraud. In a long-firm fraud the deviant establishes a 'firm' that places orders for goods which are then sold, but never actually pays the wholesaler. To secure 'good will' many perpetrating this type of fraud will initially settle r debts very quickly, but the intention will be to build up to a substantial order that is never going to be paid for. For a comprehensive overview of this type of fraud, see Levi (2008).

Fraud by organizations against the public and other organizations

This category highlights the phenomenon of Corporate Fraud which have been characterized as illegal acts Corporate Fraud committed by individuals in the 'furtherance of the operative goals of the organisation' (Box, 1983: 20–22). This could include 'cooking the books' by inflating sales, profits and assets to make investment more attractive; cheating customers by issuing short measures; substituting cheaper materials and price fixing. Businesses can also defraud other organizations (Box, 1987: 25). There are also a wide range of 'scams' that fall under this category, which, because of their extent, deserve consideration in their own right later.

Case Study 2.1

In 2008 a British water company was fined over £20 million by the regulator OFWAT for overcharging its customers and misleading the regulator. The company had misled the regulator on its performance which had enabled it to increase its charges at a higher rate than if the real performance figures had been supplied (OFWAT, 2008).

Frauds against employees and investors

A wide range of frauds have developed that specifically target investors and employees. A pyramid scheme is a plan by which a person gives consideration (usually money) for the opportunity to receive money that is derived primarily from the introduction of other people to participate in the plan rather than from the sale of a product. The arrangement often operates as an investment and invariably leaves most participants poorer. Similarly investment frauds usually involve bogus companies or individuals offering generous terms for investments only to escape with the investors' loot (see Case Study 2.2).

Case Study 2.2

In March 2008 a father and daughter were arrested in the USA after allegedly defrauding over 15,000 people in the UK – mostly elderly – of £35 million. The father and daughter cold called the victims and using high-pressure selling techniques sold shares in worthless or non-existent companies (Department of Justice, 2008; Gray, 2008; Timesonline, 2008). These frauds are often known as 'boiler room' scams.

There have also been many examples where those running 'established' companies have perpetrated frauds against their employees and/or shareholders. For example, Bernard Madoff pleaded guilty to 11 offences related to his wealth management business, including securities fraud, wire fraud, mail fraud, money laundering and making false statements and returns to the US Securities and Exchange Commission (SEC). In effect he had been running the business as a 'Ponzi' scheme where, instead of investing his clients' money legitimately, he deposited it into his own bank account at the Chase Manhattan Bank, and later with JP Morgan, earning an estimated personal gain of nearly $500 million. Estimates of the losses incurred by his investors vary from $18 billion to $65 billion. In June 2009, he was sentenced to serve 150 years in a US federal prison (Department of Justice, 2009; Findlaw, 2009).

Financial fraud: Insider trading/dealing

The US Securities and Exchange Commission (2001) define insider trading as ' ... buying or selling a security, in breach of a fiduciary duty or other relationship of trust and confidence, while in possession of material, non-public information about the security'. Both people working for companies and company auditors may have privileged information which, they know, might affect the share price were it to come into the public domain. Someone trading in shares with this knowledge can generally make a lot of money. Using this information to trade shares or to supply information to others to do so is known as insider trading and is against the law. This is one of many types of abuse that can be perpetrated on the financial markets.

Case Study 2.3

In March 2008 a father and son were convicted of insider trading. The son had been undertaking work experience for an investment bank and was feeding information to his father to purchase shares on deals the bank was advising clients on. His father had made over £110,000 from these forbidden stock market deals. The father was jailed for 2 years and the son 1 year (*Daily Telegraph*, 2009b).

Counterfeit products

There is a global industry dedicated to counterfeiting virtually any product that has value. Products counterfeited range from clothes to drugs, works of art, mechanical parts and even eggs! Fraudsters will counterfeit anything that can be produced at less cost than the real product and can be sold near to the real product's price.

Case Study 2.4

In August 2007 a Chinese pharmaceutical manufacturer was forced to remove 20,000 doses of an anti-malaria drug in Kenya after discovering that a criminal syndicate had been counterfeiting its drug and offering it for sale throughout the country. The counterfeited drug, one of many anti-malaria drugs to have been done so, is ineffectual, thus thwarting Kenya's efforts to tackle a disease that kills over 35,000 of its people each year (BBC News, 2007a).

Tax and excise fraud

Since most people dislike paying taxes and some will illegally try to evade them, fraud against tax and excise liabilities is a major problem for the public sector in the majority of countries. Typical examples of such fraud include non-declaration of income by individuals and under-recording of profit by companies. One major fraud committed by companies is the attempt to evade full or partial payment of Value Added Tax (VAT) often through some element of false accounting. HM Revenue and Customs (HMRC) regard this as a serious problem and their investigations identify businesses which

- are bogus and set up to steal VAT from the system;
- lie about transactions made and as a result the tax they owe; and
- claim refunds to which they are not entitled.

Case Study 2.5

Two businessmen were each found guilty on 17 counts of VAT fraud and were sentenced to 5 years' imprisonment. They developed their VAT scam by producing false expenses invoices on their home computer and putting them through the books of their video shop to claim back the tax. The suspicions of customs officers were aroused and an investigation was launched. They checked the books at the shop, raided the home address and found computers used to produce the bogus invoices and paperwork. John Powell, Customs spokesman for East Midlands, said the following:

> This was a major VAT fraud which was unearthed by the thorough efforts of our investigation team. The Jury at trial accepted the evidence that the [businessmen] were falsifying invoices to 'cook the books'.

They had attempted to defraud Customs and Excise of over £241,000 (Government Information, 2002).

Additionally, a large number of businesses do not meet their legal responsibility to register for VAT. These form part of the so-called 'informal' economy, constituting an underworld of hidden trade. The second major form of fraud against HMRC relates to the duty liable on goods. Roque (2000) identified four main types:

(i) *Bootlegging*: smuggling tobacco and alcohol across the channel;
(ii) *Drawback fraud*: where supposedly duty-paid goods are exported and the tax paid in the home country is remitted back to the trader;

(iii) *Diversion fraud*: where false documentation is used to avoid payment of duty; and

(iv) *Commercial fraud or smuggling*: where goods are concealed, or misdirected without paperwork.

Fraud against the public services

Apart from collecting revenue the public sector is heavily involved in the transfer of payments in the shape of welfare benefits and the provision of services. Here again there are numerous opportunities for fraud. Many of these types of fraud fall under the categories of employee and external fraud discussed earlier. As Chapter 11 will explore social security fraud in more depth, it will not be discussed further here.

Frauds and scams against the public

Scams by confidence tricksters against members of the public have a long history (see Vaughan and Carlo, 1975; and Morton and Bateson, 2007). In recent years the availability of cheap telecommunications and the Internet have enabled scams to be perpetrated on an industrial scale through so-called 'boiler rooms' and spam e-mail (Button et al., 2009). Examples include

(i) *Prize-draw, lottery and sweepstake scams.* Fraudsters send out letters and e-mails to potential victims telling them they have won a prize or are entitled to a financial reward, but need to pay an 'administration' fee in order to secure access to the funds. Sometimes, particularly in the case of overseas lotteries, victims are asked to contact an 'agent' by telephone.

(ii) *Work at home and business opportunity scams.* Fraudsters advertise work opportunities through newspapers, magazines, shop windows and even on flyers attached to lamp posts. The 'work' (e.g. stuffing envelopes, making up home assembly kits) requires few skills or qualifications but promises to reap above-average financial rewards. The victim is required to pay a 'registration' or other fee to the fraudsters in order to obtain the necessary work materials. In reality, no work exists.

(iii) *Pyramid selling and chain letter scams.* Pyramid sellers ask victims to pay an initial joining fee, after which they are promised large sums of money for recruiting new members into the scheme. However, pyramids invariably collapse due to insufficient members joining, leaving those who have been exploited out of pocket. Consumer Direct, the Government advice service, recently estimated that pyramid scams cost UK consumers around £420 million per annum, and that around 480,000 adults are victimized each year with an average loss of £930 (Greek, 2009).

(iv) *Miracle health and slimming cure scams.* Every year around 200,000 people in the UK fall for scam 'miracle' health cures relating to a range of health conditions such as obesity, impotence and cancer. The growth of the Internet has created new opportunities for this illicit market.

(v) *Clairvoyant and psychic mailing scams.* Targets receive a letter from a clairvoyant or psychic who, for a fee, offers to make predictions. Sometimes victims are told that something bad will happen to them, their family or friends if they do not participate. Figures from the Office of Fair Trading (OFT) revealed that more than 170,000 people fell victim to psychic scams in 2006, losing an average of £240 each (Robins, 2007).

(vi) *Bogus holiday club scams.* Under these scams fraudsters persuade victims to pay large, up-front, fees to join clubs that promise cheap holidays. People, who may pay up to £15,000 for membership, often find they have no guarantees about the dates or quality of their holiday accommodation. They may also be committed to paying a fee irrespective of whether or not they take a holiday. Unscrupulous clubs will often approach people while they are on holiday or through supposed scratch card wins, after which they will be invited to high-pressure sales events (BBC News, 2007b).

(vii) *African advanced fee frauds/foreign money-making scams.* Fraudsters use mail, e-mail or faxes to target potential victims, usually with a fictitious scenario of a corrupt government official who has 'procured' a large sum of money and who needs a bank account to place it in. Frequently a fee is sought to help facilitate the transfer and often the bank accounts of victims are targeted (OFT, 2006) (for further discussion of this type of fraud, see Chapter 11).

Electoral fraud

Electoral fraud is a fraud where there is usually no direct financial benefit involved. Nevertheless, it is not uncommon, occurring both in the most corrupt countries and in those whose democratic credentials are held up as best practice. Case Study 2.6 illustrates an example of electoral fraud in the UK.

Case Study 2.6

In April 2005 six councillors in Birmingham were found guilty of corruption and of a systematic attempt to rig the 2004 local elections in their two wards. They had secured their re-election by abusing the postal votes system, which had very limited security procedures. They were sacked as councillors, they were ordered to pay the legal costs of £200,000 and their file was handed to the Director of Public Prosecution to consider a criminal prosecution (Dale, 2005).

Conclusion

Fraud encompasses a very wide range of behaviours and there is much debate over whether certain acts constitute a crime. The expenses scandal in the UK Houses of Parliament during 2009 illustrates this very well, where many members of the public would regard many of the acts of politicians as amounting to fraud, yet so far (writing at the end of 2009) only a handful risk been prosecuted in the criminal courts. Most have simply had to return monies to the parliamentary authorities with no other sanction. This is an area which will be developed further throughout this book: the very different treatment that the 'powerful' and those wearing white collars often receive.

This chapter has explored what constitutes fraud and has examined the background to the emergence of the Fraud Act 2006. It has also briefly discussed some of the criticisms of this legislation before moving on to illustrate examples of some of the most common types of fraud. The wide range of frauds, together with the varying types of victims, the different types of perpetrators, the diverse methods they employ and varied consequences arising from their actions, demonstrate the complexity of the crime. This has implications across a wide range of issues, not least the matter of measuring, investigating and prosecuting fraud. Chapter 3 will explore the first of these issues.

Further reading

- Farrell, S., Yeo, N. and Ladenburg, G. (2007) *Blackstone's Guide to the Fraud Act 2006*. Oxford: Oxford University Press.
- Law Commission (2002) *Fraud: Report on a Reference under Section 3(1)(e) of the Law Commissions Act 1965* (LAW COM No 276). London: HMSO. Available from http://www.lawcom.gov.uk/docs/lc276.pdf.
- Levi, M. (1981) *The Phantom Capitalists: The Organisation and Control of Long-Firm Fraud*. London: Heinemann.
- Mars, G. (1984) *Cheats at Work: An Anthropology of Workplace Crime* (2nd edition). London: Allen and Unwin.
- Ormerod, D. (2007) Criminalising Lying. *Criminal Law Review*, March, pp. 193–219.
- The Fraud Act 2006. London: The Stationery Office Ltd. Available from http://www.opsi.gov.uk/Acts/acts2006/pdf/ukpga_20060035_en.pdf.

CHAPTER 3

The Extent of Fraud

Overview

The aims of this chapter are to provide

- an insight into the challenges of measuring fraud
- an illustration of some official measures of fraud
- an account of some of the limitations of fraud statistics
- an assessment of some surveys of fraud
- an account of some measures of fraud used outside the UK

Introduction

In this chapter we examine the extent of fraud in society. As Chapter 2 has already illustrated, fraud is not an unambiguous concept and naturally that means it will be hard to measure because of the large grey area surrounding it. This is but one of the many challenges in seeking to gauge the extent of fraud. In January 2010 the National Fraud Authority published its first annual fraud indicator gauging the problem as costing the UK economy £30.5 billion (National Fraud Authority, 2010). This is double the next most recent sophisticated estimate from the research commissioned by the Association of Chief Police Officers (ACPO), which had conservatively estimated direct losses amounted to £12.98 billion per annum (and when the costs of dealing with fraud were added, that figure increased to £13.9 billion) (Levi et al., 2007). The Fraud Review, which had reported prior to this, had estimated fraud could cost the UK from £14 billion to £72 billion per annum (Fraud Review Team, 2006a). These are a few of the dozens of different types of measures that exist to estimate fraud. These measures will be explored in this chapter and will be critically assessed.

The chapter begins with a discussion of the challenges of measuring fraud. We then consider some of the official measures of reported fraud such as the 'fraud and forgery' component of the official crime statistics, the caseload of the Serious Fraud Office (SFO) and the statistics of certain government departments, before discussing some private sector attempts to determine fraud levels. After discussing the limitations of fraud statistics, we then consider some of the many surveys that are used to gauge the level of fraud (usually in monetary terms) both nationally and in particular sectors. The chapter ends by providing some international comparisons to illustrate the extent of the problem.

Challenges of measuring fraud

As Chapter 2 has suggested, there is much dispute about the definition of fraud, a factor which inevitably impacts on its measurement. It is worth bearing this point in mind since, although we shall discuss some of the ways in which different organizations measure fraud, these measurements, like the definitions implicit in them, are by no means uncontentious. Having said that, it is hoped that the Fraud Act 2006 will do much, along with the National Fraud Reporting Centre (to be discussed in Chapter 5), to provide a more systematic measure of fraud.

A second challenge is whether resources that are unaccounted for are the result of fraud or of some kind of error. The complexity of accounting systems and, in some cases, the sheer number of cases to deal with often make it difficult to decide whether a case constitutes fraud or error. For instance, in the field of social security, overpayments may be made to claimants, sometimes because of a mistake by the claimant or the official assessing the claim, rather than because of any deliberate dishonesty. In some large organizations such is the complexity of the finances, accounting procedures and valuation of assets that it sometimes becomes difficult to account for all resources. This might be because of fraud, but also because of flaws and errors in the accounting procedures themselves. For example, in February 2008, Portsmouth City Council was unable to account for £7.8 million of its assets, not because of any fraud but because of the accounting procedures used and the inability of staff to trace paperwork (Pykett, 2008, para. 2).

A third issue is that victims might not know they have been defrauded. Corporations with multi-million-pound budgets, employing highly paid executives, may not notice the loss of sums of money which, by their standards, are relatively small. As a result, if asked to describe their experiences of victimization in surveys, they are likely to either under-report or complete 'nil-returns'.

Linked to this, even when individuals and corporations do discover that they have been victimized, they frequently fail to report the fact to the authorities. As a result, this victimization evidence never comes into the public domain. In his interviews with directors from British and American-based firms, Levi found that American companies were more likely to report fraud than British ones. This was mainly due to a lack of confidence in the police's ability/willingness to investigate complaints. Although Levi did find that the UK companies took a 'more dainty' attitude to reporting fraud, some directors preferred to investigate the fraud first so as to present the story to the police as a *fait accompli*. Otherwise, there was a danger that the police might open a 'Pandora's box' in the course of an investigation (1987: 132).

Levi's study was published in the late 1980s before some of the more notorious city frauds were exposed. Russell (1998) found that 20 per cent of the directors he surveyed would not report a fraud automatically, and as a matter of policy, the main reason is that it would harm the firm's public reputation. Building on such research, the Fraud Advisory Panel asked Andrew Higson of Loughborough University to investigate the issue further. He discovered that most frauds were not reported, with one senior manager putting the figure reported at 1 in 30. Again the principal motive was to protect the organization's reputation, hence the much greater incidence of reporting of external frauds. Other reasons for non-reporting included the perceived cost effectiveness of reporting in terms of management resources needed, as opposed to the likelihood of the police, or regulatory authorities pursuing the claim. As one put it,

> One problem is the interaction between the civil and criminal processes. As soon as you take it to the police the criminal process takes over the civil process. People may be more concerned about getting

their money back, but this is delayed if the matter is reported to the police, as it is necessary to wait until a criminal trial is over.

(Higson, 1999: 10)

Such findings were confirmed in a 2004 survey of Australian companies by the accountancy firm, KPMG. This found that while 25 per cent of frauds were left unreported due to insufficient evidence, 12 per cent of companies did not want the adverse publicity that would be involved (KPMG, 2004a: 23).

Finally, as we later discuss, many measures of fraud are undertaken on the basis of surveys. In all surveys – even those undertaken to the highest statistical standards – there is a margin of error. Further, the methodologies used in some surveys are less rigorous than they might be. All things considered, then, many of the measures that we discuss below should be regarded not as definitive estimates of fraud but as 'guesstimates' offering indicative information about fraud trends.

Official statistics of cases of fraud

The official crime statistics (or notifiable offences as they are often called) are offences 'serious' enough for defendants to be tried in the Crown Court, or to elect for trial by jury. There are 64 types of such offences which, grouped under wider headings, include offences of violence against the person, theft and handling goods, sexual offences, fraud and forgery, burglary, robbery, criminal damage and others. There is much debate on the validity of crime statistics in general, some of which will shortly be explored. Yet, as Chapter 2 showed, in the UK until 2007 there was not even a codified set of fraud offences to assess in the official statistics; rather there was a mix of the different offences under which fraud and other crimes were prosecuted. In the official statistics 'fraud and forgery' includes fraud by company directors, false accounting, cheque and credit card fraud, other fraud (obtaining property by deception), bankruptcy and insolvency offences, forgery or use of false drug prescription, other forgery and vehicle/driver document fraud (Home Office, 2009). In 2007–08 National Statistics recorded 163,283 instances, a 5 per cent increase on the previous year (Home Office, 2009).

The official crime statistics are not the only record of the number of reported cases of fraud. Another public organization that publishes official statistics related to fraud is the SFO. The functions of the SFO are outlined in greater depth in Chapter 8. Briefly, their role is to investigate and prosecute serious and complex fraud involving amounts of more than £1 million. Thus the SFO deals only with a small number of large-scale and organized frauds. Table 3.1 illustrates the case workload of the SFO in 2008–09.

HM Treasury also conducted (now discontinued) an annual survey of government departments covering internal fraud (and theft) and providing very detailed statistics. The 2007–08 survey covered 47 such departments and revealed that 22 reported no cases of theft or fraud. The other 25 bodies reported a total of 761 cases, valued at £4,278,000. Of these 18 were classified as 'large value cases', or exceeding £20,000 or more; moreover, 11 exceeded £100,000 and involved £3,209,000, or 75 per cent of all total losses (HM Treasury, 2008: 5–6).

There are also a number of government departments experiencing substantial external fraud that keep their own official statistics. During 2004–05, for example, the Department for Work and Pensions (DWP) detected 150,651 cases of fraud, which led to 8670 prosecutions and 8573 convictions (House of Commons Written Answers, 2006). The vast bulk of these frauds were dealt with by the DWP's internal systems of justice. NHS statistics for 2006–07 showed that a total of 409 cases were investigated during the year, resulting in 62 criminal prosecutions and 66 civil and disciplinary sanctions (NHS CFSMS, 2007a).

It is not just public bodies that record fraud statistics. There are a variety of private organizations that do the same, some of

Table 3.1 Workload of the SFO in 2008–09

	Number
Active cases at start of year	65 (sum at risk £6.8 billion)
Referrals accepted during 2008–09	18
Cases worked on during year	112
Investigations closed/not prosecuted	10
Cases completed at court	18
Total cases concluded	28
Cases ongoing at year end	84

Source: Adapted from Serious Fraud Office (2009).

which we discuss later. For example, the Association of British Insurers (ABI) collects statistics on insurance fraud. Private organizations include trade or industry bodies, such as UK Payments Administration, which record cases where their members are victimized, and there are organizations that compile statistics as part of a broader range of services for their clients, such as the KPMG's annual fraud barometer. Let us consider each of these, briefly.

The Association for Payment Clearing Services (APACS) is the trade association for companies that provide payment services to customers. It compiles detailed statistics from members on a range of issues that include fraud. It publishes annual statistics on the total costs of fraud experienced by its members which, in 2008, amounted to £609 million (APACS, 2009). This constituted a rise on the previous year where it had amounted to £535 million.

KPMG produces an annual fraud barometer which provides statistics on the number of fraud cases coming before the courts (criminal or civil) in the UK valued at £100,000 or more. As the barometer has been running for over 20 years, it provides a good means of identifying trends in fraud. This shows that in recent years the number of frauds has increased with the growing threat of organized crime. For example, in 2009 the barometer reported £1.1 billion of fraud coming to the courts in the UK nationwide in 239 cases (the second highest in 21 years), compared to £1 billion in 197 cases in the previous year (KPMG, 2008a, 2009).

Limitations of fraud statistics

Notwithstanding the factors mentioned above, there are some problems with the recorded crime statistics (notifiable offences), in general, which apply particularly to fraud.

The use of official statistics in criminological research has been a subject of debate among academics for decades (see for instance Bulmer, 1977 and 1984; Jupp, 1989). In terms of measuring crime the most obvious point to make is that the official statistics exclude offences which are only triable in the magistrates' court. This means that the statistics do not cover the majority of offences that are dealt with in the courts, something which could have implications for measuring fraud.

The second problem is that the majority of crime is not reported at all. There are many reasons why people and organizations do not report crime including the perception that the offence is too trivial. Skogan (1984) identified a series of factors leading to non-reporting including the perceived seriousness of the offence; the possibility of claiming insurance; the past behaviour of victims and the nature of offender–victim behaviour. Carcach (1997), looking at an Australian national survey, found a similar pattern for the non-reporting of breaking and entering, robbery and assault. He concluded as follows,

> The decision to report crimes is affected by inter related complex factors, such as the personal characteristics of the victim; perceptions about the seriousness of the crime incident; previous crime experiences; victim–offender relationships; the likelihood of compensation, and attitudes towards the police and the justice system generally.
>
> (Carcach, 1997: 3)

Non-reporting of fraud is linked to the fact that it involves acts of deception. As outlined earlier, it is likely to be invisible, with some victims unaware that it is being committed. Thus Barnes and Allen (1998), in their survey of fraud in the UK and Europe, revealed that most frauds are discovered by accident. Bankers believed that they discovered 73 per cent of frauds; but respondents from insurance, construction, manufacturing and retailing reported uncovering only 30 per cent, 33 per cent, 36 per cent and 38 per cent, respectively, of frauds eventually discovered. The other issue is the fact that fraud is continuous until discovered, making it difficult to know what impact a single offender has had in terms of financial damage. However, the firms surveyed believed that only around half of all frauds were discovered in the first 12 months. The authors also found that the probability of fraud being discovered was inversely related to an organization's size, with smaller firms being more likely to discover fraudulent behaviour.

A second reason for fraud going unreported – and later being unrecorded – is the lack of a settled definition. Higson (1999) reinforces the point that fraud is essentially an umbrella phrase that covers a multitude of offences. Also, because of its secretive nature, the recording of a fraud goes through a number of stages before it can be ascertained as such. Higson characterizes this as the 'anatomy of a fraud':

- a deception/misappropriation occurs;
- an anomaly is discovered;

- the suspect perpetrator(s) are identified;
- evidence is gathered;
- the matter is reported externally;
- the evidence is strong enough to support a prosecution; and
- the offender is found guilty.

At each of these stages there is the possibility that the process will halt. Not least of the problems surrounding the subject is the distinction between what could be regarded as 'sharp practice' from an individual with a reputation for 'cutting corners to get things done' and fraud.

Another element is the attitude of personnel within organizations, including auditors and directors, towards reporting. The Cadbury Report (1992) noted that since directors are obliged to maintain adequate records, there needs to be a system of internal controls in place in order to minimize fraud. The Statement of Auditing Standards (SAS) issued by the Auditing Standards Board concluded that if external auditors discover a fraud, they should report it as soon as practicable to appropriate levels of management, the board of directors or the audit committee. Moreover, if this should implicate senior figures in the organization, they had an additional duty to inform an appropriate authority outside that organization if they considered it to be in the public interest. Such 'exceptional circumstances' include cases when auditors suspect that directors are aware of the fraud and have not reported it to a regulatory authority. However, there is confusion as to what directors are required to do in industries that are not subject to financial regulation. In his interviews with external auditors, Higson (1999) found their overwhelming response to be that the 'client decides' whether fraud is reported or not. As one respondent stated, 'Auditors are rarely in a position to report it themselves – often it is mainly suspicions of fraud, or it may be material to the accounts' (Higson, 1999: 15).

On the other hand, reporting a crime does not ensure it will be recorded, and this is something that may reflect the different agencies that deal with fraud offences, including the police, the SFO and bodies such as the Financial Services Authority (FSA). Consider, for example, how the police record crimes. Here, there are several stages, or 'filters', that a reported incident has to go through before being recorded, or not recorded, as a crime (Doherty, 1997). At each of these stages the police have considerable discretion as to what action to take. Initially, for example, the officer may consider that no crime was committed or may decide to take 'no further action', in which case the incident will not be recorded. Recording is also dependent both upon police priorities at the time the event occurs and upon the particular recording practices found in different police areas. These factors are, in turn, affected by external influences. For example, the drive to improve performance indicators may lead police in different areas to target different offences during crime initiatives.

Changes may also occur in the way offences are recorded. In 1999 certain offences, including common assaults, were counted for the first time. In terms of fraud, the Home Office Counting Rules require that, for any particular incident, the police record the single most serious offence attributed to each individual victim (Levi, 2000). For multiple offences the rules are more complicated. For example, in a credit card fraud, if the offences are committed against a number of department stores, they will be recorded separately. However, if there are multiple offences in the same store, these will be recorded as a single offence. NERA (2000) notes that the Home Office now requires the police to report not only frauds reported to them but also any frauds uncovered as part of a subsequent investigation, whether they involve other victims or not. Yet problems remain with the way known fraud is recorded, with different police forces recording it in different ways. Thus the City of London Police present fraud in terms of value per type of fraud; the Metropolitan Police rank the actual numbers of fraud by type; and West Yorkshire Police, which have one of the major fraud squads outside London, record them on a 6-monthly basis and by value of cases.

Surveys and estimates of fraud

Given the limits of the measures used to record crime, in general, and fraud, in particular, attempts have been made to gauge the size of the problem by using surveys.

The annual British Crime Survey (BCS) interviews around 50,000 people aged 16 and more to gain information about their experience of crime during the previous year. For property crimes such as theft, burglary and robbery, the BCS is considered to be one of the best barometers of trends. In terms of fraud, however, its use is limited. Though the Survey does cover certain types of fraud against individuals, such as mobile phone theft, plastic card fraud and identity theft, it does not include organizations, a significant source of fraud victimization. The 2008–09 survey found that 6.4 per cent of respondents had been victims of plastic card fraud during the previous 12 months (Home Office, 2009). Yet given its limitations, the BCS can only provide a very limited picture of fraud victimization.

Partial, though limited, compensation for this shortcoming is provided by the Home Office's Commercial Victimization Survey (CVS). This is based upon over 6000 telephone interviews with retailers and manufacturers. The last survey, carried out in 2002 and published in 2005, found that 18 per cent of retailers and 7.6 per cent of manufacturers had been victims of external fraud and 3.7 per cent and 1.6 per cent, respectively, of internal fraud (Shury et al., 2005). The average cost of these incidents for retailers was £1278 (external) and £7398 (internal), and for manufacturing £10,146 (external) and £12,759 (internal).

Some government departments conduct or commission research on the financial costs of fraud. DWP estimates of social security fraud range from £1.5 billion to £4 billion per annum (Doig, 2006). HM Revenue and Customs statistics are much more complicated due to the diverse frauds the department experiences (e.g. income tax avoidance, smuggling of tobacco and alcohol and VAT 'carousel' fraud). However, the report by NERA did estimate tax evasion at £4.04 billion in 1998–99. The Inland Revenue report for 2001 stated that in 1999–2000 tax evasion was worth £5.4 billion and for 2000–01 it was £4.5 billion (NERA, 2000).

There are also some private organizations that conduct surveys of members. The British Retail Consortium carries out an annual review of the costs of crime, including fraud, which, in 2004–05 cost retailers £68.1 million (Levi et al., 2007). Insurers also conduct surveys, the most recent suggesting losses of £1.6 billion in the UK in 2006 (ABI, 2007). Insurance fraud will be explored in more depth in Chapter 9.

Surveys have also been conducted to ascertain the extent of public victimization in respect of scams. In the USA, a nationwide survey for the National Institute of Justice found that 58 per cent of respondents had been victims of a fraud or attempted fraud (cited by Deem, 2000: 34). In the UK the Office of Fair Trading (OFT) (2006) has estimated that 48 per cent of the population have been targeted by a scam and that 8 per cent of people would admit to having been a victim of one. The OFT (2006) study also provides a detailed breakdown of the experience of victimization by type of scam.

International comparisons

This chapter ends by considering some estimates of the extent of fraud in other countries and of the challenges faced in measuring fraud there. The large professional services provider, Ernst and Young, conducts a global fraud survey every few years and in 2006 published its 9th edition. The survey covered 586 respondents from 19 countries, some of which, such as Brazil, China, India and Russia, are considered to be 'emerging markets'. It found that, in the previous 2 years, one in five respondents had experienced major fraudulent activity and that, despite increased investment in anti-fraud strategies, the levels of fraud remained similar to those found in previous reports. It also noted that, of those who had experienced a fraud, 75 per cent had done so in a developed country compared to 32 per cent from an emerging market (Ernst and Young, 2006). This survey was focused upon larger corporations and, as such, does not represent the broader private sector as a whole.

The USA experiences similar challenges to the UK with regard to fraud measurement. However, in the USA, these problems are further compounded as a result of the federal system. The result is that each of the states may define crimes, such as fraud, differently, and these definitions may, in turn, differ from those offered at the federal level and by legal case histories. Further complication will be added by the varied reporting and recording practices of the many different police and criminal justice agencies across the country. Perhaps not surprisingly there is no central repository of fraud statistics in the USA (ACFE, 2007a), with the only meaningful data on the size of the problem being that produced by organizations such as KPMG and the Association of Certified Fraud Examiners (ACFE). The KPMG survey is conducted periodically with the last survey having been completed in 2003. This is based upon telephone interviews with executives from companies with annual revenues of $250 million or more. The survey found that 75 per cent of those surveyed had experienced a fraud, up from 62 per cent in the previous 1998 survey. The most common type of fraud experienced was employee fraud (60 per cent), followed by consumer fraud (32 per cent), vendor-related/third party fraud (25 per cent), computer crime (18 per cent), misconduct (15 per cent), medical/insurance fraud (12 per cent) and financial reporting fraud (7 per cent) (KPMG, 2004b). The survey also examined the costs of these different types of fraud. The most expensive was financial reporting fraud which amounted to nearly $258 million per company on average, followed by medical/insurance fraud at more than £33 million, consumer fraud at $2.7 million, vendor-related/third party fraud at $759,000, employee fraud at $464,000, misconduct at $432,000 and computer crime at $67,000. As a survey of major private corporations, its use in estimating the extent of fraud in the USA, or even in the private sector, is limited. However, it does provide a brief snapshot of fraud trends among these types of corporations.

Another major longitudinal study of fraud in the USA is the annual ACFE *Report to the Nation*. This report, which is based upon a survey of Certified Fraud Examiners (CFE), focuses only on 'occupational fraud' and thus excludes all external frauds. In 2008 they estimated that occupational fraud cost the USA $994 billion with 7 per cent lost from corporate revenues (ACFE, 2009). This compared to 2006 where the median estimate of losses from corporate revenues stood at 5 per cent which, if replicated across the USA, amounted to £652 billion (ACFE, 2007a). Again, despite its obvious limits, this survey provides some useful trend evidence. For example, the headline figure of 7 per cent represents an increase from 5 per cent loss of revenue in the previous survey, but this had fallen from 6 per cent in the survey before that.

Australia is another federal country where jurisdictional differences conspire to make accurate statistics on the number of fraud cases very difficult to find. As with the USA there are the federal, state and territorial legal definitions, case histories and varying reporting and recording practices. In total there are nine separate jurisdictions which could contribute data (Smith, 1997). Despite these problems one estimate suggested fraud was the most expensive crime in Australia costing between AU$3 billion and AU$3.5 billion in 1996 (Walker, 1997). KPMG has conducted a biennial survey of fraud in Australia and New Zealand since 1993 which provides some trend data. As with the

American survey it focuses upon large corporations. The 2006 report found that 47 per cent of those surveyed had experienced a fraud, 2 per cent more than in 2004. Total reported fraud, from 65,000 incidents, amounted to AU\$154.9 million, with an average cost per organization experiencing at least one incident of AU\$714,000 (KPMG, 2006). This compared with the situation in 2002 when 27,657 instances produced total losses of AU\$456.7 million, with an average loss per organization experiencing at least one incident of AU\$2.1 (KPMG, 2004c).

Conclusion

Central to effectively tackling fraud, whether at an organizational level or at national level, is accurate measurement. Only by knowing the size of the problem measured over a longitudinal basis can one judge whether measures implemented to reduce it are having any effect. Most organizations and countries do not measure fraud with enough accuracy (Gee et al., 2009). This is a problem. In the UK the creation of the National Fraud Authority (NFA) with many responsibilities – one of which is more accurate measurement – may stimulate greater interest in the wider economy in measurement. There are challenges, but greater accuracy on trends is possible. It will be interesting to observe the UK as the NFA unfolds its strategy to assess the impact upon wider measurement and the strategies that then evolve to tackle it.

This chapter has examined various attempts to measure the extent of fraud in society and has illustrated that it remains a significant challenge. This is because, as the first two chapters have shown, fraud is often difficult to define and identify, let alone detect. Fraud shares with other 'white collar' crimes elements of low visibility and can often involve several victims, not all of whom will be aware that it is happening to them. This means that frauds are often uncovered only after they have been happening for a significant length of time and causing untold damage to organizations and individuals. It is also possible that some frauds will never be discovered. Even if they are detected, there is often reluctance on the part of the victims to report their losses. All these factors mean that any attempt to assess the true extent of fraud remains elusive. It also has implications for attempts for criminologists and criminal justice agencies to gain a wider understanding as to why people commit it: the subject of Chapter 4.

Further reading

- Association of Certified Fraud Examiners (ACFE): http://www.acfe. com/resources/publications.asp?copy=rttn for the ACFE *Reports to the Nation.*
- National Fraud Authority Annual Fraud Indicator: http://www. attorneygeneral.gov.uk/nfa/GuidetoInformation/Documents/NFA_ fraud_ indicator.pdf.
- Fraud Review Team (2006b) *Final Report.* Available from http://www. lslo.gov.uk/pdf/FraudReview.pdf.
- Levi, M., Burrows, J., Fleming, H. and Hopkins, M. (2007) *The Nature, Extent and Economic Impact of Fraud in the* UK. London: ACPO. Available from http://citeseerx.ist.psu.edu/viewdoc/download?doi=10.1.1. 108.8217&rep=rep1&type=pdf.
- Office of Fair Trading (OFT) (2006) *Research on Impact of Mass Marketed Scams.* London: Office of Fair Trading.
- HM Treasury for statistics on the extent of reported frauds in the UK Government. http://www.hm-treasury.gov.uk/psr_managing_risk_ of_fraud.htm.

CHAPTER 4

Why Do People Commit Fraud?

> ## Overview
>
> The aims of this chapter are to provide
>
> - an account of why people commit fraud
> - an introduction to some of the theoretical explanations relating to fraudulent behaviour
> - an introduction to attempts to profile typical fraudsters
> - an explanation of corporate fraud

Introduction

The variety of people who are fraudsters and the circumstances in which fraud happens mean that attempts to create a general explanation of why people offend are inadequate. As Dittenhofer puts it, 'There does not seem to be a specific class of people, nor a meaningful profile of the individuals who commit these crimes' (1995: 9). This mirrors similar problems when explaining white collar crime and, indeed, crime in general. Those engaged in plastic card and cheque fraud often have a history of petty offending, whereas substantial frauds in organizations may be undertaken by people with no offending history (Gill, 2005; KPMG, 2007a). Some of the case studies discussed in Part III will illustrate this issue further. However, this does not make it impossible to comment on the reasons people engage in fraudulent behaviour. Levi (1988) states that the majority of fraud occurs in the course of an occupation. Accordingly, the focus of this chapter is on the research that has been conducted on employee fraud. In what follows we examine some of the different theoretical explanations put forward to explain employee fraud as well as some of the typologies of different offenders. The chapter ends with a brief examination of corporate fraud where organizations, as a whole, become corrupt and, in so doing, 'breed' fraud.

Employee fraud

The study of fraud has largely been conducted within the category of white collar crime. This can be justified on two counts: that it shares many of the same characteristics as white collar crime; and that the element of trust is a determining factor in separating fraud from theft. As Levi (1988: 12) points out, 'Many of the most scandalous affairs of the 1980s have been generated by persons of impeccable social background and no previous record of dishonesty: that is why they were allowed to do such large frauds.'

Comer (1985) separated out clerical or administrative fraud from so-called 'blue collar' crime, on the basis that there was more opportunity for fraud in the clerical sector and for it to have a greater impact. Allen (1998) concludes that the most likely offenders within organizations are middle managers. Benson and Moore (1992) argue that employees who commit white collar variations of fraud, such as embezzlement, have different backgrounds from those committing 'street crime'.

However, it would be erroneous to conclude that fraud and white collar crime may simply be equated. Wells (1997), summarizing his own 1996 *Report to the Nation on Occupational Fraud and Abuse*, pointed out that 58 per cent of frauds were committed by employees of non-managerial status, 33 per cent by managers and 12 per cent by the owners of organizations. Moreover, if we accept Croall's definition that white-collar crime 'is committed in the course of legitimate employment and involves the abuse of an occupational role', then 'blue collar' crime should also be included in any analysis of why employees commit fraud (1992: 9).

Fraud as opportunity

There has been a great deal of research to illustrate how deviant acts are related to opportunity. During the 1970s Home Office research found that when toxic town gas was replaced by non-poisonous natural gas, suicide rates fell since, rather than using an alternative method, many potential victims chose not to take their lives. It was concluded that if a fundamental decision of life or death could be based upon opportunity, a lesser decision to commit crime might, similarly, be affected (Clarke and Mayhew, 1988). This and other factors led to extensive research into opportunity reduction which showed, among other things, how the compulsory wearing of helmets for motorcyclists led to a reduction in the number of motorbike thefts and how fitting compulsory steering locks to cars in Germany reduced the number of car thefts (see Mayhew et al., 1976). The idea that people make 'rational choices' (rational choice theory) and that these choices can be affected by manipulating the opportunities available to them generated a second theoretical approach: routine activities theory. This argues that three elements are required for a crime to occur: a motivated offender, a suitable victim and the absence of a capable guardian (Cohen and Felson, 1979).

Of course, this is only a brief summary of an extensive body of research which may be applied to fraud. Some fraudsters will be career offenders who actively search out opportunities. Others may be law-abiding citizens who, because of some personal circumstance, stumble upon an opportunity to commit a fraud and choose to do so. Many motivated offenders will commit a fraud because of the conjunction of a suitable target (victim) and an opportunity (the absence of capable guardian). However, opportunity only provides part of the picture since we need to consider explanations as to why many people, when presented with opportunities to commit fraud, fail to do so.

Individualistic explanations

Usually, these explanations seek to discover the underlying characteristics or motivations that set the offender apart from others, including pathological factors (Smegal and Ross, 1970: 1). By contrast, others stress the 'normality' of employees who commit fraud, arguing that there is little to separate them from law-abiding, or honest, colleagues (Coleman, 1999).

Dittenhofer (1995), summing up 40 years of research into fraud committed by white collar workers, points to the 'Fraud Triangle' of 'pressure', 'opportunity' and 'rationalization' as the requisite elements for committing fraud. Pressures may be financial, psychological or social and result from a confluence of opportunities in the workplace, such as employees being allowed discretion and autonomy in their working conditions, and 'distal' factors, away from the workplace such as an individual's present or past circumstances (Gill, 2005). Cressey's (1973) study found that this manifested itself in the form of problems that were 'unshareable' with others. He classified these as inability to pay debts; personal failure, either actual or perceived; business downturns; worry over status within the organization; and relations with employers. A financial element was found to be involved in all of these categories, something that is especially 'unshareable' given that managers, and others in positions of trust, are regarded by employers and others as being honest.

The notion of the fraud triangle has also been adopted and adapted in studies undertaken by KPMG, whose publication series on fraud headline this as the reason why people commit fraud against major private sector companies (KPMG, 2007a). Albrecht et al. (1984) reinforced the presence of a combination of situational pressures, opportunities and individuals' rationalizations and identified motivating factors such as living beyond their means; an overwhelming desire for personal gain; high personal debt; excessive gambling debts; close relations with customers, including pressure from family and friends; a feeling that pay does not reflect their position, or responsibilities; a 'wheeler dealer' attitude; and a desire to challenge the system. Some of these could be classified as 'instrumental', whereas others might be regarded as 'expressionist'. This mixture of motivations is reflected in Dittenhofer's (1995) classification of syndromes, which we shall consider in more depth.

(i) *The need/temptation syndrome.* This is both the most straightforward and common motivation for fraud: financial need/greed. It can arise from a variety of causes such as an addiction, a desire to enjoy a lifestyle beyond one's means, greed or family problems. In this context, Zietz (1981) points to men embezzling to sustain lifestyles, whereas women do it, primarily, to support families. People in this situation may be responding to short-term pressures, but could eventually come to rationalize their behaviour as 'normal'. Wheeler's (1999) analysis of embezzlers suggests another element: that their actions arise from fear due to external pressures such as threats of redundancy.

(ii) *The borrowing syndrome.* Here again the fraud starts as a short-term measure in response to an immediate financial problem, with the intention – whether realised or not – of paying back the sum at a later date (Dittenhofer, 1995).

(iii) *Injustice/'due me'/dissatisfaction syndromes.* Unlike the first two syndromes, fraudulent behaviour in these categories is a function of a sense of injustice felt by the employee outweighing the scale of the fraud being committed. Zeiltin suggests that dishonesty is partly due to staff compensating for the nature of their job – for example, as a reaction to a highly regulated job with little opportunity for self-expression. Mars (1982, 1984) regarded these as 'donkey' jobs (see later). Similarly, it can be a result of dissatisfaction with their employers because, for example, they have been passed over for promotion. As Tucker puts it, 'Taking property is one way employees express grievances against their employers .... It is a form of self-help' (1989: 323). The same author also points to the relationship between theft and marginality, stating that 'employees who are marginal members of an enterprise tend to be more likely to steal employer's property as a way of handling grievances' (1989: 324).

Such marginality is determined by a person's organizational status and their conditions of employment – whether, for example, s/he is permanent or short-term staff. In a 3-year study investigating fraud in the retail, hospital and manufacturing sectors, Hollinger and Clark (1983) pointed to the relationship between fraud and age, with a greater likelihood of younger employees, having less attachment to the organization, committing theft. The other factor is the degree to which the employee is socially isolated in the organization. For example, if organizations are structured so as to differentiate employees by salary and function, the result may be a sense of competition between employees, rather than a sense of community. In this context, Zeiltin has noted that fraudulent activity may not only benefit the fraudster; by relieving employee frustration, it may also allow management to turn a blind-eye, thus avoiding responsibility for improving salaries and the working environment (2001: 352).

Connected to this is the 'due me' syndrome where a long-serving employee feels that his/her contribution has not been fully recognized. Mars (1982, 1984) found that dock workers justified their fiddling by seeing it as 'an entitlement from exploiting employers' and as, therefore, legitimate behaviour (Hollinger and Clark, 1983: 77). Frauds of this type and the need/temptation types are usually small and designed primarily to make up a perceived shortfall in salary.

(iv) *The ego syndrome.* Here financial imperatives are mixed with a sense that offenders need to be recognized as achieving something more than they actually have. This links in with Maslow's (1943) hierarchy of needs which posits that once people feel secure they focus on esteem needs that promote a positive self-image where their contributions are recognized. This is reflected, for example, in the need for status among colleagues or the need for appreciation from employers (Mullins, 1992: 304).

 (v) *The Robin Hood syndrome.* This can be seen in relation to Maslow's (1943) third category of need: the need to be loved. Individuals will steal/defraud in order to give to good causes, or to disadvantaged groups, deriving little benefit themselves.

Case Study 4.1

In November 2009 an employee of a German bank was found guilty of transferring funds from affluent customers' bank accounts to those of poorer customers. The 62-year-old woman initially granted overdrafts to customers who normally wouldn't have qualified for them. In order to cover this up, she moved more than $11 million (£7 million) in 117 transfers. The bank lost a total of £1.5 million, as customers couldn't repay the loans. The woman, nicknamed the 'Robin Hood Banker', received a 22-month suspended sentence. Asked why she had done it, she replied: 'I must have helper syndrome' (Benedictus, 2009; BBC, 2009c).

(vi) *The 'it won't be missed' syndrome.* This is where the individual's motives are primarily concerned not with money, but in beating the system, or the company, in the knowledge that only a comparatively small amount is involved.

(vii) *The challenge syndrome.* Categories 4–6 describe cases where the financial aspect is less important than the satisfaction of psychological impulses. The challenge syndrome describes employees who see management systems as, in some way, a challenge to their skills or intellect in response to a need to have their achievements confirmed or recognized. Examples might include hackers who see no harm in beating computer security systems. Albrecht (1984) states that these employees are likely to commit greater frauds than those lower down the organizational ladder who are prompted primarily by financial gain.

Social explanations

Individuals in occupations rarely operate in isolation and organizational influences play a part in creating the situation within which they may offend. Such explanations point to the culture created inside organizations as a crucial determinant for law breaking to happen, with the tone being usually set by senior management and transmitted downwards (Croall, 1992: 64).

Similarly, Tucker (1989) and Zeiltin (2001), in their studies, point to the influence of the social mores of the workplace on the propensity to offend. Looking at 'blue collar' work, Horning (1970) also stresses the role of employee sub-cultures playing a role in determining the dynamics of pilfering:

> The work group subculture includes a set of norms which prescribe the types of property pilferable, the conditions under which pilfering should occur, as well as the conditions under which the workers can expect the support of the group.
>
> (Horning, 1970: 62)

In this context, the norms of the group prescribe the boundaries within which pilfering can take place. Specifically, it is permissible to pilfer property – in this case, a metal tube – from an anonymous employer. As one interviewee stated,

> When you are working for someone you can't see...I think you're
> more likely to not feel guilty...[gives name of company]...is just a
> building; it doesn't mean nothing to me except it's a place where
> I work. I don't mean nothing to them. What's a little tube to them
> they've got millions.
>
> (Horning, 1970: 56)

Mars (1982, 1984, 2001), looking at the workplace from an anthropological perspective, posited that many workers do not see activities such as pilfering, fiddling and stealing as theft at all. Perpetrators' justifications for theft arise from a combination of the desire for personal gain and factors relating to social interaction between members of a social group. In this way, it can be described as 'amateur theft' (Henry and Mars, 2001).

Goods that are taken are sold on to the group, or to 'mates', at less than an economic price, the rest of the 'payment' being in exchange for expectation of favours, or payment in kind. Thus a system of deferred 'social' debt is established among the group where favours are expected and acknowledged. Mars (1984: 172) characterizes such theft as a parallel market where 'By doing a customer a favour [the perpetrator] assures himself of a future supply of reciprocal favours...he opens an account...with social credit.' Mars goes further and seeks to classify jobs and the potential for employee theft. In *Cheats at Work* (1982, 1984) he adopted the principles of cultural theory to propose a grid-group paradigm to classify and examine varieties of occupations and their associated opportunities for dishonesty.

In Mars' analysis, the grid represents the degree to which a work culture imposes a set of behavioural characteristics on how workers interact with each other. The group measures the degree of interaction and interdependence workers have with each other in performing their work. The extent to which a culture or the grid imposes itself on individual workers is dependent on a number of factors. These include the following:

- the degree to which workers' activities are governed by rules and regulations;
- the degree to which workers in occupations are distinctive from other workers by means of symbols, such as uniforms, or the degree to which they are physically isolated from other groups;

- the degree to which employees are reliant on each other and support each other; and
- the degree to which workers compete against each other.

By way of illustration, Mars presented two extreme situations: privates in the army and sales representatives. Uniform distinguishes army privates both from other occupations and from other ranks in their own organization. Additionally, privates are subject to a series of strict regulations and defined procedures. By contrast, sales representatives are judged by their performance, and not by the degree to which they observe rules. They are also likely to be very competitive in their attitude to other sales representatives.

The group dimension involves the degree to which workers work collectively. The determinants of the strength or otherwise of the group on the individual depend on

- the degree to which workers work together in completing tasks, or the degree to which their work is complementary. An example of a strong group here would be workers on an assembly line; and
- the degree to which workers share non-work activities and the degree to which they regard themselves as separate and distinctive from outsiders.

On this basis Mars proceeded to classify occupations and the opportunities they present for dishonesty into four main types: donkeys, wolves, hawks and vultures.

(i) *Donkeys*. Donkeys are seen as occupations where there are strong grid/weak group relations. Here, workers are located in a hierarchy, but they are relatively isolated from each other in the workplace. Examples would include checkout operatives in supermarkets or train conductors. Here the usual victim is the company, rather than the customer. So, for example, the checkout operative may ring up less than the full cost of the item and pocket the difference, or may not charge friends and relations for all of their purchases. These actions would conform to Zeiltin's (2001) and Tucker's (1989) classification of employees asserting some autonomy over a highly regulated environment.

(ii) *Hawks*. Hawks are weak grid/weak group occupations where there is little regulation/supervision and little sense of interdependence or collective identity. Here fraudulent opportunities are wider than for donkey jobs and can include fiddling expenses and under-reporting of income. In some cases senior management may condone such actions as long as the job is done.

(iii) *Wolves*. Whereas donkey and hawk jobs offer opportunities for dishonesty that are essentially individualist in their nature, 'wolves' operate as a pack, or closely knit workgroup, often with a defined hierarchy. Examples include dockworkers, baggage handlers at airports and so on. Such groupings limit the opportunity for individual dishonesty.

(iv) *Vultures*. Occupations that can be classified as vulture jobs exhibit opportunities that arise out of the nature of the job and the acquiescence of management. Mars (1984) and Gill et al. (1994) place jobs such as waiters and bar work in this category, a type of work which exemplifies Zeiltin's view of theft as a form of employee control. In that regard, Mars (1973, 1982, 1984) depicts fiddling in hotel catering as a part of the industry's culture which is 'passed down' the generations. Typically, these sorts of jobs are competitive: employees working for the same employer or at the same location.

If Mars stresses the social organizational aspects of 'blue collar employee crime', Bamfield (1998) sought to explain employee theft through constructing typologies, based on research into the retail industry. In his studies he found that perpetrators

- made bogus refunds to themselves using customer receipts;
- over-charged customers;
- directed customers' points to their own loyalty cards;
- failed to enter transactions; and
- misused customers' credit cards in order to create false transactions.

There were also acts of collusion between customers and staff against the company. These included

- paying refunds to an accomplice when no previous transaction has taken place;
- making false markdowns;

- making fictitious two-for-one offers;
- allowing family members to use staff discount cards;
- providing discounts to friends by keying in a cheaper product to the till.

Following on from this, Bamfield put a series of questions to retail staff in order to ascertain the prevalence and pattern of theft/fraud and their attitudes to it. On this basis he identified four main types of employees: angels, baboons, jackdaws and crocodiles:

(i) *Angels* were opposed to all theft and did not participate in it;
(ii) *Baboons* were those who committed low-value but frequent frauds for friends and family members;
(iii) *Jackdaws* usually acted alone and for personal gain, seeing such activities as 'perks' of the job; and
(iv) *Crocodiles* represented the end of the evolutionary ladder as far as retail staff fraud was concerned. They were almost semi-professional thieves whose employment position gave them the opportunity to steal more than was the case in the other categories.

As well as constructing typologies, academics and accountants have also attempted to build up profiles of the characteristic behavioural patterns that could indicate fraudulent behaviour by employees.

Offender profiling and characteristics of fraudulent behaviour

The image of offender profiling presented to the public through the media is of a psychologist being called in to solve a crime – usually a murder. In reality, it can be used across a range of offending, using methods based on the study of behaviour observed when offenders commit crimes and applying them when investigating offences such as fraud (see, e.g. Rainbow, 2007).

In the absence of an agreement on the causes of fraud, academics and accountants have tried to construct a profile of characteristics and patterns of behaviour that could alert companies to the possibility of employees defrauding them. The

Wells Report (1997) received 2608 replies from a survey of 10,000 Certified Fraud Examiners (CFEs) in the USA. On this basis the author made some general observations about losses, mostly revolving around opportunity. For example, men were four times as likely to be involved in fraud as women were, though probably because males typically hold more senior positions than do females. However, Weisburd et al. (2001), looking at typologies of fraud offenders, found that at all levels within their classifications – including even 'medium'-level offences such as credit card fraud – men accounted for around 80 per cent of the totality of fraud. Only in one offence category – bank embezzlement – were the ratios between the sexes more or less even. In terms of age, the median loss from older employees' frauds was 28 times higher than for younger employees. Similar differences were found in respect of married men (for whom the median value of fraud committed was three times greater than for single men) and for college graduates (for whom the median value of fraud committed was five times that of high school graduates – again a reflection of greater opportunities to commit significant frauds).

KPMG (2007a) has recently published research based upon 360 cases of fraud from 700 investigations in their European, Middle Eastern and African regions. Their profile of a typical fraudster describes a male (85 per cent), aged between 36 and 55 (70 per cent), who, acting alone (68 per cent), commits a fraud against his own employer (89 per cent), for whom he has worked for at least 6 years (51 per cent). Two-thirds of all primary perpetrators were from top management. The research found that greed and opportunity accounted for 73 per cent of the 360 cases studied and that there had been no prior suspicion in more than half of the cases. In 49 per cent of cases the fraudsters had been able to exploit weak internal controls. The Report argues that three factors are connected to the commission of fraud: opportunity, arising from weak internal controls (security measures); motivation, where financial pressures cause perpetrators to commit fraud in order to fill the gap between salary and lifestyle; and rationalization, where fraudsters justify their actions on the basis that they are 'owed' the money by their employer.

In another study, Kapardis and Krambia-Kapardis (2004: 197) were able to identify the typical fraudster as a male, aged

35–45, with high educational status, who had experienced serious financial problems and who would be convicted of multiple offences. He would have no prior criminal record, would be in possession of a position of trust and would rationalize his deviant behaviour. Specializing in fraud, he would act alone, using false documents, and victimizing two or more people previously known to him. They also concluded that frauds are rarely isolated events as many offenders will stop only when found out.

Davies's (2000) study created ideal types of fraudsters. *Boasters* brag about their abilities and contacts, giving the impression that they are wealthy and successful, often entertaining guests and friends lavishly. They are also liable to inflate an individual company's prospects. *Manipulators* are in positions where they deal exclusively with a company's suppliers, or attempt to restrict other employees' access to accounts, or records. *Deceivers* try to pass responsibility on to someone else and use delaying tactics if asked awkward questions about their performance or behaviour. Finally, *Loners* rarely, if ever, take a holiday and, if they do, make sure that any work accumulated is left for them to deal with. Also, while seemingly conscientious, they are reluctant to involve others in their work.

The second factor in predicting fraudulent behaviour is to assess the environment in which it can occur. Here Davies (2000) outlines the conditions in commercial and financial organizations that are both conducive to and predictive of fraud. One such factor is an autocratic management style where a chief executive retains significant control, meaning that accountability at board level is limited. Directors' attitudes are also important and the belief that 'the ends justify the means' will soon trickle down to middle management and impact on behaviour. Individuals may also exercise power and influence greater than their formal status would enjoy, and having a forceful person in charge of a department may lead to regulations and procedures being ignored or over-ridden.

Other predictors are concerned with the quality of the staff and the degree of staff turnover. The greater the turnover, the less sense of attachment individuals feel for the organizations (see Tucker, 1989). There are also other issues such as the degree of managerial control and whether the parts of the organization are physically separated from each other.

Welfare fraud

This chapter has identified the various motivations and causes for fraud and crime by individuals in occupations. However, much of the fraud against, say, the public sector takes the form of social security fraud. Very little research has been done in this area, but comment can be made on a small number of such studies.

Social security fraud can be said to be primarily prompted by financial necessity. Thus, Renooy (1990) found that the biggest motive for participating in the 'twilight' economy was the need for money. However, there were other factors uncovered, including personal disposition to commit fraud or, indeed, to evade tax on undeclared earnings. These included whether the individual's income had fallen to below what it had been previously. Mitton (2009), in her literature review on the subject, quotes several studies from the UK that reinforce the Dutch experience. Thus, Kempson and Bryson (1994); Dean (1998); Dean and Melrose (1996, 1997); and Rowlingson et al. (1997) all support the thesis about the sudden loss of income, rather than necessarily the low level of incomes being a determining factor. Similarly, Katungi et al.'s report into people on low incomes working in the UK informal economy concluded that the main reason why people worked in the informal economy was poverty and/or as a response to a domestic crisis, such as debt. As they stated,

> At these times of crisis, being caught for fraud seemed a less threatening prospect than the immediate risks of being without food, heating or being threatened by debt collectors.
>
> (Katungi et al., 2006: x)

Mitton found that the social aspect of working was also a factor and that 'working on the side' wasn't caused by greed but as means of 'getting by' (2009: 14). However, welfare fraud does share some elements with employee fraud in that an important factor is the opportunity to commit it. Thus Dean and Melrose (1997) and Rowlingson et al. (1997) found that benefit fraudsters took up offers of jobs in casual, unskilled trades, rather than actively looking for them. Finally, as with all fraudsters, individuals' personality traits are a determining factor in the decision to commit welfare fraud.

(Hussain, 2014).

Hessing et al.'s 1993 research into benefit fraud in the Netherlands sought to extend Rooney's research by identifying a 'population' of known benefit fraudsters as opposed to an honest 'population' claiming benefit. They were then asked a series of questions designed to establish specific personal traits and get their opinions on benefit fraud and tax evasion. This found that personal traits were also seen as important, such as whether they were competitive and risk takers, factors. They also found that fraudsters were much more tolerant of all types of fraud, not just their own. In terms of personal and social influences, both Hessing et al. and Mitton (2009) found that the degree to which fraudsters were integrated/alienated into social groups that reinforced attitudes towards participation in the 'twilight' or 'hidden' economy was also an important determinant.

Explaining corporate fraud

It is also important to consider why corporations act in fraudulent ways since, in the last 20 years, several have collapsed leaving huge debts. One of these, the American energy provider ENRON, left debts of over £18 billion following systematic accounting malpractice. A similar-sized collapse occurred with the demise of Worldcom. Large-scale corporate fraud has also occurred in the UK with the collapse of BCCI in 1991 at a cost of £760 million, Polly Peck in 1991 (£450 million) and Barings Bank in 1995 (£800 million). What is striking about these collapses is the systemic nature of the fraud that precipitated them. For that reason it is worth exploring theories that seek to explain corporate fraud.

In order to understand the problem, a distinction needs to be drawn between crime committed in the course of an occupation and corporate crime, the latter being 'a form of collective rule breaking in order to achieve the organisational goals' (Braithwaite, 1985). An obvious riposte is that since organizations cannot think or act, corporate crime, including corporate fraud, cannot, by definition, exist. However, Coleman (1999) argues that although corporations are run by individuals, it is the collection of roles and functions which individuals occupy that shape conduct and constitute the structural reference point for understanding behaviour. As such an individual's morality is of less importance than the structure within which he/she operates.

Looking at the Challenger shuttle disaster in 1986, Boisjoly et al. concluded that the organization – in this case, NASA – had indeed become the 'acting unit' through which the attitudes and moral standards of the individual technicians, engineers and managers became subservient. Thus, as Boisjoly argued,

> It is no longer the character and virtues of individuals that determine the standards of moral conduct, it is the policies and structures of the institutional settings within which they work and live.

(1995: 208)

Coleman said that 'organisations are in a sense machines for controlling human behaviour' (1999: 369). Edwin Sutherland (1949) was the pioneer in the exposition and debate over white collar crime. One of his motives in discussing what he called the 'crimes of the powerful' was to extend his existing theory of 'differential association' to such offences. Differential association states that all crime can be explained in terms of a preponderance of 'criminal norms' over non-criminal ones and that an individual can learn or be 'socialized' into criminal norms by coming into contact with those individuals with a balance of criminal norms. This is fine as far as it goes, but it does not explain how and why these other criminals learned their norms. Indeed, Braithwaite (1985) went so far as to denounce differential association as a 'platitudinous attempt' to explain organizational crime. However, it did focus attention on groups and organizations as sub-cultures and as sources of crime.

Braithwaite (1985) looks at the organization itself as the source of criminality and states that whether an organization is criminal or not will depend upon the degree to which there are legitimate and illegitimate opportunities to achieve its goals. If legal avenues block an organization's goals, then it will resort to illegal ones. He further asserts that while most organizations will be structured and run to be law-abiding, there will be organizations that are 'criminogenic' by the way they exercise 'concerted ignorance' where senior management demand results, whatever the means (Slapper and Tombs, 1999: 126). Box (1983) adapts anomie theory to argue that corporate crimes such as fraud are a response to economic, financial and legal pressures and uncertainties. Consequently, he was able to demonstrate that corporate fraud increases with recession (Box, 1987). Taylor (1999) also places the major corporate frauds in the context of the de-regulation of capital markets in the 1980s and 1990s. Roberta Karmel, a former commissioner of the Securities and Exchange Commission (SEC), stated that, for US corporations, the 1980s was a 'decade of greed' where market-based solutions to economic and social problems became synonymous with greed (Pomeranz, 1995). Why are individuals driven to illegal behaviour in this context? Here Sutherland's work is useful since it relates to culture and sub-cultures within organizations. Thus Taylor (1999) sees the origin of the city scandals of the 1980s and 1990s as the growth of a culture of competition and a daily struggle for advantage. Combined with the notion of 'playing with other people's money' this created an ethic of individual irresponsibility (Taylor, 1999: 141).

Individuals are socialized into putting the corporation's objectives before their own, with the emphasis on success and peer recognition. Messerschmidt (1994) adds to this the element of gender as a determinant, with masculinity expressed in terms of the struggle for success, as he puts it:

> The corporate executive's masculinity, then, is centred around a struggle for success, reward, and recognition in the corporation and community. The image of work rooted materially in the corporate executive's gender/class position helps to create the conditions for corporate crime. Devotion to achievement and success brings about the need to engage in such crime.
>
> (Cited in Levi, 1994: 247)

Conclusion

In this chapter we have explored some of the theories that have been put forward to explain why people and organizations commit fraud. As far as individuals are concerned, studies have shown that there is no identifiable type, or class of individual, that is more prone to fraud than any other; this put into question the notion of fraud as an exclusively 'white collar' crime, as discussed in Chapter 1. The studies have also shown that fraud is committed for a variety of reasons, highlighting the importance of opportunity as well as looking at individualistic and social explanations. When considering corporate fraud, it was shown again that such frauds are committed for more than one reason and are often a result of the culture fostered by senior members of organizations and transmitted to middle and junior management. However, the further complexity of the explanations for committing fraud is illustrated by insurance fraud (which will be considered in Chapter 10). Many normally law-abiding citizens are prepared to and do commit insurance fraud. This illustrates the importance of opportunity and the different perceptions people have towards different frauds. This is highlighted further in Chapter 5 when we consider the politics of fraud.

Further reading

- Coleman, J.W. (1999) Motivation and Opportunity: Understanding the Causes of White-Collar Crime. In M. Levi (Ed.) *Fraud: Organization, Motivation and Control (Vol. 1: The Extent and Causes of White-Collar Crime)*. Aldershot: Ashgate.
- Cressey, D. (1973) *Other People's Money*. Montclair, NJ: Patterson Smith.
- Dittenhofer, M.A. (1995) The Behavioural Aspects of Fraud and Embezzlement. *Public Money and Management*, January–March.
- Kapardis, A. and Krambia-Kapardis, M. (2004) Enhancing Fraud Prevention and Detection by Profiling Fraud Offenders, *Journal of Criminal Behaviour and Mental Health*, 14(3), 189–201.
- KPMG (2007) *Profile of a Fraudster 2007 Survey*. Available from http://www.kpmg.co.uk/pubs/ProfileofaFraudsterSurvey(web).pdf.
- Mars, G. (1984) *Cheats at Work: An Anthropology of Workplace Crime* (2nd edition). London: Allen and Unwin.

CHAPTER 5

The Politics of Fraud

Overview

The aims of this chapter are to provide

- an account of the low priority generally given to fraud
- an outline of the key policy-related developments occurring in respect of fraud in the UK over the last decade
- an overview of the main 'players' in the politics of fraud

Introduction

There are a wide range of different crimes that secure the attention of policy-makers and politicians, but until the recent Fraud Review, fraud was not one of them. As Levi argues, '...there is little political impetus to devote resources to fraud, which (social security fraud excepted) has largely been excluded from the "law and order" focus of tough on crime policies in the UK' (2003: 38). Yet fraud is a major problem. Chapter 3 illustrated that UK fraud – at a very conservative estimate – could account for over £30 billion of losses per annum. Despite that, there is only one police force in England and Wales – the City of London Police – that has fraud as a performance indicator consistently. Though many areas of deviance, including terrorism, anti-social behaviour, street robbery, gun crime, people trafficking and illegal immigration, are the focus of attention for politicians and policy-makers, fraud – with the possible exception of benefits fraud – has not received the attention it warrants. At last this is beginning to change and later we shall discuss some of the most significant initiatives to have emerged during the last few years. To begin with, however, let us consider why fraud is such a Cinderella issue.

Value given to fraud

One reason why fraud has not been given a higher priority in the past is that certain crimes lend themselves more easily than others to public outrage, thereby provoking a political response. Sex offenders do not represent a threat to the vast majority of the population, but media reaction to this type of crime, particularly when it involves a child, frequently whips the public into a frenzy. By contrast, fraud – with the exception of benefits fraud – lacks a significant public profile and generates minimal popular concern. Thus, the fact that millions of pounds are lost to the exchequer through VAT fraud has not led to the tabloid newspapers running campaigns to demand instant and tough government action. At a more mundane level a headmaster who fiddles £20k from the school budget or a pensioner who is tricked into parting with a few thousand pounds in a scam generally do not raise public outrage demanding tougher sentences for fraudsters and greater police resources to tackle the problem. Indeed, many 'frauds' are considered neither serious crimes nor crimes at all. For example, in January 2008 a British MP was suspended by the House of Commons and ordered to pay back over £13,000 following the discovery that he had employed his son as a research assistant while the latter was a full-time student, supported from public funds. To compound this matter, no evidence existed to show that the MP's son had actually done the work for which he had been paid (BBC News, 2008, para. 12). In many occupations the fiddling of expenses on such a scale would result in termination of employment and a referral to the police for prosecution. A fellow MP stated the following in the debate on this matter:

> If this example of what I would see as embezzlement had occurred on this scale in, say, the Refreshment Department, we would expect the person involved to leave the employment of this establishment on the day it was discovered. I believe that we should treat ourselves in a similar manner to how other people employed by this House would be treated.

> (Hansard, 31 January 2008)

Yet in this case, the Standards and Privileges Committee did not consider it worthy of referral to the police, considering their punishment sufficient. The much larger scandal concerning the expenses of dozens of MPs and Lords which broke a year later provoked even greater outrage and, at the time of writing (March 2010), only four decisions to prosecute were taken by the Crown Prosecution Service (CPS) (3 MPs and 1 Peer) (CPS, 2010).

In fact, there is much evidence to suggest the public is ambiguous in its attitude to fraud. In a survey carried out in 2005, respondents were asked to rate different types of fraud by their severity, and scores of 5 (very wrong) and 4 (wrong) were at the top of the scale. The fraud rated as most serious was credit card fraud which was rated 'very wrong' or 'wrong' by 96 per cent of respondents. This was followed by housing benefit fraud, 89 per cent; unemployment benefit fraud, 84 per cent; NHS prescription charge fraud, 83 per cent; TV licence fraud, 77 per cent; insurance fraud, 64 per cent; and finally VAT fraud, 61 per cent (NHS CFSMS, 2007b). In another study for the Association of British Insurers (ABI), members of the public were asked how far they considered certain behaviours 'acceptable' or 'borderline acceptable'. The results are ranked as follows:

- Knowingly taking too much change from a shop – 55 per cent
- Smuggling and selling alcohol and cigarettes – 48 per cent
- Exaggerating an insurance claim – 40 per cent
- Knowingly buying stolen goods – 36 per cent
- Not paying road tax – 36 per cent
- Making up an insurance claim – 29 per cent
- Shoplifting – 29 per cent
- Using someone else's credit card – 6 per cent (ABI, 2003)

What this and other surveys appear to show is that the public are generally less concerned about taxation frauds than they are about benefit frauds or about frauds that might affect them directly, such as credit card fraud.

One factor explaining the public attitude to fraud is its ambiguous status. Some acts of deviance – possessing a handgun or plotting to blow up a train – are obviously criminal. Yet the legal and moral ambiguity of some acts make their categorization as frauds uncertain – something which is often exploited by defence barristers to bewilder juries. For example, the 2005 trial into allegations of fraud and corruption relating to the London Underground Jubilee Line extension failed to produce a verdict, the collapse of the proceedings costing the taxpayer an estimated £60 million. Similarly, the 1995–96 Maxwell Trial cost £30 million and led to two acquittals (Timesonline, 2005). When doubt can be cast on the nature of alleged frauds – as to whether they were mere 'mistakes', the result of marginal, but non-fraudulent, business practices, or a product of complex fund movements – attitudes and responses may become blurred.

It would be wrong to suggest that UK policy-makers have paid no attention to fraud. However, policy intervention has tended to be fragmented, being dealt with as an 'add on' to other policies and rarely treated as an issue in its own right. Levi (1987) identifies dozens of statutes, including the Theft Act of 1978 and the Banking Act of 1979, which have made provisions relating to commercial fraud. Yet, he also notes the power of business to influence proposals in its own interests rather than in the interests of law enforcement. This powerful lobby is far more likely to be listened to than other interest groups located in less powerful or more deprived communities. Consequently, this may also explain the limitations of past government activity in respect of fraud.

The key fraud developments in the UK

Given the above discussion, it is no surprise to find that legislative and political developments relating to fraud in the UK have been relatively sparse over the last 25 years. There have been pockets of activity, notably in respect of social security fraud, but in terms of general government-backed reviews and legislation, the field is limited.

Chapter 2 explored the background to the 2006 Fraud Act and identified the two Law Commission reviews that ultimately led to that legislation. In 2003 the Criminal Justice Act was passed. This would have enabled the judge to decide in complex fraud cases not to use a jury. The clause never came into force because it required activation through an additional vote from parliament and attempts to reintroduce it with the Fraud (Trials without a Jury) Bill have, so far, failed. The 1987 Criminal Justice Act created the Serious Fraud Office (SFO), which arose from the recommendations of the Roskill Committee in 1986. These are the only statutes of note that have been directed at fraud generally and even here it could be argued that the SFO has a very narrow brief.

In terms of large government investigations into dealing with general fraud, there have been two major reports. The first was the Roskill Committee that reported in 1985 and was initiated by the Home Office and the Lord Chancellor's Department. The impetus for the review aroused from a desire to explore the replacement of jury trial in complex fraud cases, although its terms of reference and the final report were much wider. Its terms of reference were as follows,

> To consider in what ways the conduct of criminal proceedings in England and Wales arising from fraud can be improved and to consider what changes in existing law and procedure would be desirable to secure the just, expeditious and economic disposal of such proceedings.

> (Roskill, 1986: 5)

The Report made 112 recommendations, many of which – including the creation of the SFO – were implemented. However, many were not. For example, the Committee recommended the creation of an independent Fraud Commission which was to have a central responsibility for monitoring the efficiency and effectiveness with which fraud cases are dealt with. The Commission was also to publish an annual report, make recommendations for improvements in dealing with fraud and act as a co-ordinating body for the various relevant agencies (Roskill, 1986). Other significant recommendations that were never implemented included creating a career structure for fraud officers and providing greater resources for them (Doig, 2006).

Since Roskill there have been various reforms and initiatives aimed to enhance anti-fraud capacity. These include better prevention through the creation of Credit Industry Fraud Avoidance System (CIFAS), reforms to enhance the fight against social security fraud (to be considered further in Chapter 11), the creation of the NHS CFSMS and numerous reports making recommendations for enhancing best practice from bodies such as the Audit Commission and the National Audit Office (Levi, 2003). Gaps still exist, however, most notably, declining police resources, differing approaches to fraud across the public sector, continued failure to secure convictions in some high-profile frauds and the lack of a national co-ordinating body. It is within this context that on 27 October 2005, the Attorney General (AG) announced the establishment of the Fraud Review. This created a review team tasked to report jointly to the AG and the Chief Secretary to the Treasury by late spring 2006. It was headed by Jenny Rowe and colleagues from Attorney General's Office (AGO), but supported by experts from the NHS CFSMS, the City of London Police, the SFO, the Home Office and the CPS. The press release announcing the review defined its terms of reference as follows:

> to consider the scale and costs, both direct and indirect, to the country of fraud, the role of Government and industry in tackling it, as well as its prevention, detection, investigation and prosecution or punishment. It will also look at the scope for improving the current arrangements, with the aim of reducing the amount of fraud and minimising the harm it causes to the economy and wider society.
>
> (Criminal Justice System Press Release, 2005, para. 2)

After an interim report the final report was released in July 2006 (Fraud Review Team, 2006a, 2006b). This set out 62 recommendations including the establishment of a National Lead Force (NLF) for fraud (to be based on the City of London Police), the creation of a National Reporting Centre (NRC), the creation of a National Fraud Strategic Authority (NFSA) (subsequently the word 'Strategic' was dropped from the title), the extension of sentencing provisions, recommendations on information sharing and the establishment of a group to consider the introduction of plea bargaining. At a conference organized by the AGO in March 2007, it was announced that all the recommendations would be implemented.

Some of these recommendations merit further discussion. For example, the role of the NLF (established in April 2008 in the City of London Police's Economic Crime Department) will be to act as a centre of excellence in fraud investigation disseminating best practice, providing advice to investigators and assisting other forces in the most complex and challenging cases. The NRC – which was to be housed by the City of London Police, but has subsequently moved to the National Fraud Authority (NFA) – will accept reports from individual and corporate fraud victims, provide a service to victims, allocate cases to the most appropriate body and undertake analytical services. In November 2009 it was announced the NRC was to be called Action Fraud.

Another recommendation was for the creation of the NFSA (now NFA). The NFA was formally established on 1 October 2008 as a new Executive Agency of the AGO. The Authority was charged with the development of a national fraud strategy, the first such strategy being launched on 19 March 2009. It will also be required to measure fraud (as well as to encourage other organizations to do so) and to monitor the performance of all bodies, public and private, in tackling fraud. It will also disseminate best practice in tackling fraud, promote anti-fraud strategies and seek to resolve problems and conflicts arising between some of the many organizations with an interest in fraud. The Fraud Review also recommended that the NFSA should establish a national system of accreditation for fraud investigators and that the police should consider greater use of civilians in fraud investigation.

The Report also suggested that the Department of Constitutional Affairs (DCA) and NFSA should work to identify guidance and measures to improve data sharing, that more data matching of multiple sets of data should be carried out, that the National Fraud Initiative (NFI) (a data-matching exercise undertaken by the Audit Commission) should be widened to include all public authorities and that, in order to aid this, there should be faster release of data on deceased persons.

There were also a series of recommendations relating to trials and subsequent sanctions. It was advocated that a plea bargaining system should be considered for serious cases, that there should be measures to allocate judges to cases with more expertise in the area of fraud and that specialist training should be offered to judges. Possible changes over disclosure were also advocated, as well as the greater use of electronic documents in trials. The Review also proposed that new sentencing guidelines be issued with the Fraud Act 2006 and that the maximum sentence in most serious fraud cases should be increased from 10 to 14 years. Other measures advocated on sanctions included a proposal for the range of non-custodial sentences to be extended; and for powers to be put in place to wind up companies, award compensation to victims and appoint a Receiver to recover misappropriated property. Linked to this, a power to prohibit/restrict an offender from engaging in profession/commercial activities was also advocated. Finally, the Review proposed that a Financial

Court jurisdiction should be established to link the Crown Court with the division of High Court and that greater use of administrative and civil court options should be considered (Fraud Review Team, 2006b).

It is also worth noting two implications of the Fraud Review. The establishment of the NFA, with a remit to measure fraud more robustly, is likely to encourage more active measurement within organizations. This may change organizational attitudes to fraud which, in the past, have tended to regard it as 'the price of doing business', the financial penalties of which should be transferred to consumers where possible. As Gee (2007: 9) argues,

> The future promises to be a more professional one where business decisions in respect of fraud are more rational and more focused on the bottom line – reducing losses to fraud and freeing up money for better systems and services.

Accurate measurement on a regular basis is likely to turn fraud into a business cost, with greater pressures coming from shareholders, taxpayers and governing bodies to bring about its reduction. This is likely to mean more investment in counter-fraud capacity, one element of which will be investigative resources. Many larger bodies already have investigative capability through their own in-house or contracted resource, but capacity does vary and more resources are likely to be required. However, this will still not eliminate demands being made of the police when investigations are coming to a conclusion and assistance is required in conducting searches and interviewing reluctant suspects under caution when they are unwilling to cooperate with fraud investigators voluntarily. There may also be a 'trickle down' to smaller organizations unable to afford a counter-fraud resource who see the benefits in more accurately measuring fraud and as a consequence place greater demands upon the police for help in tackling it.

The second implication concerns the capacity of the police to deal with the likely increase in demand for investigative services. Even with the changes proposed, there is still going to be a lack of capacity for many individuals and small organizations becoming victims of fraud. Larger organizations and better-off individuals have always been able to hire their own counter-fraud capacity or turn to private investigators or forensic accountants.

Others, however, will continue to rely upon already-limited police resource. Though the Fraud Review suggests that police fraud squads should be ring-fenced, this is likely to be inadequate and, ideally, more resources need to be dedicated to the investigative infrastructure. In addition to this, however, resources might be made more effective were they to be centralized in one national body (Button et al., 2008).

The 'players' in the politics of fraud

At this point, it would seem appropriate to consider how the new organizations proposed by the Fraud Review will fit into the broader field of counter-fraud, a field made up of a wide range of statutory and non-statutory bodies.

Government departments and statutory central bodies

For most crimes in England and Wales one would consider the Home Office as the main government department for co-ordinating policy and practice. In that regard it has been central in new developments to tackle anti-social behaviour, enhance security, reduce the risk of terrorism and reduce street crime and burglary. Yet it was the AGO, not the Home Office, that led on the Fraud Review. Even so, with its central role in protecting the public from terrorism, crime and anti-social behaviour, the Home Office is of central importance in fraud, its influence and control extending to the 43 police forces and to the Serious Organised and Crime Agency (SOCA). The Home Office also compiles the main crime statistics in respect of fraud, sets the main perfor-mance indicators relating to crime, in general, and has also led on numerous statutes concerning fraud.

The most important government department relating to fraud in recent years has been the AGO, which serves the AG and Solicitor General, who are appointed by the Prime Minister. The AGO acts as guardian of the public interest and as chief legal adviser to the government. It also has overall responsibility for the Treasury Solicitor and supervises the Director of Public Prose-cutions (DPP), the Director of the SFO, the Revenue and Customs Protection Office, HM Crown Prosecution Service Inspectorate and the DPP for Northern Ireland. It is the AGO's responsibility for the SFO which makes its role in fraud so important. However, the AGO is also responsible for the CPS, the Treasury Solicitor's Department, the Department of the Director of Public Prosecutions of Northern Ireland, the CPS Inspectorate and the Revenue and Customs Prosecution Service, all of which are also important components of the counter-fraud infrastructure (AGO, n.d.). The work of the AGO in the Fraud Review has also enhanced its credibility and leading status in counter-fraud work. The establishment of the NFA, discussed earlier, which the AGO will oversee as an Executive Agency, will also cement its position as the most important government department in this area.

Various other government departments are also important in the fraud infrastructure. HM Treasury has an interest in the reduction of fraud as a means of controlling public expenditure and it publishes an annual survey of fraud in government departments. HM Revenue and Customs (HMRC) employs staff to tackle numerous forms of tax fraud. The Department for Work and Pensions has the largest group of fraud investigators (3000+) and one of the biggest fraud problems (£2 billion plus per annum). However, its desire not to engage in the broader policy-making process was exposed by its exclusion, along with HMRC, from the remit of the Fraud Review. Another important player is the NHS Counter Fraud Service (which is part of the Business Services Authority and was formerly known as the NHS CFSMS). With its central unit setting policy and co-ordinating the fight against fraud, its staff and the 300 plus Counter Fraud Specialists (CFS) employed by NHS trusts have been very successful in the fight against fraud. The NHS CFSM (as it was then) has also been very influential and played a key part in the Fraud Review.

The final two central bodies that are important in this field are the Audit Commission (AC) and the National Audit Office (NAO). The AC is charged with ensuring that public money is spent economically, efficiently and effectively in local government, health, housing, criminal justice and fire and rescue services. The AC is a quasi-independent non-departmental public body within the sphere of the Department for Communities and Local Government. It undertakes a range of functions that are important in countering fraud. All the public bodies in its sphere have an auditor from the AC who can be contacted regarding allegations of fraud, abuse of office and misuse of funds. Indeed, the AC under the Public Interest Disclosure Act 1998 is a recognized 'whistleblower' for employees in local authorities and the NHS (Audit Commission, n.d.). Depending upon the allegation, the auditor will pursue action which may involve bringing in other bodies such as the police. The AC also proactively tackles fraud through the NFI where data from the different bodies it supervises are brought together for analysis. Finally, the AC also publishes a wide range of reports, some of which cover issues relating to fraud and corruption.

The NAO audits the accounts of national government, agencies and other public bodies in England and Wales (Accounts in Scotland and Northern Ireland are covered by Audit Scotland and Northern Ireland Audit, respectively. Devolved issues in Wales are covered by the Wales Audit Office). The NAO reports directly to parliament and works very closely with the House of Commons Public Accounts Committee. Its functions relate to financial audits and reports concerning value for money. Though the NAO's auditing functions give it an important role in tackling fraud, it is the reports the organization produces, exposing good and bad practice, which make it particularly significant.

Investigative and prosecution agencies

We now turn to some of the main investigative and prosecution agencies in England and Wales. The SFO, which was discussed earlier vis-à-vis the Roskill Committee, is actually a government department, even though its role is as an investigative and prosecution agency for serious fraud. The Director of the SFO is accountable to the AG and its jurisdiction extends to England, Wales and Northern Ireland. Its workload focuses upon complex and large frauds. Generally, a number of issues influence its decision to accept a case. Does the value of the fraud exceed £1 million? Is there a significant international dimension? Does the case raise issues of widespread public concern? Does it require highly specialized knowledge? Is there a need for the SFO's special powers? Writing in 2003 the then head of the SFO, Rosalind Wright (2003: 10), argued, '[The SFO] has been a signal success.

In the 15 years of its existence, it has investigated over 1000 allegations of major and complex fraud and has prosecuted hundreds of defendants.' The 2006–07 Annual Report revealed that over the last 5 years the SFO had dealt with 166 defendants of whom 102 had been convicted to produce a conviction rate of 61 per cent (SFO, 2007a). Nevertheless, the SFO has had a controversial history, largely due to its failures to secure convictions in some very high-profile fraud cases such as Maxwell (at a cost of £30 million) and the Jubilee Line Extension (at a cost of £66 million). More recently, it has drawn criticism for its decision not to continue its investigation into BAE systems regarding allegations of bribery to Saudi Arabian officials in pursuit of a major arms contract. In 2007 the SFO's future was under ministerial review with rumours of its disbandment and suggestions that its constituent parts might be moved to SOCA and the CPS (Bowers and Wintour, 2007). A subsequent review by Jessica De Grazia was published which was very critical of the SFO and in July 2009 it was announced the SFO budget was to be reduced from £51.5 million to £43.4 million in the forthcoming financial year, a 15.7 per cent cut (Mason, 2009).

It has already been suggested that the police capacity in respect of fraud is weak, the total strength of police fraud squads having been estimated at 524 officers (Fraud Review Team, 2006a). There is also the Dedicated Cheque and Plastic Crime Unit drawn from the Metropolitan and City of London forces but funded by the banking industry through APACS. Historically the most important body in this field is the City of London Police because of its location in the centre of finance. Indeed, the City force was the only one to have fraud as a priority. As a result of the Fraud Review it is now the National Lead Force on fraud. In 2005 the SOCA was established as a result of the amalgamation of the National Crime Squad, National Criminal Intelligence Service, part of HMRC (dealing with drug trafficking and criminal finance) and part of UK immigration (organized people smuggling). Its main functions relate to investigating and disrupting organized crime, but in doing so 10 per cent of its resources are suppose to be allocated to fraud (SOCA, 2006).

In addition to the traditional law enforcement community there are a number of specialized public bodies investigating and prosecuting fraud focused upon protecting government revenues. The DWP and HMRC have already been discussed, but there are other bodies with sizeable numbers of investigative staff as well. The Financial Services Authority (FSA) is responsible for regulating the financial sector and there are number of areas where different types of fraud fall within the ambit of its investigative staff, such as insider dealing, market abuse and money laundering. Similarly, there are a number of divisions within the Department for Business, Enterprise and Regulatory Reform (formerly the Department for Trade and Industry) that deal with fraud. The Insolvency Service within this department has responsibility for fraud relating to bankruptcy and the Companies Investigation Branch investigates trading malpractice by companies. The Office of Fair Trading (OFT) also conducts campaigns aimed at vulnerable consumers who may fall victim to scams, such as bogus prize draws, and has a small investigative capacity. Other departments with small numbers of counter-fraud staff include the Ministry of Defence (MoD) with the MoD Police Fraud Squad and Defence Fraud Analysis Unit focusing upon procurement fraud; the Department for the Environment, Food and Rural Affairs (DEFRA); and the Rural Payments Agency which has a small group investigating fraud relating to agricultural subsidies.

There is also a strong investigatory framework in local government. Housing benefit is administered by local authorities and the occurrence of substantial fraud in this area has led most local authorities to employ dedicated counter-fraud staff or set up counter-fraud departments. The investigation of fraud relating to the payment of council tax is also a responsibility of these or other fraud investigators within local authorities. Local authorities also have responsibility for trading standards and their duties include countering forgery, counterfeit products, enforcing weights and measures and consumer protection.

It is also important to note the substantial numbers employed by the private sector dedicated to the investigation of fraud. In the financial sector many organizations have their own in-house counter-fraud staff. The Fraud Review Team's (2006a) first report estimated that the six largest banks alone employed 2500 investigators. On top of that there are firms of private investigators which offer counter-fraud services as well as professional services firms such as KPMG and Ernst and Young who offer both investigative and forensic accounting services.

National NGOs

In order to deal with fraud various non-governmental organizations (NGOs) have been established to help tackle the problem or provide forums to further the cause of countering fraud. One of the most prominent examples is CIFAS which is a member-based organization largely rooted in the banking and financial sectors, though now offering services well beyond these. It was founded in 1988 and has grown to provide a range of fraud prevention services. The most significant is the fraud avoidance system which enables organizations to share information on fraudulent applications. This enables data on names, addresses, telephone numbers and the like to be marked up, thus triggering further investigation should they arise again in an application. CIFAS also provides training services (CIFAS, n.d.). Another important NGO is the charity Public Concern at Work which provides independent whistle-blowing services for individuals and organizations. For many employees not confident in their own organization's whistle-blowing mechanisms, this provides a free service where suspicions can be reported and expert advice offered (Public Concern at Work, n.d.). There are also some examples of sector-based NGOs that play a key role in tackling fraud, such as the Insurance Fraud Bureau (IFB) which is funded by insurers and will be discussed in greater depth in Chapter 11.

Some NGOs pursue more policy-orientated aims. The Fraud Advisory Panel, a charity initiated by the Institute of Chartered Accountants in England and Wales in 1998, could be described as a think tank dedicated to fraud. It has developed proposals in a number of areas including legal reform, investigation, education and training (Fraud Advisory Panel, n.d.). Most of the UK is also covered by Fraud Forums which bring together key stakeholders to share best practice, enhance partnerships and provide training. One of the most successful is the North East Fraud Forum which was founded in 2003 and has since run eight conferences, 20 master classes and three 6-day training courses for over 2500 delegates. It has also run campaigns, produced DVDs and helped other regions to establish forums (North East Fraud Forum, n.d.). There are also forums based upon particular sectors such as the Telecommunications UK Fraud Forum (TUFF) – as its name suggests, TUFF brings together telecommunications companies.

Major interest groups

The fraud problem has also generated a wide range of interest groups keen to influence policy in government and in investigative and prosecution agencies. One type is made up of groups that have wide-ranging interests, of which fraud is one. Examples include the ABI, the British Bankers Association, the Chartered Institute of Public Finance and Accountancy and the other accountancy professional bodies and practices. Some of these, such as KPMG, offer fraud services and also seek to influence policy – in this case by conducting research on fraud and working with key bodies to ensure that the most effective policies emerge.

A second type is made up of organizations exclusively concerned with fraud, most of which are representative associations. The largest in the UK is the Institute of Counter Fraud Specialists (ICFS) which has about 300 members drawn from both public and private sectors. It holds conferences and seminars, it has an informative website and it is emerging as a key voice for the 'profession'. Only accredited CFSs (who secure their award from the Counter Fraud Professional Accreditation Board) can join this body and if it is to become a dominant voice on par with some of the other interest groups, it needs to penetrate further into the 11,000 plus CFSs (Button et al., 2007).

The Association of Certified Fraud Examiners (ACFE) is an American-based organization with a worldwide membership (100+ countries) that represents over 45,000 members. It provides training, organizes conferences and seminars and also provides a range of other professional services (ACFE, 2007b). Central to its existence is its professional award of Certified Fraud Examiner (CFE) which is a key qualification for many accountants, auditors, fraud investigators and loss adjusters. The UK Chapter of the ACFE has a few hundred members. Another representative association is the Local Authority Officers Investigators Group (LAIOG). It represents several hundred investigators working in local government, providing a forum for sharing best practice through seminars and conferences. There is also a body dedicated purely to insurance fraud investigators known as the Insurance Fraud Investigators Group (IFIG), which is considered in Chapter 10.

Conclusion

The expenses scandal, relating to the UK Houses of Parliament and the financial crisis have potentially raised the profile of fraud in both policy-makers' and the public's mind. Combined with the creation of new institutional infrastructure such as the NFA is beginning to make its mark on the public and private sectors (and even more importantly has the potential to have an even greater impact). We may, therefore, be on the verge of a major change in the way fraud is dealt with in the UK. Greater research, more awareness of the problem, superior investment in counter-fraud capacity and more fraudsters being caught and punished could all become more common in the public sector. However, there are also risks to the movement towards this agenda. The economic downturn and its impact upon public finances may lead to cuts, or perhaps even the abolition of some of the structures created and already in existence. In the pre-election skirmishes there has been much talk of culling quangos, which many counter-fraud bodies are. There are also many industry funded bodies and associations which may struggle in the more difficult economic circumstances. Many companies and organizations may also be tempted to cut counter-fraud capacity, which is often seen as a luxury and not the essential it should be, in trying times. And research funding – which is so badly needed into many aspects of fraud – is always one of the first casualties of budget cuts. There are therefore many risks to fraud growing to become the issue of importance it should be.

This chapter has examined the politics of fraud. It began by exploring the value given to fraud by the public, policy-makers and politicians. In doing so it highlighted the generally low priority given to the problem. The chapter then went on to review the small number of major initiatives that have been pursued by the government to tackle fraud over the last 25 years. These included the Roskill Commission of 1985, the Fraud Act of 2006 and the recent Fraud Review (2006a and 2006b). It focused in particular on the Fraud Review and the many recommendations that have been made which will substantially change the way fraud is countered in England and Wales. Finally, we explored the multiple government bodies, NGOs and interest groups with a stake in fraud in England and Wales.

Further reading

- Fraud Review Team (2006b) *Final Report*. Available from http://www. aasdni.gov.uk/pubs/FCI/fraudreview_finalreport.pdf.
- Levi, M. (2003) The Roskill Fraud Commission Revisited: An Assessment. *Journal of Financial Crime*, 11(1), 38–44.
- Button, M., Johnston, L. and Frimpong, K. (2008) The Fraud Review and the Policing of Fraud: Laying the Foundations for a Centralised Fraud Police or Counter Fraud Executive. *Policing*, 2(2), 241–250.

Some key bodies:

- National Fraud Authority: http://www.attorneygeneral.gov.uk/nfa/Pages/default.aspx.
- Serious Fraud Office: http://www.sfo.gov.uk/.
- City of London Police: http://www.cityoflondon.police.uk/citypolice/.
- NHS Counter Fraud Service: http://www.nhsbsa.nhs.uk/fraud.

Tackling Fraud

CHAPTER 6

Preventing Fraud

Overview

The aims of this chapter are to provide

- an analysis of the importance of opportunity in committing fraud
- an outline of the principles of situational crime prevention and how it can be applied to fraud
- an assessment of the effectiveness of situational measures
- an introduction to other preventative measures

Introduction

In the next three chapters we examine how fraud is tackled by organizations, focusing in this chapter on its prevention, then considering its investigation (Chapter 7) and its prosecution/regulation (Chapter 8). In this chapter we draw upon some of the issues discussed previously. For example, in order for prevention to be effective it is vital to understand fraudsters' motivations (see Chapter 4). We also examine the different strategies used to prevent fraud, dividing them into a number of discrete types: situational strategies, cultural strategies and deterrence.

Before embarking upon this, however, it is important to re-emphasize that fraud has a diversity of forms and, because of this, the strategies required to prevent it need to be equally diverse. Thus, internal frauds perpetrated by employees of an organization require the mobilization of particular strategies such as the screening of staff, the modification of internal procedures and campaigns to change culture. Conversely there is a wide range of external frauds, particularly against ordinary members of the public, where prevention rests largely with state agencies, rather than the victims. For example, local trading standards organizations and the Office of Fair Trading (OFT) take a lead in campaigns that seek to prevent people becoming victims of scams.

Fraud as opportunity

Chapter 4 demonstrated the important role of opportunity in fraud. Realization of this fact has generated a considerable body of research illustrating the benefits of situational crime prevention techniques in the minimization of opportunities. That is not to say that other factors – psychological, social and so on – are unimportant in explaining fraud, but as Farrell and Pease (2006: 187) argue,

> This does not mean that other social problems should not be tackled – they should – but they are primarily tackled for reasons other than crime prevention. In contrast, influencing the immediate circumstances and context in which crime takes (or does not take) place is the avenue with greatest chance of preventative success ...

The importance of prevention to remove opportunities is further illustrated by fraudsters' accounts of how and why they were able to pursue their frauds. In a study based upon interviews with 16 fraudsters convicted of stealing 'large sums' of money ranging from £65,000 to £25 million, it was found debts, greed, boredom, blackmail, temporary insanity, desire for status and corrupt company culture were some of the motivations for fraud (Gill, 2005). Central to the fraudsters' accounts of how they were able to commit their frauds were weak organizational controls (i.e. poor security). Typical of such weak controls was the tendency for only small samples of financial transactions under a specified cost level (e.g. £750) to be reviewed. Another was for not enough staff to be employed to undertake appropriate checks. These accounts also revealed the weakness of auditing arrangements. It is worth quoting the perspective of one fraudster, 'Eric', who defrauded his company of several million pounds.

> Accountants can only work on the figures they have got, audit the same. Auditors came to see me and I just lied to them and gave them false pieces of paper and that was that. The checking process was abysmal. I was not worried because I have 20 years experience of auditors. Had they been better at their job I would have been in trouble. What I was doing was simple, but the lack of process enabled me to do what I did, the absence of systems, the lack of attention to detail, the lack of knowledge in auditing and accounting. I had three audits in those 18 months .... I gave the auditor the information and he said, 'thank goodness for that', and my thought was, 'you complete muppet'... There was no interrogation from audit and that was good for me.
>
> (Cited in Gill, 2005: 40)

It is also interesting to note that most of the offenders did not consider what they were doing to be high-risk and, as a result, had little fear that they would get caught. Most were caught as a result of a change beyond their control, such as the appointment of a new auditor able to spot anomalies.

In profiling fraudsters from multiple studies Kapardis and Krambia-Kapardis (2004: 197) concluded that frauds are rarely isolated events and that many fraudsters will only stop when found out. Therefore, in cases where controls are weak and the chances of apprehension low, strong accounting controls and security procedures could have an impact upon the incidence of fraud. They argued,

> ... effective preventative measures against fraud are undoubtedly strong internal accounting controls and stringent staff employment-screening procedures to minimise opportunities for fraud to occur, and better vetting of job applicants by employers to screen out the predator, career fraud offender with a criminal record, often for deception offences.

However, in the majority of cases studied fraudsters did not have prior criminal records; what was more important was the opportunity to commit fraud, the crises in the lives of the fraudsters and the nature of the organizational culture. Indeed, it is interesting to note that the collapse of Barings Bank, the result of an £850 million fraud by an employee, started with a £20,000 fraud undertaken to cover a fellow employee's mistake. The controls, management and auditing arrangements of Barings were extremely poor and, at one stage, when the losses were relatively manageable they could have been stopped easily (Leeson, 1996: 93). Instead, over 3 years, the losses culminated in the collapse of the bank.

Preventing fraud

The first stage in any preventative strategy is to identify all potential fraud risks and their likely severity. Following that, risk management strategies will be enacted to remove or reduce those risks (Jones, 2004). Central to this process is the accurate measurement of fraud losses so that preventative and other strategies can be monitored in order to assess their impact upon levels of fraud.

Fraud risk reduction strategies encompass a wide range of preventative tools. A useful starting point for analyzing the different tools used by those seeking to prevent fraud is Ronald Clarke's distinction between increasing the effort, increasing the risks, reducing the rewards, reducing provocations and reducing excuses. Originally this was applied to preventing 'volume crimes' such as burglary, theft and robbery. However, the same principles can be applied to preventing fraud. Figure 6.1 illustrates some of the strategies that can be used to prevent internal fraud distinguished by these three headings. The discussion that follows will focus largely, though not exclusively, on internal fraud.

Increasing the effort

These are measures that seek to make the effort of commissioning a fraud more difficult. One of the most important is access control which, in the context of fraud, relates to who gets to key positions of responsibility and who the organization does business with.

Access control

Access control in Clarke's original model refers to measures to restrict access to the protected area to selected people with the

Increasing the effort	Increasing the risks	Reducing the rewards
Access Control Vetting of staff Vetting of vendors/contractors Restricted access – via more extensive vetting – to positions of responsibility where there is a high risk of fraud **Target Hardening** Rigorous internal controls Strong audit	**Increasing Surveillance** Rigorous internal controls Rigorous audits Independent whistle-blowing lines for employees Post-employment vetting Information sharing Drug tests Integrity tests Data-mining and matching	**Target Reduction and Removal** Making accounts of size that is small as possible Removal of accounts, products where risk of fraud. **Deterrence through Sanctions and Redress** Pursuit of criminal, civil and employment sanctions Seeking return of monies lost through courts
Reducing Provocations Workplace relations	**Reducing Excuses** Rules Alert conscience	

Figure 6.1 Clarke's situational crime prevention strategies applied to internal fraud [adapted from Clarke (2005: 46–47)].

aim of making it harder for criminals to go about their work. In the case of fraud these same principles can be applied. Vetting (or screening) of staff, contractors and vendors can be pursued to minimize the risk of potential fraudsters securing access to places (whether physical or online) where they are able to pursue frauds. It can also mean procedures that restrict certain trusted employees to positions where there are greater opportunities to commit frauds.

Vetting of staff is seen as a major strategy in the prevention of internal fraud. It can also be used to protect against external frauds through application to vendors and contractors, although in the main it is an internal tool. The profile of fraudsters and the discussion of their motivations examined in Chapter 4 revealed many who were not career fraudsters but 'ordinary' people presented with an opportunity that, because of personal circumstances, they chose to pursue. For these people vetting will be of limited use – bar post-employment vetting which will be discussed shortly. Nevertheless, vetting can help to prevent fraud by stopping those bent on committing it, or those with a propensity towards it, from joining an organization in the first place. This does not mean that anyone with a slight blemish should be rejected. Rather, information may be secured that enables a risk-based decision on employment to be made.

Case Study 6.1

In October 2007 a woman was convicted of defrauding her company of over £2 million. She spent over £120,000 on an entertainment system for her home, £110,000 on a luxury kitchen and thousands on eating in top restaurants and top-of-the-range holidays. She had been employed as a Finance Director for a Marketing Agency. In her previous job, however, she had been convicted of stealing £25,000 from her employers and sacked and punished with a community service order. She was also a 'lapsed trainee accountancy student'. This is a very good example of where vetting by the employer could have saved them a great deal of money and embarrassment (Edwards, 2007: 7).

Vetting of staff consists of several elements. The first is the verification of information contained in an application form (or CV). Some studies have shown that significant numbers of people lie and embellish their CVs. One study found that a third of people questioned made false claims about their qualifications, experience, interests and past jobs. It also found 20 per cent of the 1000 workers surveyed had exaggerated their CVs (BBC News, 2001a). Therefore, checking the qualifications claimed by applicants, writing to previous employers to confirm previous jobs and periods of employment and checking references form the foundation of most vetting strategies. Yet, in the study just cited, a third of the 350 managers surveyed did not check applicants' CVs, because the task was considered too time-consuming. In circumstances where identity theft is reported to cost the British economy around £1.3 billion per annum (Cabinet Office, 2002), however, the need to check documents for veracity is vitally important.

There are various additional checks that an employer can undertake on prospective employees. These include checks of criminal records, credit records and company directorships.

In England and Wales the Criminal Records Bureau will disclose criminal records in respect of certain occupations such as accountancy, legal services, gaming, medicine and the like. Some organizations mandate additional tests, such as drug testing of prospective employees; and particularly extensive background checks will be made on people applying for sensitive positions in the civil service, the police and security services (Murray, 1996). There are also specialist services offered by bodies such as Credit Industry Fraud Avoidance System (CIFAS). This is a fraud prevention body that holds information from its members companies on past applications which are considered fraudulent. This enables names, addresses and so on to be cross-checked to assess if they have been previously logged by CIFAS which then enables the organization to conduct further enquiries or simply reject the application (CIFAS, n.d.). 192.com Business Services also offer data on fraud risks related to specific addresses/persons which is extensively used by the retail sector (192.com Business Services, n.d.).

The most extensive vetting involves the interviewing of friends, colleagues and previous employers about a prospective employee. This occurs most commonly in the public sector on behalf of bodies such as the police, the military and the Security Services. Some private sector organizations also carry out vetting for the most senior appointments, usually employing specialist screening or private investigative companies to do so. Typical of the services offered by the many firms engaged in this expanding market are the three levels of vetting offered by Carratu International set out in Figure 6.2.

In the UK there is also a British Standard (BS) 7858 Security Screening for persons employed in a security environment. This sets out procedures for screening which include providing proof of identity, past record of education and employment, character references, criminal convictions and evidence of any bankruptcy and court judgements. Misrepresentation or failure to disclose are grounds for dismissal (British Standards Institution, 2006).

Target hardening

In mainstream crime prevention, target hardening encompasses items such as locks, bolts and barriers, the purpose of which is to

Level 1	Level 2	Level 3
Confirmation of address and other contact details	Level 1 +	Usually for the very highest appointments and includes Level 1 + 2 +
Credit referencing and history including bankruptcy search	Property ownership search	
	Search of judicial and legal data	Additional relevant research to confirm the probity of the applicant
Confirmation of employment history and references	Company directorship search	
	Full media/database search	
Validation of relevant educational qualifications and membership of professional bodies		

Figure 6.2 Carratu's employee vetting services [adapted from Carratu (n.d.)].

make it more difficult for the offender to attack the target. Target hardening for purposes of fraud prevention usually involves the deployment of various internal management controls.

Many fraudsters will get past the vetting controls of an organization and many others will have no obvious blemishes in their character to expose the threat they may pose. In those circumstances, as Levi (2006: 274) argues, '... the focus shifts to internal management systems and compliance monitoring (for internal frauds), and creditworthiness checking ...'. Organizations use a wide range of controls and compliance procedures for these purposes. Jones (2004) provides a comprehensive list of internal controls set out in Figure 6.3. Some of these can be considered as not just target-hardening measures but also methods that increase the risks of getting caught through surveillance.

A vital part of control lies in the organization's audit function. The importance of this aspect was highlighted earlier with the examples of 'Eric' and the Barings Bank fraud. Audit falls into two parts: internal audit and external audit. In the latter the audit is usually undertaken by an external firm of accountants or by one of the public accounting bodies such as the National Audit Office (NAO) or Audit Commission. Internal audit is conducted by employees of the same organization, usually under different line management arrangements. Traditionally audit was the process of checking the accuracy, validity and disclosure of the

Control	Description
Physical	Strong-rooms, locks on cabinets, controls on keys, access codes, etc.
Accounting	Financial reconciliation. For example, does the salary list reconcile with the actual staff members on personnel records, do invoices reconcile with actual services and products purchased? When cheques are written, does the writer have the appropriate invoice? These require systems to undertake cross-checks.
Authorization	Certain transactions should require authorization by a supervisor. Does this take place and are the authorizations monitored to ensure compliance with the system? This is sometimes done by a signature, a stamp or, in a computerized system, often by a password.
Structural	Are duties clearly distinguished with structures of decision-making mapped?
Supervisory	Are day-to-day decisions monitored and checked to ensure overall compliance with the system?
Separation of Duties	Are separate people responsible for undertaking functions where there is a risk of fraud if only one person does so? For example, are the purchasing and payment functions separated? Ideally separation should occur between decision to purchase, placing the order, checking of goods and payment of supplier.
Managerial	This is a catch-all and covers the regular monitoring and updating of the system.

Figure 6.3 A traditional classification of internal controls [adapted from Jones (2004: 55–56)].

financial accounts presented and signing them off as 'true and fair'. With the computer age, however, the process has evolved into 'systems based audit' (SBA) which, once higher risk areas have been identified, allows more targeted sampling in the audit to take place (Jones, 2004). Despite the advances in technology there have been some prominent examples of failure of both internal and external audit. The most spectacular was the collapse of ENRON which, despite some fundamental problems in its finance and governance, was signed off by Arthur Anderson (its auditors). The subsequent collapse also led to the end of Arthur Anderson. The example of 'Eric', cited above, also reveals how weak and familiar auditors can lead to failures in audit. To combat such risks it is often advocated that external auditors should be periodically changed. Audit would also fit under the next category of increasing the risks and, in particular, increasing surveillance.

Increasing the risks

These are strategies that seek to make the risks of offending greater and the perpetrator more likely to get caught.

Increasing surveillance

In the traditional model of crime prevention, surveillance involves appropriate design techniques, the use of CCTV and the employment of security staff. These all have a role to play in the prevention of certain frauds. For example, an attempt to use a stolen credit card might be aborted if CCTV is directed at a check-out. However, as with other fraud prevention strategies, increasing the risks encompasses diverse strategies. Some of the target-hardening measures discussed above are also forms of surveillance. For example, a manager checking a payment against an invoice constitutes an act designed to increase the chances of getting caught, serving as a barrier to perpetrating a fraud.

There are also various data-mining and data-matching programmes that can be applied to databases of information to identify anomalies that can be investigated further. Although these are primarily used as a pro-active investigative tool, these can also be used as a surveillance tool. For example, KPMG claims in their promotional literature:

> We can use sophisticated, market-leading data analytics to sift through large volumes of company information to test controls and highlight fraud 'red-flag', trends and anomalies. This is a faster, more efficient and reliable way to find possible control weaknesses and suspicious activity and save costs through reduced fraud.
>
> (KPMG, 2007b)

There have been a number of high-profile frauds where the mechanisms available to expose fraudsters have been weak (Levi, 2006). In such a situation, an employee making allegations against a superior may be put at risk. To combat this problem legislation such as the Public Interest Disclosure Act 1998 has encouraged organizations to set up so-called 'whistle-blowing' hotlines to raise concerns anonymously and in confidence (Borodzicz, 2005). In the National Health Service (NHS), where the majority of fraud and corruption is committed by it's own employees, there is a very well-publicized hotline 0800 028 4060 staffed Monday to Friday 8 AM–6 PM dedicated to fraud and corruption. Other organizations simply have a telephone number they can ring, though the smaller the organization the less effective this is. To combat social security fraud in the UK, the DWP has set up the National Benefits Hotline, which anyone suspecting someone of committing benefits fraud can ring 0800 854440. Alternatively, some organizations opt into bodies such as Public Concern at Work, which offers independent whistle-blowing services.

Some organizations, as well as vetting new staff, vet existing ones, including those whose risk factors have risen, thus requiring further investigation. There have been numerous examples of fraudsters who, in a personal crisis, start defrauding the organization they work for. There have also been cases, once discovered, that have revealed staff living well beyond their means. Therefore, post-employment vetting offers an opportunity to discover potential problems before they precipitate fraud. Some organizations employ private investigators to look into the lifestyles of employees whom they consider to be potential risks. Vetting strategies include searching for property and credit data and may also involve private investigators observing staff outside working hours, looking at the car they drive, the restaurants they eat at, whom they visit and so on.

Case Study 6.2

A school headmistress was convicted of defrauding the school of £500,000 in 2003 and was jailed for 5 years. She spent the money on luxury trips, holidays in exotic locations, jewellery, designer goods, electrical gadgets, top restaurants and even £7000 on shoes using the school credit card. She dominated the school and bullied any person who challenged her. In 1 year, 26 teachers left the school. An independent whistle-blowing mechanism would have provided an opportunity for one of the teachers to raise concerns. Post-employment vetting may also have raised concerns on whether the luxury lifestyle she pursued could be afforded by even a well-paid headteacher (BBC News, 2003a).

Case Study 6.3

A Deputy Director of Finance with Metropolitan Police was convicted after defrauding £5 million over 8 years from the his employers to fund a lifestyle as the 'Laird of Tomintoul' in Scotland. His lavish lifestyle was well beyond his means and there was no scrutiny of it. There were also very poor controls over the accounts he was responsible for in the Metropolitan Police, which had been highlighted by external auditors but not acted on. He had also been hired to his post with no formal accountancy qualifications! (Jones, 2004: 248).

Linked to post-employment vetting some organizations may also impose mandatory drug tests. As the example below illustrates, there are a range of changes in behaviour which are associated with drug problems. Most significantly, drug habits are expensive and difficult to fund from one's salary (Figure 6.4)

Some organizations also use integrity testing where members of staff are given the opportunity to commit frauds by corrupt employees or clients – in reality investigators play fraudster's roles.

Repeated drug use is associated with:

- Mood swings
- Unusual irritability and aggression
- A tendency to become confused
- Abnormal fluctuations in concentration and energy
- Impaired performance
- Poor timekeeping
- Increased short-term sickness
- Deteriorating relationships with colleagues, customers and management
- Dishonesty and theft (associated with funding an expensive habit)

Figure 6.4 The impact of repeated drug use on an individual [adapted from Health and Safety Executive (n.d.)].

Reducing the rewards

If the previous measures fail, the third strand to Clarke's model comes into play. This consists of strategies aimed to minimize potential rewards and make offenders weigh up the costs and benefits associated with the commission of fraud.

In mainstream crime prevention, target removal and reduction involves things like replacing coin-operated electricity meters with those operated by payment cards. Comparable techniques can be used for dealing with internal and external fraud. For example, in 1997 the incoming Labour Government set up a scheme to encourage training through the establishment of Individual Learning Accounts (ILA). Under this scheme an individual could buy a course for a fee of £250 to include a £200 subsidy from the Government. Some training providers claimed that people were on courses when they were not and the system led to the emergence of non-existent courses, non-eligible courses and eligible courses with inflated fees. The result was fraud amounting to £110 million and the termination of the scheme and replacement by a new one with greater preventive capacity (Doig, 2006). Similar preventive techniques can be used to address problems of internal fraud. For example, payroll fraud – where ghost employees are added or inflated salaries are paid – is relatively common. To combat this some organizations simply contract out the payroll function to an external body.

Deterrence is an important part of preventative strategy. As Hollinger and Davis argue, 'Perhaps the single most important factor influencing employees' decisions to steal involves whether they will get caught or not' (2006: 218). Getting caught, however, is only one aspect of deterrence; the other is what the punishment is likely to be. Historically, the criminal justice system has been poor at dealing with fraudsters: if apprehended, they were unlikely to face criminal prosecution; if prosecuted, they were unlikely to be convicted; and, if convicted, their sentences were likely to be relatively light (Hollinger and Davis, 2006; Levi, 2006; Fraud Review Team, 2006b).

Thus, it is vital that those who perpetrate frauds are detected as soon as possible and, where appropriate, the detection is publicized to staff to discourage others from wrongdoing. In addition to this, the punishment must fit the crime. In the past, many fraudsters have simply been dismissed, thereby avoiding criminal prosecution (Levi, 2006). By contrast, in the NHS, a policy of 'parallel sanctions' is pursued. This involves a combination of criminal prosecution, disciplinary procedures and – where a licence to practice is involved – attempting to have the fraudster struck off. In addition to this, the NHS will also pursue a civil action to recoup its losses. In 2006 a former NHS dentist was disbarred by the General Dental Council after being convicted of defrauding the NHS of almost £200,000 by making claims for work he had not done. He was jailed for 18 months and proceedings were pursued to recover the monies lost (BBC News, 2006a).

Reducing provocations and excuses

Earlier, in Chapter 3, the importance of workplace relations in facilitating fraud was noted. Research by Hollinger and Davis (2006) suggests that the more positive employees' views are towards their organization, management and supervisors, the less workplace deviance there is likely to be. Therefore, measures to combat negative attitudes in respect of pay, working conditions, participation, workplace relations and the like can have a positive impact. In other words, strategies to improve workplace relations can also tackle some of the underlying causes of fraud, though doing this is usually beyond the remit of counter-fraud specialists.

There is also much that can be done to remove potential excuses and rationalizations for fraud. For example, it is important to have clear rules about acceptable behaviour and the sanctions that will follow from their breach. Thus, if it is made clear that fiddling travel expenses will be treated as fraud, staff will have no excuses when sanctions ensue. Central to reducing provocations and excuses is changing organizational culture, which will be discussed shortly.

The effectiveness of situational prevention

The main critique of situational measures is that because they do not tackle the underlying causes of the offending behaviour, they merely displace the crime elsewhere. Reppetto (1976) has identified five forms of displacement:

  (i) *Temporal*. The crime is committed at a different time.
 (ii) *Tactical*. The crime is committed using a different method.
(iii) *Target*. The crime is committed against a different target.
 (iv) *Territorial*. The crime is committed in a different area.
  (v) *Functional*. A different type of crime is committed.

Barr and Pease (1990) have added a sixth category:

(vi) *Perpetrator displacement.* Prevented crimes are committed by different offenders.

However, when applied to fraud, rather than to traditional 'volume' crime, the relevance of some of these categories seems less strong. As was said previously, many fraudsters have no previous criminal background and may commit fraud because of a personal crisis or because of a fraudulent opportunity presenting itself. If preventive techniques are strong, such people are unlikely to engage in functional displacement (e.g. robbery or burglary) or to target another part of the organization or another territorial location. Arguably, then, these various categories of displacement might be more appropriate to persistent organized fraudsters though there is very little research to assess the displacement effects of different fraud-prevention measures (Levi, 2006). Given this situation, alternative methods need to be considered. One of these involves trying to change organizational culture.

Changing the organizational culture

It was noted in Chapter 4 that internal fraud – and some external fraud – is linked to cultures of dishonesty within organizations. In some organizations, sub-cultures emerge that subvert and undermine formal organizational rules. In their definitive study of workplace dishonesty, Hollinger and Clark (1983) found that workmates' perceptions of theft could have a stronger influence on employee behaviour than organizational rules. In another study, Horning (1970) found that employees regarded different types of theft with varying levels of acceptability. For example, the theft of small items was seen as acceptable, the theft of larger items less so and stealing personal property was considered definitely off limits!

Changing cultural attitudes towards fraud is therefore an important preventative strategy. The NHS has been at the forefront of this approach to countering fraud. In order to change the culture of staff and patients to wrongdoing, various techniques are used. First, the NHS publicizes its activities in order that potential fraudsters, whether patients or staff, know that there is an active and effective body that can apprehend and punish them. Accordingly, maximum publicity is given to successful investigations and to the sanctions fraudsters have received. Campaigns are also pursued with posters, advertisements and articles in newsletters; and each year there is a high-profile 'fraud awareness month'. Finally, presentations are given to staff about the impact of fraud and the potential sanctions fraudsters might face (NHS CFSMS, 2007a).

There are also campaigns targeting external fraud. In the UK, benefits fraud has been the subject of repeated advertising campaigns. However, a critic of one DWP campaign ('We're on to you') suggested that it pandered to myths about social security fraudsters funding luxury lifestyles when the reality, for most fraudsters, was simply securing enough money to get by. For that reason, it was claimed, such campaigns would have little impact on claimant attitudes towards fraud (Grover, 2005).

It is also worth trying to identify the signs when an organization's culture makes it prone to fraud. Jones (2004) identifies a range of signals that might be indicative of such a state of affairs and suggests that it is worth trying to develop techniques to prevent them developing (Figure 6.5).

Signals illustrating organization prone to fraud:
- Climate of stress/fear
- Unquestioning acceptance of superiors
- Unquestioning acceptance of 'practice and custom'
- Unreasonable perks
- Lack of recording
- Immoral/unethical work practices
- Open tolerance of petty crime

Figure 6.5 Signs of organizational culture prone to fraud [adapted from Jones (2004: 188)].

Conclusion

The opportunity-driven motivations of many fraudsters mean there is significant scope to have an impact upon fraud using the appropriate tools. The five strands of situational prevention advocated by Clarke can be adapted to fraud to create effective tools and, when combined with strategies to change organizational culture, set the foundations for substantial resilience to fraud, particularly in organizational settings to counter internal fraud. There is also a part to play in prevention for many external frauds and frauds against the general public. Many of the latter type of frauds, however, prevention falls largely upon state and corporate bodies such as the police, OFT and banks who do not have enough time and resources to spend on this, although there is a role for the victim too. Here in areas such as identity fraud and mass marketing frauds there has been some work done in the UK to enhance prevention by bodies such as OFT, but much more could be done. This is also the case with many organizations. One of the many ambitions of the National Fraud Authority (NFA) is to enhance prevention. Given the potential and the relatively low cost of many strategies, there is much scope for enhancing the resilience of UK Plc to fraud through better prevention.

This chapter has explored the issue of fraud prevention. It began by revisiting the motivations and explanations of how and why fraudsters commit fraud. This illustrates the importance of opportunity. The chapter then examines the situational crime prevention model and applies it to fraud. It identifies a range of strategies that fit within this model such as the screening of staff and contractors, audit and whistle-blowing. The potential risk of displacement is then discussed before we move on to consider other preventative strategies, such as changing an organization's occupational culture and addressing problems of workplace relations. Prevention has a major part to play in a counter-fraud strategy, but there will always be those who slip through the net. This is where it becomes important to detect and investigate fraud, the subject of Chapter 7.

Further reading

- Association of British Insurers (ABI) Website and publications at http://www.abi.org.uk/Publications/Publications_Product_List.aspx.
- Kapardis, A. and Krambia-Kapardis, M. (2004) Enhancing Fraud Prevention and Detection by Profiling Fraud Offenders, *Journal of Criminal Behaviour and Mental Health*, 14(3), 189–201.
- Levi, M. (1998) *The Prevention of Plastic and Credit Card Fraud Revisited*. HORS Paper 182. London: HMSO.
- CIFAS http://www.cifas.org.uk/ Website of Credit Industry Fraud Avoidance System.

CHAPTER 7

Investigating Fraud

Overview

The aims of this chapter are to

- review the wide range of organizations and agents involved in investigating fraud
- introduce the wide range of strategies used to investigate fraud

---

Introduction

This chapter will explore the investigation of fraud. In the first part of the chapter, we identify the wide range of organizations involved in fraud investigation and demonstrate the limited role of the police. In the second part of the chapter, some of the strategies used to investigate fraud are considered. In doing this we shall focus on conventional civilian-led fraud investigations directed at internal fraud. It is also important to note the very important role played by the police, Serious Organised Crime Agency (SOCA) and the Serious Fraud Office (SFO) in some of the most serious frauds and that some of the more sophisticated strategies for dealing with the most serious and organized frauds are beyond the scope of this chapter.

The investigative infrastructure

In recent years there has been a growing recognition of the extent to which policing has become pluralized or fragmented

(Bayley and Shearing, 1996; Johnston, 2000). This process is particularly evident in respect of fraud investigation where pluralization has a long history and where public police organizations have only a minor investigative presence. This was made clear in the Fraud Review (2006a) which found there to be only 524 police officers in England and Wales dedicated to the investigation of fraud. This compares to around 8000 Accredited Counter Fraud Specialists (ACFS), themselves only a portion of those actively involved in fraud investigation (Button et al., 2007). Some of the main groups of fraud investigators in the public sector are listed in Table 7.1. The largest number is employed

Table 7.1 Largest groups of fraud investigators in the public sector

Organization	Type of fraud investigated	Approximate staffing
Her Majesty's Revenue and Customs (HMRC)	Excise and tax	7500 (including drugs investigators)
Department for Work and Pension (DWP)	Benefits	3250
Local Authorities	Housing benefit fraud	2000
The Police	High-volume fraud + economic crime	524
National Health Service (NHS)	All fraud against the NHS	344
Serious Fraud Office (SFO)	Serious and complex fraud	300+ contractors
Department of Trade and Industry (DTI)	Companies/Insolvency Acts Offences	150
Financial Services Authority (FSA)	Insider trading/market abuse, misleading statements and practices	46
Office of Fair Trading (OFT)	Cartels	32
Serious Organised Crime Agency (SOCA)	Organized fraud by criminal gangs	Yet to be determined

Source: Adapted from Fraud Review Team (2006a).

by HM Revenue and Customs, although the figure of 7500 staff listed in the table overestimates the actual number of fraud investigators because many focus upon drugs, smuggling and more general administrative work. By comparison, the 3250 DWP staff listed in the table are all actively engaged in the investigation of social security fraud. For that reason, it can be said that the DWP employs the largest single group of fraud investigators in the country. Indeed, this number is greater than the operational strength of many police forces. The third largest group is made up of local authority fraud investigators. Here, there are around 2000 staff spread across the 450-odd local authorities in the UK, though this is a conservative estimate, NAO (1997) research estimating that, on average, each local authority employs around five fraud investigators. Their work focuses mainly on housing benefit fraud, council tax fraud and internal fraud, and many of those working on housing benefit fraud work closely with DWP investigators. In fourth place, with 524 fraud squad officers comes the police, followed by the NHS with over 300 staff employed in its central NHS CFSMS and throughout the various NHS Trusts. The rest of the table lists some of the other major groups. As well as those listed, however, there are pockets of investigators spread throughout the public sector in government departments and in agencies such as the UK Identity and Passport Service (UKPIS), the UK Charities Commission, the Department for International Development and the Driver and Vehicle Licensing Agency.

In addition to the state sector there is substantial private sector involvement in fraud investigation. This takes two forms: in-house investigators employed by commercial companies and contract private investigators. The bodies employing most fraud investigators include financial institutions, credit reference agencies, insurance companies and telecommunication firms, most of which have dedicated in-house fraud investigators. The Fraud Review Interim Report (2006a: 71) identified the six largest UK banks as, alone, employing 2500 investigators.

The contract investigative sector is also sizeable. It has been estimated that there are as many as 15,000 private investigators in the UK and most either offer or specialize in fraud investigation (George and Button, 2000). In recent years private investigators have been joined by a growing number of prestige accountancy practices offering investigative services as well as forensic accounting. For example, KPMG Forensic has a fraud investigation and dispute advisory team of over 300 people. This consists of ex-police officers, forensic accountants, expert witnesses, data-mining consultants and fraud risk management specialists. The team investigate and advise on suspected fraud and deception cases. They have clients across the globe and take on frauds ranging from less than $50,000 to major international crimes costing in excess of $1 billion (KPMG, 2008b).

The types of staff engaged in fraud investigation also vary as Figure 7.1 illustrates. Police fraud investigators generally hold constabulary powers and are trained as detectives, although some police forces are beginning to experiment with civilians (HMIC, 2004; Fraud Review Team, 2006b; Button et al., 2008). As constables they have powers of arrest, search and, subject to regulation, the ability to undertake intrusive surveillance. These powers, which are not held by the vast majority of fraud investigators, mean many have to co-operate with the police on certain investigations to undertake searches and arrest uncooperative suspects. Next, there is a group of fraud investigators with varying special powers in HM Customs and Excise, the DWP and local authorities. Many of these powers concern access to information in respect of suspects. For example, the Social Security Fraud Act 2001 (otherwise known as the Fraud Act) provided an extended framework for the investigation of fraud in the UK and Northern Ireland. It did this by increasing the powers of benefit fraud investigators under the Social Security Administration Act 1992,

Type of staff	Background	Powers
Counter fraud specialists	Civilian fraud investigators largely employed in the public sector, but growing in the private sector trained according to common packages overseen by the CFPAB.	Most have no special powers, although some in the DWP have special powers to secure information.
Civilian fraud investigators	Diverse range of fraud investigators found in some public sector bodies, but largely in-house private bodies and private investigators utilizing wide range of different training packages.	Generally have no special powers, although some public bodies may have specialist powers to secure information.
Police fraud squad officers	Police officers who have undergone basic detective training and specialist fraud training.	Powers of constable.

Figure 7.1 Investigative fraud staff.

to be able to gather personal information on benefit claimants. For almost all other fraud investigators there are no special legal powers.

The discussion so far has illustrated that the largest group of fraud investigators are civilians. Up until the late 1990s there were no common standards on training or education, and no professional associations. However, over the last decade there have been attempts to professionalize fraud investigation, the majority of them in the public sector, with the most significant development being the emergence of the Counter Fraud Specialist (CFS). Counter Fraud Specialists are civilian fraud investigators (largely employed by the DWP, local authorities and the NHS) who are professionally trained and accredited in techniques relating to the prevention, detection, investigation and prosecution of fraud. CFSs are united by undergoing a common training package accredited by the Counter Fraud Professional Accreditation Board (CFPAB) and the University of Portsmouth, a package that leads to the award of Accredited Counter Fraud Specialist (ACFS). There is also a career route provided through the CFPAB leading to higher awards of Certified Counter Fraud Specialist (CCFS) and Graduate Counter Fraud Specialist (GCFS) (Button et al., 2007). The CFPAB has also sought to set a code of professional conduct for CFSs. In addition there is a professional association that has formed to represent CFSs, the Institute of Counter Fraud Specialist (ICFS). There have been over 11,000 accreditations of CFSs, but there are more likely to be about 8000 active CFSs (Button et al., 2007).

One of the core functions of the CFS is the investigation of fraud and related offences. Most frequently cases will be referred to a CFS through whistle-blowing facilities, data-matching exercises or anomalies thrown up by audits. A CFS has knowledge of the law relating to fraud and, in some cases, will also have specialist legal knowledge on a particular area such as benefits law. Drawing upon this knowledge, the CFS will be expected to plan and initiate the investigation of suspected fraudsters. Investigations arise from a variety of sources in the different organizations, from intelligence-led referrals in the DWP to high-risk applications in the United Kingdom Identity and Passport Service (UKIPS). Nevertheless, a CFS would be expected to use the appropriate databases, documentary evidence, transcripts of interviews, witness statements, surveillance evidence and other relevant information to conduct an investigation. Central to this role is the ability to interview suspects and witnesses according to Police and Criminal Evidence (PACE) Act 1984 and other regulations (or equivalent in Scotland). Nevertheless, the extent to which a CFS conducts interviews under caution varies. It happens rarely in organizations like the Abbey and UKIPS (where invitations to attend interviews under caution by suspected fraudsters are rarely accepted) but is quite commonplace in local authorities and the DWP (where the disincentive of losing benefits may apply if co-operation in interviews does not occur).

Another common function that distinguishes the CFS from traditional fraud investigators is pursuing preventative work, though commitment varies between organizations, with the NHS probably being the most committed. Making presentations on fraud to enhance an anti-fraud culture and focusing upon intelligence gathering and analysis or data matching and sharing are common tasks undertaken. Surveillance is not a core function of all CFSs, although most are trained in it as part of their accreditation process. In some organizations, such as Abbey, no surveillance occurs; and there are others where its occurrence is rare or where, as in the NHS, it is entrusted to specialist sections. For the DWP and local authorities the ability to conduct surveillance in compliance with the Regulation of Investigatory Powers Act 2000 and other relevant legislation is a key part of their role. The preparation of cases for criminal prosecution or lesser sanction is another important responsibility. However, the number of cases that end up in court varies between the different CFS-employing bodies. All CFSs would be expected to be able to prepare a case for handover to their own prosecution department (as with the DWP, and the NHS) or to the police for criminal prosecution (as with UKIPS). CFSs are also required to prepare cases for the pursuit of civil recovery, the termination of employment, the application of some other sanctions specific to the organization or, ultimately, criminal prosecution. CFSs are also expected to give evidence in court in order to facilitate successful prosecutions where deemed appropriate.

Finally, it is important to note that there are many civilian fraud investigators working in the public and private sectors who are not CFSs and there are many working in other occupations who become involved in fraud investigation. For example, both uncover fraud and in some cases, will conduct fraud investigations. Computer forensic specialists can also play a significant role. Having outlined the infrastructure of fraud investigation we shall now examine how fraud is investigated.

Investigating fraud

We now consider some of the strategies used by CFS and civilian investigators to investigate fraud bearing in mind what we said earlier – that police play only a minor role and many fraud investigations do not result in criminal prosecutions. The variety of organizations involved in investigation, the different types of fraud being investigated and the varying powers available to those involved make generalization difficult. Bearing that in mind, we shall generalize where appropriate but remember to point out organizational differences where that is necessary. In doing this, our main focus will be on internal frauds. It is also worth re-emphasizing that in many private sector organizations, the aim of the investigation is not to invoke the criminal justice system but rather to secure the return of any monies lost. The fact is that private sector organizations have learnt several things from experience. The first is that it is impossible to recover all losses incurred through criminal prosecution, and that the costs involved may not be financially justifiable. The second is that prosecution may involve several interviews with the police, detailed analysis of financial records and lengthy involvement in court hearings for staff, all factors bearing economic and organizational costs. The third is that admitting fraud victimization in public may have negative consequences for corporate reputation. It may also expose security weakness that could provoke further attacks (Smith, 2005: 8).

Detection of fraud

Many frauds are detected through proactive strategies. The proactive approach involves scanning the organizational environment through the analysis and testing of organizational systems, situations and operations to identify areas of risk for the purpose of developing or improving measures and systems of control that would pre-empt wrongful acts (Fox et al., 2000: 8). It is about probing the organizational systems to find out about potential areas susceptible to fraud. A very common way frauds are uncovered is through the general auditing process. There are more specialized forms of proactive auditing. For example, the Audit Commission National Fraud Initiative (NFI) undertakes proactive exercise once every 2 years for over 1300 public sector bodies (including the NHS, Local Authorities, The Pensions Service and Companies House) by data-matching such things as known dead persons against lists of claimants. The results of the data matching are fed back to the respective public bodies for further investigation. NFI was launched in 1996. Due to its success in 1998 (detected fraud and overpayments to the value of £42 million), the Audit Commission decided that NFI should form a regular part of the statutory audit and it is now conducted every 2 years. The total detected fraud and overpayments to date (including pre-1998 exercises) are estimated to be over £450 million (NFI, 2009: 1–2).

While NFI takes place once every 2 years, there are other public sector bodies undertaking proactive exercises as and when it suits them. For example, the NHS undertakes its own local and national proactive exercise as part of risk measurement and this is directed by the NHS CFSMS. The national proactive exercise is usually undertaken to measure, for instance, the risk of fraud in procurement or the presence of 'ghost' names on payroll records or agency time sheets across the NHS. Results from the national proactive fraud exercise are distributed across the NHS with guidance on how to improve systems and stop future fraudulent activities occurring. In addition, NHS local CFSs undertake fraud awareness campaigns and develop news articles for Primary Care Trust (PCT) newsletters. Local authority fraud investigators also undertake anti-fraud drives when, for instance, intelligence suggest that organized benefit fraud is taking place within an organization. Fraud is also detected through traditional reactive work via tip-offs, incidents and referrals received from members of the public, staff and third parties.

Albrecht et al. (2006: 158) suggest that 'most corporate frauds are detected by management and employees by accident through tip offs or complaints of wrongdoing rather than proactive effort by auditors or fraud investigators.' The most common method of detecting fraud is through tip-offs on hotlines. According to the ACFE's (2004) Report to the Nation on Occupational Fraud and Abuse, fraud losses are reduced by nearly 60 per cent when a hotline is present, with fraud being discovered via tip-offs 40 per cent of the time. Internal audit procedures were the second most common method of fraud detection accounting for 24 per cent of discoveries (Slovin, 2006: 45). In addition, there are a number of banking and finance industries having the ability to detect fraud using real-time systems. For instance, private sector organizations that are members of CIFAS are able to see 'red-flags' on their systems indicating potentially fraudulent applications. Similarly, Equifax, a credit reference agency, has recently introduced a new system called SIRAN which allows lenders to evaluate the effectiveness of their fraud strategies, something which is crucial in reducing the risk of fraud on an ongoing basis. As fraudsters are known to target their activity across the lending industry, SIRAN facilitates the sharing of data from all sectors, including banks, retail credit providers, credit card issuers, mobile telecommunications and mail order suppliers (Equifax, 2006: para. 5).

Investigation strategies

Once a fraud has been detected, either through a proactive or through a reactive measure, the task is to investigate it. How this is undertaken varies significantly according to the sector and the size of the fraud. Some organizations might try and entice the police to investigate, though their lack of interest in investigating what can be quite substantial frauds is well documented. The recent Fraud Review Team (2006a: 69) cite the following response from a Chief Constable to an organization that had discovered a £100,000 employee fraud:

> The investigation of fraud is extremely expensive in terms of hours spent obtaining statements and preparing a prosecution case. The Constabulary is required under the Crime and Disorder Act to produce a crime reduction strategy. Our strategy identifies priority areas and police resources are directed to those priority areas. Fraud is not one of them.

For most organizations that discover fraud the most common outcome is either to use in-house fraud investigators or to contract the initial investigation to an external private company. Evidence may then be secured which is then enough to entice either the police to intervene or, if it is a substantial fraud that fits their criteria, the SFO. However, even for an organization seeking a criminal prosecution, the investigation will remain the responsibility of that organization and police involvement – if any – will not arise until there is case file to hand over with all necessary work done. The resources dedicated to fraud investigations also vary. Some large-scale frauds investigated by the SFO cost millions of pounds and involve dozens of staff over long periods of time. At the other extreme some expenses claim frauds might take one investigator less than a day to investigate and are relatively simple to pursue. However, investigations usually draw upon a range of common strategies some of which are considered below:

(i) *Desk-based strategies*. Many volume fraud investigations start with 'desk-based' strategies for reconciling paperwork. Investigations often arise from discrepancies arising during the normal audit process. Common examples include inflated overtime claims, 'ghosts' on the payroll and inflated payments to contractors for goods and services, all of which can be reconciled by cross-checking the relevant documents (e.g. time sheets against overtime claims, staff lists against salary lists and goods against actual purchasing lists). In short, organizations produce large numbers of documents that fraudsters often exploit. The challenge is for the investigator to find the appropriate documentation and link a person to it. The investigator may also use various databases to secure further information on a suspect. Statutory bodies such as the DWP and HM Customs and Revenue access private records held by other statutory bodies and by organizations such as banks. Other investigative bodies may utilize other private information sources provided by CIFAS, Companies House or the Land Registry. Public sources, such as the electoral roll and personal web pages, can also be used.

Case Study 7.1

An example of 'desk-based' investigation is a midwife supervisor who worked for the NHS. She was contracted to work for 15 hours a week solely on the parent craft sessions within the NHS Trust. However, she submitted falsified time sheet for over a period of 4 years costing the NHS more than £63,000. The discrepancies became known when the Local Counter Fraud Specialist

---

Case Study 7.1   (Continued)

carried out an exercise for the Trust she worked for by comparing time sheets to ward rotas. She was charged with theft and fraud, with 15 months' prison sentence, and was ordered to pay £63,812 in compensation (NHS BSA Press Release, 2009).

(ii) *Interviewing*. One of the primary strategies used by investigators is to interview suspects and witnesses to secure information. Some organizations always start investigations on the presumption of a criminal prosecution – even when it might be unlikely – meaning compliance with all the PACE codes of practice is required to ensure any evidence secured is admissible. Other bodies do not start with such a presumption, so they are not regulated by PACE. Under the former where investigators have reasonable grounds for suspecting that fraud may have been committed, they will arrange for the suspected offender(s) to attend an interview under caution which will be tape recorded on a dual tape machine and used as evidence for any subsequent criminal prosecution. It is important to note that the vast majority of fraud investigators do not have special powers of arrest and cannot compel a suspect to be interviewed. For that reason, some organizations may use any leverage they have with a suspect, such as the threat of disciplinary action by an employer for non-cooperation or, in the case of the DWP, the withdrawal of benefits. If such leverage is not available or does not work, the investigator is left with the task of securing enough evidence to gain the co-operation of the police in arresting a suspect and then conducting the interview under arrest.

The purpose of interview under caution is to give the alleged fraudster the opportunity to talk about the suspected allegation. The interviewer has to be objective when conducting interviews and the interviewee has the right to a legal advisor or Solicitor present at the interview. Also, friends, family members and other relatives could be present at the interview so long as they are not part of the investigation and their presence is to provide moral support. The interviewing process is characterized by a ritual whereby the investigator explains the 'suspect(s) rights … including the right to leave the interview room at any time as they are not under arrest, the Police and Criminal Evidence (PACE) Act guidelines within which the interview will be conducted and the reasons for being asked to attend the interview' (Tunbridge Wells Borough Council, 2006). The investigator may follow the PEACE model of ethical interviewing as a guiding principle (Shawyer and Walsh, 2007: 114). The mnemonic PEACE stands for the following:

P: Plan and prepare – prior to the commencement of interview;

E: Engage and explain – at the commencement of the interview;

A: Account – this is the stage where suspects give their version of the facts;

C: Challenge – the investigator confronts the suspects with the known facts where they differ; and

E: Evaluate – the investigator evaluates the information obtained during the interview (London Borough of Hammersmith and Fulham, 2005: 40).

In the course of the interview, suspects may be asked open and closed questions while the investigator observes their body language and the other forms of verbal and non-verbal communication.

(iii) *Surveillance*. Fraud investigation in both the private and the public sectors may involve using surveillance techniques, although the extent and the type of its use vary significantly. At one end of the spectrum are organizations like the police and HM Revenue and Customs which, when conducting an investigation, may utilize – subject to regulation – the full range of surveillance techniques. At the other end some private sector organizations might be highly reluctant to use surveillance, and when they do it might be only surveillance in public using a camcorder. The methods used by private and public sector investigators include

- Foot or mobile surveillance – following the suspect on foot or by car.
- Technical surveillance – the use of covert audio recording, video and photographic equipment.

- Electronic surveillance – the use of bugging or listening devices, e-mail intercepts, telephone and communication wire tapping and real-time systems to record and count keystrokes.

Surveillance is used widely by both public and private bodies for investigations of varying severity. For example, the DWP may use it to ascertain if someone who is claiming to be unemployed is actually working (see Case Study 7.2). In the insurance sector persons who are making a claim for a serious back injury might be kept under surveillance to check if the disabilities they claim are apparent in their day-to-day activities. A more serious organized fraud committed by a criminal gang might necessitate covert surveillance by the police or by HM Revenue and Customs using telephone tapping or interception of communications.

Surveillance by public bodies, particularly in its more covert and intrusive forms, is subject to extensive regulation through statutes such as the Regulation of Investigatory Powers Act 2000, the Data Protection Act 1998 and the Human Rights Act 1998 (Comer, 2003). By contrast, the controls for private sector investigators – particularly when criminal prosecution is not being sought – are much less defined. Yet, despite an overall increase in legal control, surveillance is becoming much more prevalent due to new developments in information technology. Two other trends are noteworthy. First, there is a shift away from reactive to proactive policing strategies. Second, because surveillance can provide high-quality evidence that is tantamount to a confession, interviews are often unnecessary (Taylor, 2003, cited by Clark, 2007: 428). Overall, then, there are clear benefits from using surveillance in investigations, but there are also some risks. For one thing, exposure of those doing the surveillance can jeopardize an entire investigation. For another, breaching regulations can render any evidence collected useless.

Case Study 7.2

Benefits fraud investigators regularly use surveillance to observe suspected cheats during their daily lives. One example typical of many was the conviction of a man for

---

Case Study 7.2   (Continued)

more than £22,000 of benefits fraud over a 5-year period. He claimed to be disabled yet by surveillance technique fraud investigators observed that he was regularly going to the gym and working as a doorman in a swingers' club. He was charged with benefits fraud and jailed for 18 months (BBC News, 2009d).

(iv) *Searches.* The search of a person or of a person's home requires an investigator to have appropriate statutory powers and an appropriate warrant. Police are the main instigators of these types of searches, though other bodies will work with the police. For example, having secured sufficient evidence to enable the police to obtain a warrant, DWP and NHS CFSs may carry out the search under police supervision.

Case Study 7.3

A postman was sentenced to 3 months in jail after been convicted of offences relating to the dumping of mail he was supposed to be delivering. Suspicions had been aroused when a bag of mail he was supposed to be delivering was found dumped on a railway line. A search of his home found a bag of mail under his bed with both opened and unopened mail (BBC News, 2002).

Searches may also be carried out without co-operation from the police. For instance, many organizations have codes of practice linked to contracts of employment that make an employee's failure to consent to a search grounds for termination of employment (Button, 2007). It is also important to remember that not all searches are physical. Some organizations may have access to an employee's personal e-mails and other electronic files which, subject to appropriate employment protocols, they can also search. A more controversial form of search is so-called 'dumpster diving' where investigators examine the rubbish thrown out from a suspect's home. This may yield evidence of credit cards, banks' statements,

receipts and payments for services rendered that can incrim-
inate the suspect. Where investigators search rubbish bins,
records have to be kept on how the search was conducted
and on when and how the materials were returned. According to Comer (2003: 59), the aim of such recording is to show
that there was no intention of permanently depriving the
owner of the trash.

(v) *Forensics*. Forensics or forensic science is the acquisition and
analysis of scientific data for application to the study and
resolution of crime, investigation, civil and regulatory issues
and criminal identification (Camenson, 2001: 1). From a
fraud investigation perspective, forensics may involve examining normal or conventional documents or the use of
computer forensics to examine digital evidence and even
DNA samples. Computer forensics is the analysis of data-
processing equipment to determine whether that equipment
has been used for illegal or unauthorized purposes (Kanellis
et al., 2006: 269). Within public and private sector organizations, there are fraud investigators who are specially trained
in computer forensics with the skills and ability to retrieve,
analyze, retain and reveal electronic evidence when needed
in court. They may obtain digital evidence from computer
hard disks and networks by examining corporate transaction
databases, accounting systems and electronic spreadsheets,
Internet/weblogs, internet chat logs/chat rooms, e-mail logs,
CD/DVD disks, flash drives/pens, personal digital assistants
(PDAs), fax machines and even mobile phones. Specialist
software is also available for obtaining digital evidence. By
examining these digital sources, there is the potential to
identify fraudulent activities, crime trends, critical behaviour
patterns and the transactions of money-laundering and
insider-trading operations (Westphal and Blaxton, 1998: 8).

Uncovering a computer user's past activities is one of the
most common tasks for a computer forensics investigator.
Often, this task is straightforward and can be accomplished
primarily through a detailed analysis of the relevant data and
application files present on a system. However, a tremen-
dous amount of information can also be discovered which
might otherwise be thought lost or hidden. By discovering data on a computer which a suspect has tried to hide
or destroy or by uncovering information in the depths of

the operating system (or even in areas no longer used by the operating system) an investigator may be able to gain valuable incriminating evidence.

In addition to using digital sources for obtaining fraud evidence, forensic work may involve examining conventional sources, most frequently relating to document analysis. This might include assessments of whether documents are forgeries, contain changed details (such as adding a 0 on a cheque or altering a name), exhibit fingerprints or need to be subject to handwriting analysis. Although the analysis of DNA is relatively uncommon at present, the expansion of DNA databanks offers future potential for fraud investigation and there is a far greater chance of identifying a suspect where DNA evidence is available (Mennell and Shaw, 2006).

Case Study 7.4

In 2003 two men were charged in connection with a £2 million fraud at a Belfast company. The fraud related to false invoices that were submitted. A major part of the investigation involved a forensic accounting firm assessing the 'false invoices' (BBC News, 2003b).

(vi) *Information technology*. The role of information technology in investigations has already been mentioned in the previous discussion. However, the importance of information technology in investigations deserves mention in its own right. Data matching is the computerized comparison of two or more sets of records which relate to the same individual, and it is becoming a popular method used by both public and private sector organizations in their attempt to reducing fraudulent activities (Rogerson, 1997: para. 2). There are a number of government departments and agencies involved in data-matching exercises including the NHS, local authorities, the DWP, the Home Office and the Foreign and Commonwealth Office. The NFI discussed earlier is one of the most important of these initiatives. Given that data matching involves drawing together information about people who are not subsequently identified as being involved in fraud, its use raises concerns regarding data protection and privacy. Following NFI experiences drawn from four national exercises, the Audit Commission has issued a new code of data-matching practice reflecting changes in the law since 1997 (NAO, 2006: 2).

In addition to taking part in NFI, local authorities have their own data-matching system using the Housing Benefit Matching Service (HBMS), now joined with the Housing Benefit Data Services Team (based in Newcastle) to form the Housing Benefit Database and Matching Service (HBDMS, bringing together those areas within the Information Directorate that interface with local authorities (HBMS Newsletter, 2007)). In addition, they may undertake data matching where benefit claimants have failed to declare their work, savings and private pensions. Similarly, the NHS may use SAS software or crime pattern analysis to identify 'hotspots'. So, for instance, it might look at 10 million prescriptions and analyze where all the exempt ones have been used, or where certain drugs – particularly high-value ones – have been consumed. Another common tool in fraud investigation is the use of Voice Recognition Analysis (VRA) in analyzing telephone calls. Here, the principle is that certain vocal features might be indicative of stress – and therefore of lying – thereby warranting further investigation. This technique is commonly used in the insurance industry, as well as by the DWP.

Conclusion

There is much debate and focus upon the police capacity to investigate fraud. They are very important in the investigative infrastructure, but as this chapter has shown, they represent the tip of the iceberg in the investigative infrastructure. There are substantially more civilian investigators in the private and public sectors, a significant proportion of which are ACFS. However, even with the bigger 'iceberg' exposed, the problem still remains that many frauds are never investigated. A challenge for policy-makers will be to marshal these diverse resources to work together more effectively to investigate fraud. This will require common training, vetting and perhaps even a form of licensing to create stronger bonds among the different investigators. Again the formation of the NFA provides an opportunity to develop this area so there are stronger partnerships, more investigations and, ultimately, more fraudsters being caught. Indeed, one of the many areas the NFA is investigating is the training and accreditation of fraud investigators.

This chapter has explored the investigation of fraud. It started by examining the investigative infrastructure and identified a wide range of agencies involved in fraud investigation, with the largest group as civilian fraud investigators, employed largely in the public sector. They have been professionally trained and accredited with recognized qualification as ACFS. There has been increasing growth and demand for CFSs, particularly in the public sector. The chapter then went on to examine some of the core functions of CFSs that distinguish them from the traditional fraud investigators. Finally, the different strategies for the detection and investigation of fraud were explored. The investigations conducted may or may not lead to a criminal prosecution, but ultimately there will be some form of sanction. This aspect of the process will be the subject of Chapter 8.

Further reading

- Comer, M. (1985) *Corporate Fraud* (2nd edition). Aldershot: Gower.
- Comer, M.J. (2003) *Investigating Corporate Fraud*. Aldershot: Gower.
- Doig, A. and Greenhalgh, S. (2009) *Handbook of Fraud Investigation and Prevention: A Guide to Legal and Procedural Strategies*. Aldershot: Ashgate.
- Further information on investigators can be found at http://www.icfs. org.uk/ and LAIOG: http://www.laiog.org/.
- Gill, M. and Hart, J. (1997a) Exploring Investigative Policing, *British Journal of Criminology*, 37(3), 549–567.
- Lyer, N. and Samociuk, M. (2008) *Fraud and Corruption: Prevention and Detection*. Aldershot: Ashgate.
- Newburn, T., Williamson, T. and Wright, A. (2007) *Handbook of Criminal Investigation*. Cullompton: Willan.
- O'Gara, J.D. (2004) *Corporate Fraud: Case Studies in Detection and Prevention*. New Jersey: John Wiley and Sons.

CHAPTER 8

Prosecuting and Regulating Fraud

Overview

The aims of this chapter are to provide

- an overview of the main prosecuting agencies in England and Wales
- a synopsis of the many challenges to successful prosecution of fraud
- an indication of the types of sentences received by fraudsters
- a summary of regulatory and compliance-based approaches to tackling fraud

---

Introduction

The discussion, so far, has illustrated the fragmented nature of the organizations engaged in combating fraud. This is also the case with a variety of prosecuting agencies, some of which pursue 'regulatory', rather than 'criminal justice', approaches. The chapter begins with an examination of the various prosecuting agencies and the different approaches they pursue. It then considers the problems of securing convictions, particularly in complex cases. During the course of this discussion the contentious issue of jury trial is briefly examined. Next, it explores the types of sentences convicted fraudsters are likely to face. The chapter closes by looking at issues of compliance and regulation and at how some bodies prefer to address fraud issues without invoking the criminal justice system.

Prosecuting agencies

Chapter 7 illustrated the diverse range of bodies involved in the investigation of fraud and the small part played by the police. Most volume crimes in the UK are prosecuted by the Crown Prosecution Service (CPS). However, an individual can pursue a private prosecution and there are a range of statutory bodies that also have their own prosecution service (Lidstone et al., 1980). With fraud, however, the fragmentation of agencies engaged in prosecution is much greater than for 'ordinary' volume crimes. The CPS still plays a dominant role in the prosecution of fraud – greater than the police do in the investigation of fraud – but there is still a wide range of bodies involved beyond the CPS. Some of the main organizations prosecuting fraud are listed below:

- Crown Prosecution Service
- Serious Fraud Office (SFO)
- Revenue and Customs Prosecution Office (RCPO) (recently became part of CPS)
- DWP Solicitors Branch
- Local authorities
- Financial Services Authority (FSA)
- The Pensions Regulator
- The Office of Fair trading (OFT)

Additionally, the Assets Recovery Agency (ARA), while lacking prosecutorial powers, can recover proceeds of criminal offences using the Proceeds of Crime Act (POCA). All these bodies have a mixture of civil and administrative/internal penalties, or sanctions, available to them, along with others that can be granted as a result of court action. The range of potential sanctions available to prosecutors and regulators is illustrated in Figure 8.1.

As can be seen from the figure, some sanctions are derived from the criminal courts, some from the civil courts and some from either one; others are purely internal administrative. With regard to criminal courts, fraud cases can be tried either in a magistrates' court or, for more serious cases, in a Crown Court. Both courts have the option of imposing custodial sentences, but for

Figure 8.1 Fraud penalties, criminal, civil and administrative [adapted from Fraud Review Team (2006b: 162)].

Tool/Org	Criminal court-based		Either criminal or civil court-based		Civil court-based				Internal administrative		
	Crim Pros	Crim	Conf and Restraint	Disqual/Ban	Civil debt, etc.	Injunction	Insolvency	Settle	Enf/stop orders	Caution	Admin fine
CPS	✓	✓	✓	✓						✓	
SFO	✓	✓	✓	✓						✓	
DTI/CIB/IS	✓	✓	✓	✓	✓		✓	✓	✓	✓	✓
OFT/TSO	✓	✓	✓	✓		✓	✓	✓	✓	✓	
Pensions	✓	✓	Cash								✓
Police			Cash		✓					✓	
DoH	✓	✓	✓	✓	✓	✓	✓	✓		✓	✓
DEFRA	✓	✓	✓	✓	✓		✓	✓	✓	✓	
RCPO	✓		✓	✓				✓		✓	
HMRC	✓		Cash	✓	✓	✓	✓			✓	✓
DWP	✓	✓	✓	✓	✓					✓	✓
ARA		✓	✓	✓				✓			tax

fraud cases this is generally the preserve of the Crown Courts, while the magistrates' courts deal with 'lower-level' offences (Fraud Review, 2006b: 169).

The penalties these courts can impose include imprisonment, fines and community penalties. Additionally restitution orders can be issued under section 148 of the Powers of Criminal Courts (Sentencing) Act 2000, ordering that the value of stolen goods be restored to the victim. Under the same Act (Section 130), an offender may be required to pay compensation in cases where an offence has resulted in personal injury, loss or damage. Where it can be shown that an offender has made a financial benefit from offences, the court is required by the Proceeds of Crime Act 2002 to judge whether or not to make a confiscation order. Both the Crown Court and magistrates' courts can disqualify a person from being a director or receiver of a company if the offence is related to him/her being a company director. A magistrates' court has the power to impose an order disqualifying an offender from acting as a company director for up to 5 years; the Crown Court has the power to impose an order lasting up to 15 years.

It is important to note, however, that sanctions through criminal prosecutions are only part of the picture. Many organizations pursue non-criminal sanctions as well. The prosecution process that the NHS undertakes is unique in its three-pronged approach to suspected offenders. This encompasses internal (and sometimes external through licencing bodies) disciplinary procedures, use of the civil law to facilitate the recovery of defrauded monies and the use of the criminal law, all of which work in conjunction with the seven generic action objectives of the NHS Counter Fraud Strategy (NHS CFS). As it states,

> Those who would defraud the NHS should know that it is not just a criminal prosecution which they may face, but the use of the civil law to freeze and recover assets and of the disciplinary regulations to remove them from the context in which their fraud took place.
>
> (NHS CFS, 2003: 3)

Once there has been a successful outcome, the other option the NHS may pursue is to seek redress. There are various methods by which this can be achieved both in and out of the courts. The civil penalty charge provides an appropriate sanction to deter patients from wrongly claiming financial help from the NHS to which they are not entitled in respect of patient charges, or goods or services. The Health Act 1999 inserted Sections 122A and 122B into the National Health Service Act 1977, which provided the power to introduce the penalty charge by means of regulations. The 1999 amendments also stipulate that the penalty charge shall be '5 times the recoverable amount, up to a maximum of £100'. The patient is also required to repay the original charge. In cases of non-payment, the amendments provide for a surcharge of up to £50 to be imposed.

In addition, Section 122C introduced a new specific criminal offence for trial in the magistrates' court. This criminal offence is designed to complement the penalty charge by providing a sanction for cases of repeated or persistent evasion. This offence attracts a fine, on conviction, of up to £2500. However, Section 122C (7) provides that patients are not liable for a penalty charge if they are convicted of a criminal offence for evasion of the same charges or vice versa – thereby avoiding double jeopardy. Since the introduction of the penalty charge for prescription charge evasion, the Compliance Unit has issued over 130,000 penalty notices and recovered several million pounds.

Under Section 71 of the Criminal Justice Act 1988, once the defendant's assets have been identified, an application needs to be made to the court to prevent him or her from dealing with such assets. After conviction, a compensation and confiscation order can be made. Such orders are usually proceeded in the Crown Court, as it would not normally be economically worthwhile in a case before the magistrates' court.

Another internal form of redress is through the NHS pension scheme. Under the 1995 Pension Act, the NHS can recover defrauded monies by reducing the amount of any pension scheme. Part ST5 of the NHS Pension Scheme Regulations notes that

> If a loss of public funds occurs as a result of a member's criminal, negligent, or fraudulent act, or omission, the Secretary of State may reduce any benefits or other amounts payable to, or in respect of, the member by an amount equal to the loss.

It would now seem appropriate to examine some of the most important prosecution agencies in a little more depth, beginning with the CPS. The CPS pursues the vast bulk of prosecutions in the criminal justice system. In 2006–07 it considered over 584,000 cases for prosecution (CPS, 2007). These figures include CPS prosecutions for 'lesser' offences of fraud largely referred by the police and other specialist fraud investigative bodies without a prosecution service, such as the NHS CFSMS. However, the CPS is also responsible for prosecuting approximately 65 per cent of more serious cases involving more than £250,000. This is done through the CPS Fraud Prosecution Service which was established in November 2005. Its prime focus is the handling of cases investigated and referred to them by the City of London Fraud and Economic Crime Department and the Metropolitan Police, but it also undertakes the prosecution of serious and complex fraud cases nationally, referred to them by individual police force economic crime units. As of 2006, it estimated that it would be handling 205 cases per year (Fraud Review, 2006a: 188). In January 2010 the HM Revenue and Customs Prosecution Office (RCPO) merged with the CPS, meaning all cases previously conducted by them relating to tax, drugs, customs and so on also fall within the ambit of the CPS.

The SFO has been mentioned already as it has the role of both investigating and prosecuting the most serious frauds. The cases it deals with are

- Cases in the order of at least £1 million.
- Cases likely to give rise to national publicity and widespread public concern.
- Cases requiring a highly specialist knowledge of, for example, Stock Exchange practices or regulated markets.
- Cases in which there is a significant international dimension.
- Cases where legal, accountancy and investigative skills need to be brought together.
- Cases which appear to be complex and in which the use of Section 2 powers under the Criminal Justice Act 1988 might be appropriate.
- Cases with significant impact, such as those which might damage confidence in UK financial institutions (SFO, 2007b).

The SFO was established by the 1987 Criminal Justice Act. Between 1988 and 2002, the SFO prosecuted 237 cases involving 516 defendants. Among these, 366 (71 per cent) were convicted. It was criticized by Widlake (1995) for being 'gung-ho',

Table 8.1 Sentences imposed on SFO successful prosecutions

Fraud sentences	2004–05	2005–06	2006–07
Defendants convicted	37	13	15
Custody immediate	29	12	14
Custody on appeal	0	0	1
Custody suspended	3	1	0
Fined	2	0	0
Community service order	3	0	0
Disqualifications as a director	15	4	7
Confiscation orders	17	9	8

Source: Adapted from Serious Fraud Office (2007a).

for 'grandstanding' and for presiding over a series of spectacular failures in prosecuting expensive cases (some of which will be
explored later in this chapter). According to Levi (1993, 1995),
it was soon apparent that the SFO would not have the resources
and capacity for investigating all forms of serious fraud. This criticism has continued with a damning report by De Grazia (2008)
which compared the SFO to equivalent American prosecutors
highlighting serious inefficiency. For example, in a case involving the same legislation relating to conspiracy on both sides of
the Atlantic, the Southern District of New York used a team of 8
to convict 14 defendants in a third of the time the SFO used 31
for prosecuting 4.

The types of penalties imposed on convicted fraudsters arising
from SFO cases are set out in Table 8.1.

One issue that is not immediately clear is the number of failed
prosecutions. This has been an important area of criticism of the
SFO and will be explored in depth later in this chapter. The
example described in Case Study 8.1 shows the longevity of some
SFO prosecutions.

Case Study 8.1

In February 2008 the SFO secured the conviction of two
accountants involved in a $200 million investment fraud and
conspiracy to corrupt a US official. The fraud was based
upon so-called 'Ponzi' frauds where investors are promised

Case Study 8.1 (Continued)

large returns on their investment of 40 per cent plus. In reality there was no real trading and the funds entering merely paid the interest returns on those already in. The investigation also found evidence of an attempt to bribe a US official. The investigation began in September 2002, the two accountants were charged in October 2005, the trial began on 3 July 2007 and it concluded on 22 February 2008 (SFO, 2008).

Local authorities also undertake a large number of prosecutions relating to fraud with housing benefit, council tax fraud and trading standards offences being prosecuted in the criminal courts. In many of these cases, the local authority's legal department pursues the prosecution. In some cases, the local authority works jointly with other bodies such as the police or the DWP.

Case Study 8.2

Council Trading Standards officers prosecuted the owner of a local restaurant in 2007 for replacing well-known brands of spirits such as Barcadi with unknown brands. The former owner of the restaurant was fined and ordered to pay costs amounting to £1150 (Bournemouth Online, 2007).

Problems facing prosecutors of fraud

As we have said previously, in some fraud cases – particularly complex ones – securing a conviction may be difficult. This is borne out by the SFO's failure to secure convictions in several high-profile cases. More evidence to illustrate the poor record of the SFO was provided in a study by the Fraud Advisory Panel (FAP) (2006), which found on an analysis of cases between 2002 and 2005 a conviction rate of 66 per cent. This raises the question: why is it so difficult to prosecute complex fraud? In addressing this question both Wright (2006) and the FAP (2006) point to a number of factors including:

- The under-resourced and fragmented nature of the UK's system for prosecuting fraud;
- The length and complexity of investigating serious fraud cases;
- Poor trial management leading to lengthy trials;
- The inadequacy of the jury system to try what are often complex cases; and
- Lack of a plea bargaining system.

As already noted fraud prosecution in the UK involves several agencies, each with differing areas of responsibilities and powers. The FAP is clear about the effect such fragmentation has on the ability to prosecute fraud successfully and efficiently:

> It is widely accepted that most investigating and prosecuting authorities suffer from inadequate funding and manpower ... the problem is aggravated by the existence of a large number of organisations .... Each staffed by too few investigators and prosecutors. The result is that specialist expertise and skills are spread very thin while administrative costs are duplicated.
>
> (FAP, 2006: 2)

Much has also been made by practitioners and academics of the potential length and complexity of fraud cases – especially those involving serious frauds. Thus the FAP (2006) reported that for serious cases (i.e. those involving over £1 million) the average time taken – from the SFO initiating an investigation to any case coming to Crown Court – was nearly 3 years. The FAP revealed that in 2003–04, once brought to trial, the top 30 cases lasted an average of 67 working days, at an average cost of £2.6 million each (FAP, 2006: 5–6).

The FAP argue that the rules on disclosing evidence to the defence cannot only affect how an investigation is conducted, but can also serve to lengthen any subsequent trial. Thus the 1996 Criminal Procedure and Investigation Act (CPIA) obliges investigators not only to pursue all 'reasonable lines of inquiry' but also to disclose all relevant material to the defence. If any material is withheld – albeit accidentally – there is the possibility that an appeal could be lodged later on. This leads to escalating costs and ever-lengthy proceedings. For example, the FAP quotes a 2005 Pricewaterhouse report which revealed that for fraud cases, the average prosecution involves analyzing more than 5000 e-mails and e-documents (FAP, 2006). Thus Wright (2006: 180) argues,

> One distinguishing feature that anyone who ventures into a court-room where a serious fraud case is being tried will notice immediately is the predominance of documentary evidence. Indeed the amount of time taken in consideration of the documentation ... greatly out-weighs the impact of oral evidence.

Compounding these obstacles, the FAP and Wright (2006) point to failings in the system of appointing judges to try the cases and the problems posed to prosecutors by the presence of juries. Criticisms of judges include their inexperience and their unwill-ingness to try complicated cases. Wright (2006) especially criti-cized judges in fraud trials as being inexperienced and for being unwilling to try complicated cases. As she put it:

> There are one or two (judges) who appear to have had the respon-sibility for trying these cases thrust upon them and do so unwillingly and less ably than is to be hoped ... many jaundiced prosecutors believe that some judges are obliged to take them on as a form of punishment and penance. Such judges do not manage the trial pro-cedure as well as they should, the proceeding run away with them, the jury remain confused and too often the prosecutor is the loser.

Even willing judges often have little experience, have limited knowledge and suffer from a shortage of appropriate logistical support. Yet, the real focus of those alleging poor trial manage-ment has been on the supposed problems arising from the system of trial by jury. The jury system has been attacked on a num-ber of grounds including its perceived cost; the unrepresentative composition of many juries; the returning of 'perverse' verdicts and in terms of fraud cases; and jurors' inability to understand complicated issues and evidence. For instance, the review of the justice system conducted by Lord Auld recommended that seri-ous fraud should be tried by a judge sitting alone or with lay members drawn from a panel, instead of a jury (Auld, 2002). Juries are generally regarded as an expensive way of trying cases and opponents of the system point to high-profile cases which have lasted for several years, costing tens of millions of pounds.

Opponents of trial by jury in cases of complex fraud have usually focused on the alleged lack of competence of ordinary members of the public to understand all the issues. As a result of the Auld Report (2002), the Criminal Justice Act (2003) Section 43 allowed the prosecution in a complex and serious fraud case to apply to the judge for the trial to take place without a jury. However, as a result of a political compromise, the Act contains the requirement that this clause cannot be invoked without an affirmative resolution being passed by both Houses of Parliament. The Fraud (Trials without a Jury) Bill (2006) sought to remove this condition and leave it to the discretion of a High Court Judge if the application was successful. Although the Bill was passed in the House of Commons, it was defeated in the House of Lords in March 2007.

Criticisms about juries trying fraud cases date from the 1960s and were part of general complaints made by the police about 'too many criminals getting off' (Levi, 1987). The 1970s and 1980s saw a number of major cases ending in acquittal, causing what Levi describes as 'episodic criticism of the fact that in spite of scandals in the city very few – indeed no major City figures had been convicted of fraud' (Levi, 1987: 197). The Fraud Trials Committee (also known as the Roskill Committee) started on the premise that 'The public no longer believes that the legal system in England and Wales is capable of bringing the perpetrators of serious frauds expeditiously and effectively to book' (Roskill, 1986: 1).

The Committee also asserted that juries' understanding in complex fraud trials was limited or, as they put it, 'many jurors are out of their depth'. Such a lack of competence was also a major factor in prosecutors not bringing cases to trial. Consequently, the Roskill Report argued that juries should be replaced by a judge and two 'lay members', qualified to understand such complexity to form a Fraud Trials Tribunal. This was in spite of the Committee's own conclusions that there was no evidence to suggest that there was a higher proportion of acquittals in such trials as compared to other fraud trials or criminal trials in general (Roskill, 1986: 142).

Levi (1993), looking at acquittals in serious fraud cases in the 1970s and 1980s, found that of 23 major fraud trials, only 10 were results of a jury's decision. In the others, either the prosecution dropped the charges or the judge ruled that there was no case to answer. Moreover, Levi (1987) disputed the Roskill Committee's research methodology, whereby a trial was played out in front of a mock jury that was expected to absorb the essentials in under 2 hours (Levi, 1987: 307). As Levi (1993: 188) stated,

> The research carried out for Roskill demonstrated very little of value to the debate about jury competence ... if the jury becomes more confused as the case goes on, rather than indicating jury incompetence, perhaps this is an entirely proper reflection of the difficulty in coming to a certain judgement about complex events which are very difficult if not impossible to reconstruct objectively?

In any event, Roskill's recommendations were not followed up. Instead, attention was paid to procedural and evidential reforms as contained in the Criminal Justice Act 1987.

Latterly, Wright (2006) and the Home Office have shifted the emphasis away from questioning the jurors' competence, to stressing the inconvenience and burdensome nature that such lengthy trials place on them. Thus the former Home Office Minister Joan Ryan states,

> Our trial system requires oral explanation of documents and in the most complex fraud trials there can be thousands of pages of documents so trials can last months or even for a year or more. They impose a huge burden on individual jurors. And there are always problems getting a cross-section of people who can afford to do jury service for so long.

> (O'Brien, 2006)

The final issue the FAP point to as a barrier to the expeditious resolution of serious cases is the lack of a system of plea bargaining in the UK. This is in contrast with the USA where 95 per cent of all criminal cases – including fraud – are settled by their use. As the Fraud Review noted approvingly, 'They avoid the cost and time of a full scale trial and can involve penalties that involve restitution to victims and protection of the public as well as punishment of the fraudster' (Fraud Review, 2006b: 14). The Review's final report made their introduction into the English Legal System a central recommendation.

> This is not fraudsters 'buying their way' out of justice. In plea bargains, the fraudster must admit guilt, accept a criminal record, and sometimes serve time in jail. Often the plea bargain will result in

better and faster victim restitution than awaiting the outcome of a criminal trial.

(Fraud Review, 2006b: 14)

Sentencing trends in the UK

If prosecutors are successful in overcoming the hurdles to a successful conviction, the next challenge is getting an appropriate sanction. The research by the Sentencing Review Panel set out in Tables 8.2 and 8.3 illustrates the popularity of different types of sentences given for fraud offences in the magistrates' and Crown Courts. At the former the most common sentence is a community sentence. In the latter, although imprisonment was the most popular sentence, it still accounted for less than half of cases and community sentences were not far behind.

There is a lot of evidence to suggest that fraudsters in the UK get more lenient sentences than those perpetrating other 'comparable' crimes. As part of the Fraud Review (2006a and b), Levi reviewed the sentencing of fraud in general. He found that in 2004 the average length of a custodial sentence for fraud cases tried in a magistrates' court was 3 months, compared with 4 months for commercial burglary and 3 months for theft and

Table 8.2   Percentage of all offenders aged 18 and over receiving each type of sentence for fraud and forgery offences (magistrates' and Crown Courts) 1999–2005

	1999	2000	2001	2002	2003	2004	2005
Absolute discharge	<0.5	<0.5	<0.5	<0.5	<0.5	<0.5	<0.5
Conditional discharge	16	16	16	17	19	18	18
Fine	15	14	13	13	14	13	12
Community sentences	43	43	45	47	44	46	45
Suspended sentence	2	3	3	2	2	2	4
Immediate imprisonment	22	22	22	20	19	19	19
Other	1	1	1	1	2	1	1

Source: Adapted from Sentencing Guidelines Council (2007: 7).

Table 8.3 Percentage of offenders aged 18 and over receiving each type of sentence for offences in the Crown Court, 1999–2005

	1999	2000	2001	2002	2003	2004	2005
Absolute discharge	<0.5	<0.5	<0.5	<0.5	<0.5	<0.5	<0.5
Conditional discharge	4	4	4	4	5	4	4
Fine	3	2	2	3	3	3	2
Community sentences	31	30	34	40	40	40	37
Suspended sentence	8	10	10	7	7	8	9
Immediate imprisonment	54	54	50	45	45	44	47
Other	1	<0.5	<0.5	1	1	<0.5	1

Source: Adapted from Sentencing Guidelines Council (2007: 8).

handling stolen goods. In the same year, for more serious cases of fraud tried in the Crown Courts, the average sentence was 15.4 months, compared to 24.6 months for burglary and 41.1 months for robbery. For cases involving conspiracy to defraud the length was 25.6 months, reflecting the greater likelihood that such cases would involve larger amounts of money. For frauds involving in excess of £1 million, and investigated by the SFO, between 2000 and 2005 the average sentences were 31.7 months, with the most severe sentences being 4–5 years (Fraud Review, 2006a: 235). Women were also likely to receive lighter sentences than men (BDO Stoy Hayward, 2005: 3).

As former Detective Chief Superintendent, City of London Police, Ken Farrow commented (BDO Stoy Hayward, 2005: 3) the following: 'The general level of sentencing in the UK is low considering the monetary gain derived from fraud, especially when compared to the US'. Levi (1987) notes that there has been no systematic review of the reasons why the pattern of fraud convictions and sentences is as it is and why sentences are comparatively lenient. Explanations focus on generic issues, such as the perceived seriousness of the offence and the individual offender's circumstances.

By contrast, Flood-Page and Mackie (1998: 77, 158), looking at Court of Appeal judgements in the early 1990s, pointed to a predilection to view fraud as a breach of trust, and thereby an offence worthy of a custodial sentence. This was prompted by a spate of mortgage-related frauds that had undermined public confidence in the financial sector. Flood-Page and Mackie (1998: 85) also draw on the nature of such breaches as determining factors, with professional people being punished more severely than, say, theft by postmen.

Regulation and compliance

Thus far, discussion on prosecution has been on the premise that the purpose is to secure a criminal conviction or lesser sanction. However, there are many agencies that deal with fraud offences but who pursue a very different approach: what is often called regulation or compliance. In a compliance system, an offence is called a 'technical violation' and compliance hopes to achieve conformity to the law without having to detect, process or penalize violators. Compliance systems provide economic incentives for voluntary compliance to the laws and use administrative efforts to control violations before they occur. For example, the FSA has a host of administrative mechanisms to encourage compliance with its rules. The Inland Revenue also uses such measures in addition to criminal penalties. Most environmental crimes are also controlled by these means. Numerous types of deviant trading by companies are dealt with by the Companies Investigation Branch of the Department for Business, Enterprise and Regulatory Reform. Other forms of malpractice in trading might fall within the ambit of local authority trading standards officers or the OFT. There are also some regulatory bodies that regulate 'fraudulent' practices, such as the Office of Communications (OFCOM) which regulates the communications industry and the Office of Water Services (OFWAT) which regulates the water industry.

Some of these types of bodies have the statutory ability to impose sanctions upon those they regulate without having to go to court (see Case Study 8.3), although the criminal courts may also be used as a final option. In Chapter 9 we shall describe how insurance companies, rather than pursuing a criminal prosecution, may investigate to a point that enables them not to have to pay out on a claim, the sanction being the cancellation of the policy and non-payment of the claim. Advocates of such an approach point to the higher levels of compliance achieved and to avoiding the costs and challenges associated with criminal prosecution.

Case Study 8.3

In November 2004 one of Britain's most senior accountants was struck off by the Joint Disciplinary Panel (the accounting profession's joint disciplinary panel) after it was found he had purchased a £34,000 Range Rover from a client and deducted it from their audit bill. He then fiddled his company's books to cover up the shortfall. The panel found that 'he seized the opportunity to obtain the car, confident that one way or another he could get away with it, not least because of his senior position and de facto high level of control over the relevant accounts.' At the time of this report, there was no pursuit of a criminal prosecution (*The Guardian*, 2004).

Case Study 8.4

OFCOM, the government body that regulates the communications industry, had fined television companies a total of £3.5 million up to February 2008. The fines had been imposed upon television companies for their abuse of premium rate telephone lines. In some cases television programmes had failed to count the votes of viewers in interactive programmes where they had a stake in choosing the winner. In others, viewers had been encouraged to enter prize draws by telephone when the winner had already been selected (*The Guardian*, 2008a).

Generally, prosecution is a last resort. Levi (1995), looking at non-police agencies such as the Securities and Investment Board (SIB) (the forerunner to the FIA), noted that in its first 4 years it only prosecuted one case involving unauthorized investments. One official at the SIB went so far as to admit that it deliberately distanced itself from prosecution, saying that 'the purpose of the SIB is to detect breaches of the Financial Services Act, not to put people in prison' (Levi, 1995: 191). As with the SIB, the FSA puts its resources into compliance. In similar vein, the Special Compliance Office (SCO) of HM Revenue employs 80 people while, latterly, a compliance approach has also been adopted by the DWP to complement its investigatory branch (Smith, 2007).

With regard to the last point, it is worth noting that an organization's decision to focus on 'compliance-based', rather than 'criminal justice-based', sanctions may have certain resource implications. The Inland Revenue, now part of HM Customs and Revenue, has always adopted a compliance-based approach to tax evasion. This approach contrasts markedly with the state's tendency to use criminal sanctions against those defrauding the social security system (Cook, 1989). In pursuing administrative penalties, rather than criminal prosecution, the SCO of HM Revenue and Customs employs a staff of 80 people. By contrast, more than 3000 officers work on the problem of social security fraud (Doig, 2006).

The Financial Services Authority

Let us now consider one of these regulatory bodies in a little more depth. The FSA was established in 1997 to assume the regulatory role previously occupied by the Bank of England and other self-regulatory organizations that had been established under the Financial Services Act 1986. The FSA is an independent non-governmental body, given statutory powers by the Financial Services and Markets Act 2000. Its main objectives are as follows:

- Maintaining confidence in the UK financial system;
- Promoting public understanding of the financial system;
- Securing the right degree of protection for consumers; and
- Helping to reduce financial crime.

In terms of fraud and fraudulent behaviour, the FSA has an Enforcement Division which investigates when authorized firms breach their rules, or the provisions of the Financial Services and Markets Act (FSMA) 2000. The FSMA also allows the FSA to take action such as

- Withdrawing a trading firm's authorization;
- Disciplining authorized firms and people approved by the FSA to work in those firms;
- Imposing penalties for market abuse;
- Applying to the Court for injunction and restitution orders; and
- Prosecuting various offences either civilly or criminally.

The FSMA also gives the FSA powers to take action under the insider-dealing provisions of the Criminal Justice Act 1993 and the Money Laundering Regulations 1993. However, in monitoring and enforcing regulations, not all cases are pursued. Rather, decisions about enforcement are based on a risk assessment and management approach using 'proportionate response'. Indeed, despite the apparent prominence of enforcement mechanisms (shown on their website), the FSA's focus is on educating the public to make more informed decisions on investing and on encouraging the firms they regulate to comply with regulations. When there are breaches, the emphasis is on civil process by way of recovering financial losses and fining firms. In 2001, the enforcement powers of the FSA were strengthened by empowering it to impose civil penalties against those, whether regulated or not, who commit the new civil offence of market abuse. Additionally, its remit was widened to include responsibility for enforcing money-laundering regulations and breaches of the listing rules and to bring criminal proceedings for a range of criminal offences currently the preserve of the mainstream criminal authorities.

In 2001 the FSA brought only three cases to a criminal proceeding, pointing to the 'technical' nature of the offences. Rather, the FSA's emphasis is on informing the public about errant firms, as it argues the following:

> Publicising unauthorised scams can help alert consumers to the need to be careful. Consumers have no right to compensation if they deal with unauthorised firms. If they have any doubt about the credentials of a firm, they should contact the FSA consumer helpline.
>
> (FSA, 2001)

This points to one of the main problems with the FSA: that it can take action only against authorized traders, leaving unauthorized investment and deposit takers alone. Between 2001 and 2005 the FSA initiated

- Seven civil and court proceedings
- Cancelled 44 authorizations to trade in the financial markets
- Disqualified 9 traders from continued trading
- Imposed 25 administrative penalties

The Fraud Review found this approach to be 'disappointing' (Fraud Review, 2006: 194).

Case Study 8.5

An insurance company was fined a record £1.26 million by the FSA in 2007 over failure to protect customers' personal information which put them at greater risk of fraud. The FSA found that the fraudsters were able to get hold of the personal information of 632 policy-holders. The company agreed to settle early on in the investigation and as a consequence the fine was reduced by 30 per cent (Timesonline, 2007).

The period since the Fraud Review has seen a change in the emphasis the FSA gives to prosecuting market offences such as insider trading, as well as other offences including mortgage fraud. The appointment of Margaret Cole as head of the FSA's enforcement section in 2005 was an early indication of this change. As she stated,

> At the FSA we decided three or so years ago that we should take stronger action in relation to markets offences – in particular insider dealing, a crime we have specific statutory remit to investigate and prosecute. We recognised that the history of insider-dealing prosecutions in the UK has not been a distinguished one, and that it continues to be difficult to root out and prove insider dealing. But despite the risks, we have taken steps to become a heavyweight criminal prosecutor.
>
> (Cole, 2009)

This was done by re-organizing the Enforcement Division into a new Enforcement and Financial Crime Division, recruiting financial crime specialists to investigate market offences. In 2009 three prosecutions for insider dealing were begun and two convictions resulted in custodial sentences (Spence, 2009) (see Case Study 2.3). In terms of fines, between 2003 and 2008 these averaged £14million per year, but increased to £27.3 million between 2008 and 2009 (FSA, 2009: 4).

Conclusion

The successful prosecution of Bernard Madoff and the subsequent sentence of 150 years in prison raises a number of questions in the UK context. First, would his trial have taken place yet and second, would he have been appropriately sentenced? Given the past experience of the SFO it would be reasonable to assume the case would either still be awaiting commencement or still be going through the trial stage. His sentence would have been highly unlikely to have been such that it would have meant spending the rest of his life in jail (the maximum sentence under the Fraud Act 2006 is 10 years, although other offences were also committed that he could have been prosecuted for). Given the record of juries in fraud cases in the UK, he might even have been tempted to plead not-guilty. The structures for the prosecution of fraud in the UK would also seem to be entering a period of reform. A successful merger of the CPS and RCPO and the increasing climate of budgetary restraint may also open up merger with other statutory prosecution agencies. The issue of jury trial is also unlikely to disappear now the first trial of a serious crime has commenced without a jury in the UK (the trial of Twomey et al. for a robbery at Heathrow Airport commenced in January 2010). Greater use of non-criminal sanctions may also emerge as a more cost efficient and effective sanction. There is therefore much to observe and debate in this area over the next few years.

This chapter began by examining various prosecuting agencies and the different approaches they pursue. It then went on to assess the challenges of securing convictions for fraud, particularly for the more complex types. During the course of this discussion, the debate about the use of jury trial in complex fraud cases was briefly explored. Next, it considered the types of sentences convicted fraudsters are likely to face and the extent to which these may be lenient in respect of 'comparable crimes'. The chapter closed by looking at issues of compliance and regulation and at how some bodies prefer to address fraud issues without invoking the criminal justice system.

Further reading

- Fraud Review Team (2006) chapters 8, 9 and 10. Available from http://www.aasdni.gov.uk/pubs/FCI/fraudreview_finalreport.pdf.
- Levi, M. (2006) *Sentencing Frauds: A Review*. Available from http://www.cf.ac.uk/socsi/resources/Levi_GFR_Sentencing_Fraud.pdf.
- Sentencing Guidelines Council (2007) *Consultation Paper on Sentencing for Fraud Offences*. Available from http://webarchive.nationalarchives. gov.uk/20100519200657/http://www.sentencing-guidelines.gov.uk/ docs/Fraud%20Consultation%20Paper%20-%20version%20for%20 printing%202007-08-07.DB.pdf.

Case Studies in Fraud

Part I of the book defined Fraud and its characteristics as an offence, and how it is regarded and treated by criminologists. Part II looked at the way it is investigated and prosecuted by agencies within and outside the UK criminal justice system. Part III comprises of a series of case studies of types of fraud and fraudulent behaviour, which illustrate some of the themes that have been raised so far in a particular context.

Chapter 9 focuses on insurance fraud and discusses a major, if under-researched, area of criminality. In doing so it reflects on issues raised in both Part I and Part II about the nature of fraud; how it is measured; and how it is investigated and prosecuted. Insurance frauds are consistently regarded by the general public as not being serious; these can often be difficult to establish and are often committed by individuals who otherwise wouldn't be considered as criminal types. Consequently, insurance-related frauds are under-estimated and remain largely invisible. Even when detected, they are often under-reported by the insurance industry itself. All this makes it difficult to estimate its extent and for organizations to organize measures and policies to combat it.

Similarly, Chapter 10 highlights issues raised in Chapters 5–8, on how various agencies investigate and prosecute fraud in the UK. The example discussed here is the way the Department for Work and Pensions (DWP) organize their counter-fraud activities. The DWP not only have one of the biggest counter-fraud operations in the UK – they employ far more dedicated counter-fraud investigators than the public police – they have also been instrumental in pioneering a strategic management approach to combating fraud. Their experiences also point to the problematic nature of how fraud is defined and measured, as discussed in Chapters 2 and 3, and hence the problems of controlling and countering it.

Chapter 11 examines the phenomenon of transnational fraud: an increasing challenge to both individual nation-states and international agencies, as the globalization of trade and the emergence of new economies continue. Transnational fraud can arise from the increased use of the Internet to trade in goods, or from the liberalization of trade in, for example, the EU. It can also affect and distort international trade through its association with bribery and corruption. Besides affecting trade, international fraud can also facilitate and fund terrorism and organized fraud. Agencies combating transnational fraud face some of the problems of defining, identifying and measuring fraud that other agencies do (see, e.g. Chapter 11). These are, however, exacerbated by the international nature of the offences.

Thus, just as other forms of fraud covered in the previous case studies have illustrated, its nature makes it difficult to identify and measure. But it also faces problems of difference between how individual nations' legal systems define fraud and cultural issues of how trade is conducted (a recent high-profile example has been the BAE/Saudi Arabia affair where the bribing of officials is regarded differently in the UK and Saudi Arabia). Different legal systems can also require different standards of evidence and grant investigating/prosecuting agencies different resources and powers, making co-operation problematic.

CHAPTER 9

A Very Common Fraud: The Case of the Insurance Fiddle

Overview

The aims of this chapter are to provide

- a picture of the extent of insurance fraud
- examples of different types of insurance fraud
- an assessment of some of the strategies that have emerged to tackle insurance fraud
- information on possible areas of reform to enhance the fight against insurance fraud

---

Introduction

Insurance fraud is a very common fraud with many people quite happy to exaggerate an otherwise legitimate insurance claim. Indeed, as this chapter will show, around half of those surveyed would not rule out making a false claim. It is estimated that the total costs of insurance fraud in the UK could amount to £1.6 billion (ABI, 2007), a figure almost comparable to estimated levels of benefits fraud (£2–£3 billion). Yet while there is much evidence about the nature and extent of benefits fraud, there is little information available about insurance fraud. Most significantly, with the exception of a handful of studies from criminology (Clarke, 1989, 1990), psychology (Morley et al.,

2006) and risk/mathematics (Picard, 1996; Artis et al., 1999, 2002), academic analysis of the problem is limited. This is changing, but there is still a reluctance on the part of insurance companies to discuss the problem in public. The resulting lack of public data makes insurance fraud a difficult area to research and write about. It should be a higher priority for researchers in the future.

The chapter begins by exploring the extent of insurance fraud and discussing some examples of the types of frauds perpetrated. Next, it explores the techniques used to tackle insurance fraud focusing, in particular, on some recent industry-level developments. It also discusses preventative strategies, investigative structures and the various sanctions applied. The chapter ends with a discussion of areas of potential reform. The main focus of the chapter will be the UK, but other relevant examples from around the world will be used where appropriate.

The extent of insurance fraud

Before we examine the extent of insurance fraud it is worth examining some key facts about the size and scope of insurance in the UK. The UK insurance market is the third largest in the world accounting for 11 per cent of worldwide premium income. It employs over 313,000 people and on a typical day it pays out over £239 million in pensions and life insurance benefits and £57 million in general insurance claims. Some of the most common areas of insurance include household structure and contents, motor, life, mortgage protection, pensions, medical and income protection. There are almost 1000 companies providing insurance services and in 2008 their net premiums amounted to £33.8 billion. In that same year over £22 billion was paid out in claims. This included motor £8.7 billion, property £4.8 billion, general liability £2.7 billion, accident and health £3.2 billion, marine, aviation and transport £1.1 billion, miscellaneous and pecuniary loss £1.5 billion (ABI, 2009a).

As with any service that provides monetary payments there are opportunities for people to make fraudulent claims on those payments. The extent of insurance fraud, however, is much more difficult to gauge than, for example, prescription fraud or social security fraud. This stems from the inherent difficulties in defining, detecting and reporting insurance fraud. Indeed, based upon numerous legal judgements, it has become established that claims for insurance are regarded as a business negotiation and that exaggerated claims form part of that negotiation (Clarke, 1989). As Clarke argues, 'Only if items are claimed for which clearly did not exist, nor form part of the loss, can the claim be contested with confidence as fraudulent' (1989: 4). Therefore, the many claims that are exaggerated in the first instance, which could be regarded on prima facie commonsense grounds as fraudulent, might not be classified as such. The commitment of many insurance companies to tackling fraud has, in the past, been very low-key for fear of putting off potential clients and raising possible business concerns. As a consequence, many frauds have gone undetected and/or unreported (Clarke, 1989; Doig et al., 1999). Very few cases of insurance fraud find their way to the police and the courts for reasons that will shortly be explained. This makes recorded criminal statistics relating to insurance fraud virtually meaningless.

In 2008 undetected insurance fraud was estimated to amount to £1.9 billion (ABI, 2009b). This was a rise from £1.6 billion in 2006 (ABI, 2007). The £1.9 billion included £1.2 billion of retail insurance fraud (up from £1 billion) and £0.7 billion of commercial insurance fraud (up from £0.6 billion). On top of this the Association of British Insurers (ABI) argues one must add the costs of detecting and preventing insurance fraud, which are not estimated by the report. The biggest proportion of fraud is therefore opportunistic retail fraud with over half of that fraud found in property policies and with the vast majority coming from exaggerations of genuine claims, rather than from fictitious applications. The 2007 report also estimated that the average fraud for a property claim was £800 and for a motor claim £1300. The research also offered some evidence of the profile of a 'typical' fraudster – a man, living in the North of England, having unsecured debt of £1000 plus and a household income below £10,000 per year.

It is also interesting to note the general public's attitude towards insurance fraud. In research on a small sample of claimants it was found that 1 in 10 had not been entirely honest with their claim and almost half knew of someone who had committed insurance fraud (Gill et al., 1994). In more recent research in the UK it was revealed that 7 per cent – around 3 million people – admitted making a fraudulent claim and 48 per cent would not rule out making such a claim. The research also found that 40 per cent saw exaggerating an insurance claim as 'acceptable' or 'borderline'. The same survey found that 38 per cent had used someone else's credit card, 31 per cent had shoplifted as an adult and 53 per cent had knowingly bought stolen goods. The report argued, '... there is public tolerance towards much dishonesty ... a significant number of people surveyed admitting their honesty could be severely tested in the future' (ABI, 2003: 2). This is not a peculiarly British phenomenon. In the USA it has been reported that 1 in 10 Americans would commit insurance fraud if they knew they could get away with it; 1 in 3 say it is acceptable to exaggerate claims to make up for the deductible (the excess); and 3 in 10 would not report a person they knew to have made a fraudulent claim (Coalition against Insurance Fraud, n.d.).

Types of insurance fraud

The ABI (2007) divides insurance fraud into three main areas:

  (i) *Opportunistic fraud in general retail insurance*: the exaggeration or inflation of genuine claims and, in a small number of cases, completely fabricated claims.
 (ii) *Opportunistic fraud in commercial general insurance*: similar to above but relating to the policies of firms.
(iii) *Organized fraud*: policies taken out by criminal gangs for the purpose of fraud.

It is important to distinguish between opportunistic and premeditated fraudsters. The former are largely accounted for by those who make a claim and use that opportunity to exaggerate what they are claiming for. The second group actually take out insurance policies with the aim of pursuing some kind of fraud, and in many cases such frauds are linked to organized criminals. Clearly the type of fraud committed has implications for the strategies to address it, something which is discussed later in the chapter. It is also worth noting that there are some parallels with exaggerated and false claims in respect of benefits fraud, a range of policies paying benefits upon the claimant satisfying certain conditions, such as critical illness, health and unemployment insurance.

However, not all insurance fraud relates to the payment of claims as the following discussion will show.

Providing false details

The price of most insurance policies is based upon the risk of the policy-holder: the higher their risk, the more the policy will cost. Thus a 17-year-old driver with little or no driving experience will pay more for a motor insurance policy than a 45-year-old with 28 years' driving experience and accumulated no claims. In order to secure a lower premium when buying products like health or holiday insurance, people will sometimes give false or incomplete information about themselves. Such frauds may not be perpetrated with the view to making a claim, but rather to securing insurance cover more cheaply. As such these represent a fraud to the insurer in reduced income and to innocent parties who may have to make a claim against the fraudster – most notably in motor insurance – only to discover there is no legitimate policy to claim against.

These types of frauds pose difficulties for insurers because they arise out of ambiguity and misinformation. Advice from the Financial Ombudsman, who, among other things, adjudicates on disputed claims by policy-holders, states that even where there is evidence to show a customer has lied or presented false documents to the insurer, it does not follow that the claim is fraudulent (Financial Ombudsman, 2002a). Indeed, with critical insurance cover there have been growing numbers of complaints over failures to pay out by insurers, many because the applicant has not provided accurate data (Inman, 2006). For example, the Financial Ombudsman gives the example of a pub landlord who had taken out a critical insurance policy for £10,000 and who was later diagnosed with cancer. The insurer refused to pay out because the landlord had put down that his height was 6'1", when in reality it was 5'10". The complaint was upheld and the insurers forced to pay (Financial Ombudsman, 2002b). This illustrates the continuum of completely fraudulent applications, applications with genuine mistakes and sound applications. Those claims with genuine mistakes could or could not be classed as fraudulent. This makes identifying the scale of this problem difficult and even more so because such frauds only come to light when there is a claim and investigations occur.

Case Study 9.1

A high-profile example of information that came to light on application for a claim was the case of Major Charles Ingram. Major Ingram had found fame by winning the million-pound prize on the television programme 'Who Wants to be a Millionaire', only to be refused payment because of allegations of cheating. However, unrelated to this in 2003 he was found guilty of two charges of obtaining by deception and making a claim on a falsely obtained policy from Direct Line Insurance for £30,000. On his policy he had failed to disclose earlier claims made (*Daily Telegraph*, 2003; *The Independent*, 2003, BBC News, 2003c).

Forged documents and identities

Forged documents are obviously linked to the provision of false information. At one level, this might involve a person using a false identity when applying for a legitimate insurance policy. It can also include providing false documents to support discounts on insurance premiums. So, for example, a motorist might use false certificates of past insurance in order to secure a no-claims discount. At the other end of the scale, there are those who use forged certificates to prove they have insurance. This type of fraud not only defrauds the insurer but puts at risk those who have to make a claim against someone with forged documents.

Exaggerating a claim

The most common type of insurance fraud relates to exaggerating a legitimate claim. Indeed, as discussed earlier this area of insurance fraud is complicated by the fact that, in law, a certain degree of exaggeration is a legitimate part of business negotiations (Clarke, 1989). Further the claimant might simply have a misguided view of the value of their claim. Consequently, the advice of the Financial Ombudsman is that exaggeration does not render a claim void and that the insurer must prove the applicant was seeking to gain more than he or she was entitled to.

Case Study 9.2

The Financial Ombudsman illustrated one example: after a burglary a man submitted a claim to his insurer amounting to £3000, including a DVD player, 14 DVDs, audio-visual equipment and jewellery. Investigations by the insurance company revealed some of the DVDs that were being claimed as stolen had not even been released and, on interview, the claimant revealed he had not even owned a DVD player. The claim was rejected and this was upheld by the Ombudsman (Financial Ombudsman, 2002a).

Making a false claim

False claims are perpetrated by both 'ordinary' claimants and more organized criminals. This type of insurance fraud simply involves making up a fictitious incident which is covered by insurance and making a claim for it. Such frauds might also involve false information being supplied in order to secure the policy in the first place. Such was the extent of the problem relating to claims of stolen mobile phones that one police force introduced declarations of truth for victims to sign. It was estimated 20 per cent of robbery claims for mobile phones were false (BBC News, 2003d). These types of frauds have also led to some of the most amusing and ingenious fraudulent claims (see Case Study 9.3).

Case Study 9.3

In one case a man claimed, under a holiday insurance policy, that he had dived into the sea, landing on a rock. This, he claimed, caused damage to his penis requiring him to have surgery. Investigations revealed that he had, in fact, had a pre-planned penis enlargement operation. The technique for the surgery was inspired by a Dr Long! (Blythe, 1995).

Case Study 9.4

At the end of 2007 the UK was gripped by the story of John Darwin who had turned up at a police station having 'disappeared' 5 years previously while canoeing. After his disappearance, Darwin's wife had told their two sons that their father was dead. Later, she made claims on life insurance policies amounting to several hundred thousand pounds. Subsequently, it turned out that Darwin had been living all the time in a bedsit in the house next door to their own house – one of several houses that made up their property portfolio. In July 2008 John Darwin was sentenced to 6 years and 3 months in prison. Anne Darwin was imprisoned for 6 years and 6 months (*Daily Telegraph*, 2008; *Hartlepool Mail*, 2008; Timesonline, 2008).

Staged insurance claims

Another type of premeditated fraud involves staged insurance claims. This happens when the damages claimed may be genuine, but the incident is not. There are many examples of failing businesses where the owner perpetrates this fraud in order to try and salvage the firm. The most common example is when a house, building or factory is deliberately set on fire, attempts being made to disguise the fraud as an accident, with the purpose of making an insurance claim. For example, in 2006 a fisherman admitted deliberately sinking his boat in order to finance the purchase of a new trawler (BBC News, 2006e).

Recently such claims have also proliferated with organized gangs staging motor accidents. In 2006 the Insurance Fraud Bureau (IFB) estimated that over 20,000 accidents might be staged by over 400 criminal networks during the course of the next 18 months. Typically, such cases involve fraudsters braking suddenly while driving causing the car behind to crash. After the 'accident' an insurance claim for injuries and damage is made. According to one estimate, a claim could net around £30,000 (BBC News, 2006b). Such is the extent of the problem that the IFB dedicated its whole £8 million budget to the problem for the next 5 years (BBC News, 2006c).

Case Study 9.5

In a gruesome example which occurred in 2001, a man died in a pool of blood in what initially seemed, to police, like a sadistic attack by someone with a chainsaw. However, investigations revealed that he had conspired with his cousin to perpetrate an insurance fraud worth over $500,000. The victim had taken out a series of policies relating to potential serious injury causing permanent disability. The cousin had cut the victim's leg with a chainsaw, the two believing that the blood flow would be easily stemmed. Unfortunately, an artery was severed and the victim died (BBC News, 2001b).

Countering insurance fraud

The diversity of fraud types requires a range of different means to counter it. Over the last decade in the UK there have been a variety of developments to enhance the ability of insurers to tackle fraud. At an industry level greater co-operation between companies has resulted in the establishment of bodies such as the IFB, which pursues a wide range of strategies. Many individual companies have also enhanced their capacity. Some of these industry-level and typical company-level strategies will now be explored.

Insurance industry developments

The realization of the growing threat from organized fraudsters targeting multiple insurance companies has spurred the insurance industry to work collectively together in a number of areas. The trade association for the insurance industry, the ABI, has encouraged a number of developments. As the ABI (n.d.) argues,

> Anyone involved in counter-fraud work in any sector will testify to the power of shared data and intelligence. Organised criminals will not focus their attentions on single businesses. They will target particular sectors or more likely a whole range of sectors wherever they see opportunities for financial gain. A pattern of behaviour that triggers suspicion of fraud will often only emerge when a number of organisations exchange information. Insurers who have used data mining software have seen the benefits of that increased many times over

where they share data with just one other player in the same market. If all insurers in, for example, the personal motor insurance market, shared data then it is self-evident that organised frauds within that market would be harder to perpetrate. 'Organised' fraudsters could be professional criminals working as part of a gang or individuals who, for example, made a practice of moving year on year to different insurers and regularly claiming against them.

The ABI has led on a number of initiatives to enhance the capacity of the insurance industry to tackle fraud. Central to this is an Anti-Fraud Committee that has members from most of the main insurance companies. It has provided opportunities for members to share best practice in tackling fraud. Additionally, it has facilitated the sharing of data between insurers to help identify potentially fraudulent claims. It has also acted as the lead in working with government, the police and the financial sector in seeking the most appropriate initiatives in tackling fraud. Perhaps most challenging of all, it has sought to change public attitudes towards insurance fraud (ABI, 2001).

Co-operation between insurers has also culminated in the emergence of specialist industry bodies targeted at countering fraud. The Insurance Fraud Investigators Group (IFIG) is a member-based body drawing upon insurers, loss adjusters, lawyers and investigation agencies. It also has strong ties with other anti-fraud bodies and the law enforcement community. IFIG's origins lay in the mid-1990s when insurance fraud investigators came together informally. In 1999 they decided upon IFIG as the name and in 2001 it became a body in its own right. IFIG has 160 members and its key aims are the following:

- Detecting and preventing insurance fraud
- Raising the profile of insurance fraud as a crime
- Providing a forum to discuss anti-fraud initiatives and techniques
- Sharing relevant intelligence via the National Intelligence Model (IFIG, n.d.)

Alongside IFIG is the IFB which was launched in 2006, targeted mainly at organized and cross-industry fraud. The IFB also operates the Fraud Cheatline, 0800 328 2550, a free phone number which anyone can use to report insurance fraud confidentially.

It has a staff of 10, a budget of £1.7 million and its members cover 95 per cent of the insurance industry. The IFB is chaired by the former Scotland Yard detective, John Beadle. One of its most important functions relates to the analysis of insurance claims of members using data-mining and data-matching software. From this it identifies suspicious claims, co-ordinates their investigation, oversees the recovery of monies and pursues prosecution with the police and the Crown Prosecution Service (CPS). In its first year of operation it completed six investigations with the police with a further 14 ongoing. Its work culminated in 74 arrests, issue of 370 intelligence reports in relation to 2069 claims, seizure of £5.5 million of cash under the Proceeds of Crime Act and receipt of 539 calls to the Cheatline (IFB, 2007).

Preventing insurance fraud

Preventative and deterrence measures targeted against fraudsters are pursued at both an industry and a company level. At an industry level insurers have realized, through some of the research discussed earlier, that they need to change the culture towards insurance fraud since many people do not regard it as a crime. In recent years through the Cheatline, the establishment of IFB and the publicizing of successful prosecutions there have been attempts to do this; but these have been limited in comparison with initiatives carried out in some other sectors (see Chapter 6 on preventing fraud).

The most significant preventative strategy has involved data mining, matching and sharing. Data is verified by companies against known indicators of fraud and certain levels trigger further investigations. This is done by claims assessment as well as by telephone and face-to-face interviews (Artis et al., 1999, 2002; Morley et al., 2006). The sharing of information is also central to tackling insurance fraud effectively, particularly for the more organized fraudsters, though also for the opportunist. There are various databases operated by the industry which enable identification of fraudsters and potential fraudsters. The Claims and Underwriting Exchange has details of all claims made in the last 5 years enabling identification of multiple claims. The Motor Insurance Anti-Fraud and Theft Register contains details of all vehicles stolen or written off after an accident. The Motor Insurance Database holds data on all insured drivers (including named drivers), enabling checks to be made on who holds motor insurance (ABI 2006). The industry uses a software tool called Hunter which cross-checks information from applicants of insurance fraud against data held on the system. Discrepancies lead to further investigations by counter-fraud staff as well as checks with CIFAS which holds data on known fraudsters.

The insurance industry has also sought to deter fraudulent claims by introducing voice recognition technology (Voice Risk Analysis – VRA); this aims to identify stress which, it is claimed, may suggest a person is lying. Esure was one of the first companies to introduce this technology (PR Newswire, 2003). Though its effectiveness is debatable (Vrij, 2008), the real purpose of such technologies is to prevent opportunistic fraud. For many people, the mere suggestion from an insurer that their voice will be analyzed may deter false or exaggerated claims.

Detecting and investigating insurance fraud

Traditionally the insurance industry did not seek to involve the police and public authorities in tackling fraud – apart from the most serious cases where there was clear evidence – preferring, instead, to deal with the matter itself (Clarke, 1989). However, with the growth of fraud, particularly organized fraud, insurers are demanding greater police involvement (ABI, 2006). Yet, as discussed in Chapter 7, the police's resource commitment to fraud does not inspire much confidence. In the ABI submission to the Fraud Review a number of cases were highlighted to illustrate the sometimes poor response of the police and other public bodies to insurance fraud. For example, in one case an industry-wide investigation uncovered 400 linked motor accidents in a major city in the UK where the gang 'induced' an accident with a member of the public. The insurance investigators produced evidence to prove that the crimes had been undertaken by a local gang to fund drug trafficking and clearly there was a danger posed to the public by the staged accidents. The response of the police was to request funding to investigate the crime, which was declined, and as a consequence the investigation did not go any further (ABI, 2006). The reluctance of the police to become involved in less organized insurance frauds because of the inability of insurance fraud staff to offer sufficient evidence has also been documented (Doig et al., 1999).

In part, the launch of the IFB, discussed previously, was aimed to address this shortfall in police provision; but with a staff of only ten people, it has been able to concentrate only on the most serious frauds, which probably represent the tip of the iceberg. By contrast, the largest amounts of insurance fraud relate to exaggerated genuine claims and for these, the frontline in detecting fraud is made up of claims handlers (Morley et al., 2006). In general, claims handlers examine anomalies, inconsistencies, patterns of claims and claimant characteristics (aggression, uncertainty, etc.) and, by so doing, identify claims that require further scrutiny. Usually clear indicators of fraud are specified by the company and, if a claim meets these, further action is taken. This might include cross-checking the claim on various databases, and, depending upon the company, claims are usually handed over to more experienced claims handlers, internal fraud departments or are contracted out to specialist private investigators or loss adjusters.

However, despite the important role of claims handlers in this process, research has suggested various things: that they are often inexperienced, poorly trained and subject to high labour turnover; that the indicators they use often produce large lists of false positives that clog up the system; and that where specialist databases are employed, data quality is variable, with misspellings, outdated data and missing information making detection difficult (Morley et al., 2006). Detailed observation of claims handlers at work by Morley et al. (2006) also found evidence that the organizational tactic of dealing with claims as quickly and efficiently as possible compromised the strategy for referring suspicious claims. Claims handlers would frequently not refer claims because of their own intuition: an intuition based on the claim value, whether there had been a previous claim, the term of the insurance and so on. Many would also not refer because they felt no ownership of the claim, never having been told of the outcomes of previous cases. Evidence of inadequate scripts for staff to elicit information from claimants and of fraud indicator forms being completed long after interviews had taken place was also found (Morley et al., 2006). Indications of fraud are also frequently identified by external agents such as garages, loss adjusters, engineers and the like, but this information is often not acted upon by claims handlers. Therefore, despite its important role, the overall quality of the claim handling process leaves much to be desired.

The majority of insurance companies employ in-house staff to investigate suspicious claims. Some may have previously worked in claims departments; others may be ex-police officers. Sometimes they provide investigative services for claims departments, sometimes for separate investigations departments and sometimes for counter-fraud sections or risk departments. Their orientation remains much as it was described by Clarke (1989) 20 years ago: to keep fraud 'private' by resolving it internally. In part, this is because of the difficulties of invoking public justice; but the main reason is because of the desire to protect the company's reputation and commercial interest. For the latter reason, when fraud is discovered the aim of the insurance company is either to avoid payment or, if payment has been made, to recoup it. As Gill and Hart argue,

> The object of investigating insurance claims is to verify their accuracy, the claimant's right to compensation and, if the clients are insurers or their representatives, to identify any attempt to defraud the insurance company. This normally remains a private matter between the company and the insured and need not result in any criminal or civil action, even if an attempted fraud is discovered. The purpose of the investigation is to inform the insurer's negotiations with the insured and their subsequent decision-making. The aim is often to avoid litigation because it is expensive and can damage the insurance company's reputation, even if they win the case.
>
> (1997: 555)

Significantly, despite growing calls for greater criminal justice involvement in insurance fraud (ABI, 2006), there is little evidence of the significant professionalization of fraud investigation that has occurred in many other sectors (see Chapter 7 and Button et al., 2007). A decade ago, Doig et al. (1999) found evidence of some insurance fraud investigators' inability to investigate to a level that could secure a criminal prosecution and reported doubts from the police about the quality of evidence insurers could produce. There are no available statistics on the number of prosecutions for insurance fraud in the UK, but given the evidence available, it would seem only a tiny minority end up in the criminal courts. For this reason many firms see no need to invest in more advanced training that equips staff to pursue criminal prosecutions. However, attitudes are changing and IFIG, in partnership with Bond Solon, has developed Advanced Professional Training in Investigative Practice which is being increasingly utilized in the insurance sector.

The contract sector also has an important investigatory role. Private investigators are frequently used to conduct investigations, and Gill and Hart (1997) found evidence of a growing market, one firm having doubled its insurance business each year for the previous 3 years. As well as private investigators many accountancy firms, such as KPMG Forensic, offer specialist investigative and forensic accounting services. Private investigators are also used where surveillance is required to verify claims. For example, in 2006, a man was convicted of 'conspiracy to defraud' after being exposed by a private investigator's surveillance footage. He was seeking £1 million compensation from NFU Mutual after an accident at a farm. He claimed that, as a result of the injury, he was wheelchair-bound. NFU Mutual hired a firm of private investigators who secured video footage of him walking and driving around. This and other evidence led to the rejection of his claim, criminal prosecution and a gaol sentence of three-and-a-half years (BBC News, 2006d). Sometimes, however, undercover activities breach acceptable ethical standards. In one case, a firm was found to be using prostitutes to lure a man into sex acts. The man in question had submitted an insurance claim relating to his alleged loss of sexual functioning (*Daily Mirror*, 19 October 1994).

Finally there are the insurance loss adjusters who undertake investigations into large and complicated claims and who, in the process of their work, may uncover fraud. There are just under 4000 Chartered Loss Adjusters in the Chartered Institute of Loss Adjusters (CILA, 2007). They act on behalf of insurers investigating claims and, though they will investigate fraud, sometimes contract it out to private investigators.

Sanctions and criminal prosecutions

Previously, we have referred to the police's lack of interest in fraud and the desire of fraud victims to keep their victimization private. However, if insures do want to go down the criminal prosecution route, not only do they face the challenge of securing police interest, they also have the additional hurdle of securing support from the CPS. In the ABI submission to the Fraud Review, they cited an example of a £250,000 fraud where subsequent investigation revealed a witness had committed perjury during the civil proceedings. The perjurer only received a police caution and despite the view of the police investigating officer that there was enough evidence to prosecute, the CPS refused to do so (ABI, 2006). In its submission the ABI advocated greater use of police cautions, that the police should be required to investigate when a certain level of loss is reached, and that there should be greater opportunities for the Asset Recovery Agency to become involved in frauds perpetrated in the private sector. It would seem, therefore, that in comparison to some sectors, the use of sanctions is under-developed. Sanctions, prosecutions and redress are a vital part of the broader task of changing cultural attitudes to committing fraud and, as the opening part of this chapter illustrated, there is still a long way to go on this front.

Conclusion

Insurance fraud provides similar levels of damage in terms of costs to society as social security fraud does. It is, however, considered much more acceptable by the general public. There is also evidence that many more members of the public are willing to flirt with the possibility of committing this type of fraud. Given the concept of negotiation in submitting an insurance claim – which may be exaggerated – it highlights further evidence of the blurred nature of fraud. Countering insurance fraud also demonstrates significant differences as there is much more emphasis on prevention. However, perhaps most significantly, the outcomes of investigations raise some of the most serious questions which require further debate and research. A multi-thousand pound attempt at an insurance fraud if discovered is often unlikely to result in a criminal prosecution, yet in the area of social security that would be very likely. This is perhaps revealing of another theme in this book relating to white collar criminals. Certain crimes are treated differently given who perpetrates them. Given insurance is very often a product of the better off in society (home owners, car owners, etc.), this provides a further example of how different types of fraudsters are often treated differently.

This chapter has explored insurance fraud. Despite being commonplace, the public availability of data on this subject is limited. The chapter began by exploring the extent of insurance fraud, looking at public attitudes to it and discussing some examples of the types of frauds perpetrated. Next, it explored the techniques used to tackle insurance fraud focusing, in particular, on recent industry-level developments. In doing so it highlighted the limited involvement of the state and drew attention to the prevention of fraud through the analysis of claims. It also discussed preventive techniques, investigative structures and the various sanctions applied.

Further reading

- Clarke, M. (1989) Insurance Fraud. *British Journal of Criminology*, 29, 1–20.
- Clarke, M. (1990) The Control of Insurance Fraud: A Comparative View. *British Journal of Criminology*, 30(1), 1–23.
- Doig, A., Jones, B. and Wait, B. (1999) The Insurance Industry Response to Fraud. *Security Journal*, 12(3), 19–30.
- Morley, N.J., Ball, L.J. and Ormerod, T.C. (2006) How the Detection of Insurance Fraud Succeeds and Fails. *Psychology, Crime and Law*, 12, 163–180.

Organizations with information relating to insurance fraud include:

- The Association of British Insurers: http://www.abi.org.uk
- The Insurance Fraud Bureau: http://www.insurancefraudbureau.org/
- The Insurance Fraud Investigators Group: http://www.ifig.org/

CHAPTER 10

Social Security Fraud

Overview

The aims of this chapter are to provide

- an overview of where social security fraud fits in the broader public sector
- an exploration of the nature and extent of social security fraud
- a description and evaluation of the strategies implemented to counter social security fraud

---

Introduction

Social security fraud evokes a strong reaction in the public and the media. In research published by the NHS CFSMS (2007b), which was discussed in Chapter 5, it was shown how the general public rates social security fraud as much worse than taxation or insurance frauds. The chapter also showed how politicians have generally shown more interest in tackling social security fraud than many others. Part II of the book also pointed to a number of issues in how fraud is investigated and prosecuted in the UK. One of the main points to arise was that responsibility for these is not exclusively borne by the police but rather is shared between numerous public and private sector agencies. Each of these organizations have developed their own individual responses based on what types of fraud they have to combat and their individual organizational responsibilities. One major example is the Department of Work and Pensions (DWP).

Welfare payments and transfers is the single largest category in the UK Government's annual expenditure and as such a major potential target for fraud. Consequentially, the department is involved in all aspects of countering fraud, including detection, investigating and prosecuting cases committed against them. These have been organized in the form of a strategic management approach that has evolved since 1997. This chapter explores the nature and extent of the problem, going on to examine the different approaches adopted to countering social security fraud. After evaluating the evidence on the efficacy of these strategies, the chapter closes by considering, first, recent attempts to adopt a compliance-led approach and, second, the problems of measuring social security fraud. Before we embark upon this, however, it is useful to briefly set out where social security fraud fits in broader public sector initiatives to tackle fraud.

Fraud and the public sector

Fraud committed against the public sector has become an increasingly important issue since the early 1990s. For example, the document *Public Services for the Future* (HM Treasury, 1998) explicitly cited fraud as having a major impact on the government's efficiency and productivity in delivering services. Treasury concerns about fraud began to be expressed around 20 years ago. In 1994, the following statement spelled out the responsibilities of individual government departments on preventing fraud:

> Departments should develop and maintain effective controls to prevent fraud and to ensure that if it does occur it will be detected promptly. If fraud does occur departments must carry out a vigorous and prompt investigation. They should take the appropriate legal and/or disciplinary action. In all cases where that would be justified, and they should make any necessary changes to systems and procedures to ensure that similar frauds will not happen again.
>
> (HM Treasury, 1994: para. 37.1.2)

The next significant development in countering fraud in government came with the publication of *Managing the Risk of Fraud: A Guide for Managers*, again by HM Treasury (1997). This laid out a blueprint for coherent and co-ordinated actions that government departments needed to take in order to combat fraud and to create an anti-fraud culture. One factor in doing this involved making sure that a <u>department's mission statement,</u> or 'statement of commitment', <u>promoted ethical business behaviour,</u> along the lines of the Nolan Committee's seven principles of public life. On that basis, it was proposed that departments should formulate a policy statement on fraud which would include

- allocation of responsibilities for managing fraud;
- procedures staff should follow if a fraud is discovered;
- guidance on training for prevention and detection of fraud; and
- reference to how organizations seek to deal with a fraudulent attack.

In pursuit of this, the manager's responsibility was to 'ensure that the opportunities for fraud are minimised. <u>Separation of duties, effective procedures and checks should prevent or deter fraud from occurring</u>' (HM Treasury, 1997: 6). As part of this strategy, departments were now required to make annual returns on all cases of suspected fraud within the following categories:

- fraud committed within the department by its own employees, along with cases of collusion with parties outside the department;
- frauds committed against the department by the public if the value exceeds £10,000;
- computer frauds;
- contractor frauds arising out of contracts placed by departments for the supply of goods; and
- frauds that expose weaknesses in systems or cause loss of a nature that could occur in other departments.

Such returns were subsequently published by HM Treasury on an annual basis, the results being collated and used to inform and advise departments on future procedures. This was seen as

- Contributing to a fraud-deterrence culture by illustrating control weaknesses which contribute to cases of actual or attempted fraud or theft. These aid government bodies in assessing the risks in their internal procedures.

- Promoting a wider fraud-deterrence culture by offering advice about combating fraud and theft generally.
- Acting as a warning to potential perpetrators that fraud is unacceptable and not tolerated within central government and that appropriate action will be taken in respect of all suspected cases.
- Providing information on reported fraud and theft to Parliament, public bodies and the wider public.

Departments were also required to report as quickly as possible details of any novel or unusual frauds (or suspected frauds) affecting them, their agencies or the non-departmental public bodies (NDPBs) sponsored by them. Additionally, departments, agencies and NDPBs were obliged to report frauds which, while minor in themselves, could be serious if repeated across government as a whole. By 2002, this process had been extended to the need for reporting where preliminary investigations had indicated fraud (HM Treasury, 2002: 7). By 2004, of the 103 departments and agencies surveyed by the Treasury, 76 or 73 per cent stated that they had an anti-fraud policy (HM Treasury, 2004). Such a proactive approach was not confined to central government departments, but more crucially to the 'frontline' departments and agencies responsible for government spending and distribution of public money and resources, including the DWP.

The extent and nature of social security fraud

In most countries governments offer social security payments to certain categories of people in need. The extent and generosity of these payments differ significantly between countries. In the UK social security benefits are given to a wide range of groups including the unemployed, the sick, the disabled, pensioners, the low-paid and single parents. The DWP, the department with overall responsibility for social security, distributed over 40 different types of benefit amounting to £124 billion in 2006, or approximately a quarter of government spending (Bourn, 2007). Major benefits include

- Jobseeker's Allowance (JSA);
- Income Support (IS);

- Child Benefit (CB);
- Disability Living Allowance (DLA);
- Disability Working Allowance (DWA);
- Pension Credit (PC) (formerly Minimum Income Guarantee for pensioners);
- National Insurance Credits (NIC) (via JSA or Incapacity Benefit (IB)); and
- Housing Benefit (HB).

Bourn (2007) concludes that in 2006 there were likely to have been approximately £2.5 billion losses from fraud and error. This figure is not entirely reliable, however, as the DWP's measurements are incomplete (see below). The benefits that are most consistently and thoroughly measured are in respect of JSA, IS, HB and PC. Before some of the main benefits are described and the extent of fraud against them is discussed, it is useful to list the most common types of benefits fraud.

(i) *Working while claiming.* Some claimants work in the 'black economy' for 'cash-in-hand' while making JSA or IS claims relating to having no employment.

(ii) *Living together as a couple (cohabiting) when claiming to be single.* Some people's benefits are reduced or removed if they live with a partner, so they may have an incentive to deny cohabitation.

(iii) *Exaggerating or making up fictitious injuries/disabilities.* Some falsely claim DWA or exaggerate the severity of their disability.

(iv) *Understating savings.* Some people may under-report their savings in order to qualify for means-tested benefits.

(v) *Claiming for fictitious or dead persons.* Some fraudsters steal identities in order to make claims; others continue to claim for a person who is deceased.

In the case of HB there are a series of other potential frauds because of the additional factor of the landlord. These include

(i) *Claiming for an address where one is not in residence.*

(ii) *Working while claiming benefit or understating one's income while claiming benefits.*

(iii) *Fake tenancies/claimants.* Some landlords making claims create fictitious claimants or tenancy agreements. This might include tenants who have moved on, or it might involve claiming for empty properties.

(iv) *False rents.* Some landlords collude with tenants to create inflated rents above the level actually paid.

Jobseeker's Allowance/Income Support fraud

Between April 2008 and March 2009 it was estimated that around 5.5 per cent, or £640 million, of JSA/IS (Income Support) was overpaid, either through fraud or through error (DWP, 2009). In the area of welfare provision there were already long-standing controversies about the alleged connections between the 'undeserving poor' who claim welfare, 'scroungers' and fraud (Cook, 1989, 2006; Sainsbury, 2003). These were augmented after 1998 by the belief in government that there was a need for the public to accept a re-definition of the relationship between the welfare state and the public. The new Labour Government saw the fight against fraud as crucial in such acceptance. As the then Prime Minister Tony Blair stated, 'We made the task of tackling fraud one of our early priorities. This is because public support is vital for welfare reform, and public support is eroded by the failure to stop people defrauding the benefit system' (DWP, 1998a: iii).

Pension Credit fraud

PC is an entitlement for people aged 60 or over living in Great Britain and guarantees a minimum weekly income. In 2007 this was £119.05 a week for single people and £181.70 a week for partners. Between April 2008 and March 2009 it was estimated that around 5.1 per cent, or £390 million, of PC expenditure was overpaid, either through fraud or through error (DWP, 2009).

Housing Benefit fraud

HB is a 'passport' benefit in that claimants eligible for other benefits are likely also to be eligible for it. It is administered for the DWP by the local authorities. In 1995 the then Department for Social Security (the precursor of the DWP) estimated that two-thirds of HB claimants also claimed IS and 74 per cent of the total expenditure lost through fraud occurred in this group. In monetary terms this involved £536 million, £412 million of

which related to private sector tenants. The survey also estimated
that 300,000 people were involved in fraud. In 2003–04, losses
through fraud and error amounted to approximately £600 million. Of this, fraud was estimated to account for between £150 and
£300 million, with errors by customers and officials accounting
for the remaining amount (DWP, 2006: 3). Between April 2008
and March 2009 it was estimated that around 4.9 per cent, or
£840 million, of HB expenditure was overpaid, either through
fraud or through error (DWP, 2009).

Case Study 10.1

A man was convicted of falsely claiming £46,000 in benefits
(Disability Benefit (DB), IS, HB Council Tax (CT) Benefit).
In his disability claim he stated that he was unable to stand
for a minute, turn on a tap or walk for a few paces. In reality he was running a company couriering organs around the
country which, over the same 9 years of the claim, had been
paid £200,000 from the NHS. He was jailed for 9 months and
ordered to repay the benefits (*The Guardian*, 2007).

Case Study 10.2

In 2008 a benefit claimant was jailed for 5 years and 3
months after being found guilty of a £170,000 HB and CT
fraud which had been used to fund a £4 million property
empire. Over a period of 9 years, he and his partner had
defrauded two London boroughs using 26 false applications
(*The Guardian*, 2008b).

Countering benefits fraud

The period up to 1998

Efforts to counter fraud can be divided between the period before
1998 and the years following. Anti-fraud strategies can be traced
back to the *Report of the Social Security Committee on Abuse of Social*

Security Benefits (1973), also known as the Fisher Report. This advocated a strategy of investigating fit and healthy claimants who were suspected of receiving non-declared earnings, the aim being to create a culture of deterrence through prosecutions. The 1980s saw an increase in fraud investigators, but also a change in emphasis away from prosecution to getting suspects to 'sign off' or withdraw their claim. As the then Social Security Minister Reg Prentice said, 'In the past, as many cases as possible were pursued to prosecution, but in future the cessation of a claim might be regarded in appropriate cases as being the most cost effective way of dealing with the matter' (Cook, 1989: 138).

It also saw the beginning of a more structured approach, with levels of investigations and the creation of Special Claims Control Units, which were charged with targeting claimants who were not suffering from illness. The success of these initiatives was to be measured by their reaching weekly benefits savings targets. The effect of these initiatives was an increase in investigations, but the policy of getting suspects to sign off, rather than for the department to prosecute, continued. However, not only such investigations were random in their nature, they also attracted criticism for being 'heavy handed' and for using inappropriate methods (Cook, 1989: 139). This random approach began to change under John Major. In 1993, the new Benefits Agency was created and charged with establishing the extent of the fraud problem and subsequently reducing it. To fulfill this mission statement the strategy was designed to ensure that

- The social security strategy was integrated with other strategies pursued by the then Benefits Agency.
- Procedures concerned with delivering benefits were tightened up, including ensuring that potential clients or claimants established their identity; that claimants' circumstances were verified, with any changes being recognized in a timely manner; and that claimants were paid through secure mechanisms.
- Frontline staff should be responsible for security.
- The provision and development of IT systems to assist the process of cases and to support effective management controls was implemented.

As the National Audit Office (NAO) commented in 1997:

> The Benefits Agency Security Strategy aims to establish the extent of fraud and reduce the amount across all benefits. The strategy is based on making the benefit pipeline secure, from initial claim on the system, thorough the calculation, determination and payment of a claim and the periodic review, to claim termination, and where necessary, overpayment recovery.
>
> (1997: 2.2)

Through such a strategy, it was hoped that fraud would be reduced by 70 per cent in 5 years. However, this was undermined because the amount of fraud had been underestimated; it had been calculated on the basis of the flawed Weekly Benefits Savings (WBS) scheme.

1998–2006: The strategic revolution

The period 1998–2006 saw a wholesale change in the way fraud was investigated with the emphasis being placed on a proactive approach, adopting the principles of strategic management. This was largely as a result of the 1998 Public Sector Agreement (PSA) between the Department and the Treasury which aimed to reduce losses through error and fraud in IS and JSA by at least 30 per cent by 2007, and 10 per cent by March 2002. These targets were later revised in 2000, 2002, 2004 and 2006.

In order to achieve these targets, the DWP adopted an explicit mission statement to 'minimise fraud in the social security system so as to maximise the resources available to meet need, and to enhance public confidence'. This was to be achieved by

- Developing an anti-fraud culture within the social security system and among the general public;
- Designing and operating policies and systems which were aimed at minimizing fraud;
- Creating an environment in which anti-fraud work could flourish; and
- Developing a highly skilled anti-fraud profession and professionalism among staff (DWP, 1998b).

Underpinning these aims were the principles of 'Getting it right'; 'Keeping it right'; and 'Putting it right', when dealing with benefit claims. Thus 'Getting it right' involved aiming to pay the correct benefits payments from day one by strengthening procedures for interviewing claimants at benefit offices. 'Keeping it right' meant ensuring that any changes in a client's circumstances would be detected promptly and payments adjusted accordingly. 'Putting it right' involved detecting when payments go wrong and correcting them promptly. This would involve investigation of cases of potential fraud and if necessary prosecuting or sanctioning fraudsters. Together these objectives would prevent fraud from entering the system and, if it did, minimizing its impact. Prosecution of offenders would act as a deterrent to potential fraudsters. The final part of the new strategy was to introduce a new, more sophisticated method of measuring fraud and error in the system.

Delivering the objectives: Approaches and structures

In order to achieve the new objectives, the department adopted a strategic management approach to detecting and prosecuting fraud, based on intelligence-led investigations. As Scampion stated,

> The strategic direction given to organised fraud should at least in part be determined by the risk identification carried out by an intelligence capability. That capability should be fully co-coordinated. It should cover the total anti fraud response – prevention and detection – and should be also directed by those responsible for overall strategy.
>
> (2000: para. 2.8)

This new approach placed emphasis on a proactive, intelligence-led approach to assess whether cases of reported or suspected fraud should be referred for investigation. As the National Audit Report commented,

> The high volume of potential cases means that an intelligence-led approach is required to ensure that the cases chosen for investigation have the greatest chance of finding fraud, and preferably those of higher value.
>
> (2003: 33)

Structures and investigations

The new approach was accompanied by a re-organization and re-structuring of the way the DWP investigated fraud. From now on, responsibility for investigations was to be at a national, regional and local level within the DWP. At DWP headquarters, a Fraud Strategy Unit (FSU) was created to produce and oversee anti-fraud strategies for all benefits, based on analyzing data collected from external and internal sources. Externally, the principal source was the newly created Benefit Hotline, where the general public could pass on information about suspected fraudsters. Within the DWP the principal sources were the Counter Fraud Investigation Division (CFID) via the National Intelligence Unit (NIU) and the Operational Intelligence Units (OIUs) (see below). Investigating allegations of fraud was the responsibility of the CFID. CFID also operated on a national, regional and local level within local Job Centre Plus benefit offices.

At the National level, there were six sectors: the Professional Standards Unit, the National Intelligence Unit, the Matching Intelligence Unit, the Operations Branch, the Head of Profession Office and the Joint Working Unit (see Figure 10.1). At the regional level, CFID had dedicated teams operating in each of the 13 Job Centre Plus regions. At the local level, investigators would operate with frontline benefit staff who, as part of administrating claims, would help identify possible incidences of fraud.

CFID investigations

Initially, CFID investigation activity was split into two distinct areas, the Counter Fraud Investigation Service (CFIS) and the Counter Fraud Investigation Division (Operations) (CFID Ops). CFIS investigated individuals' fraudulent benefit claims, while CFID Ops investigated organized or 'more serious' crimes against the Benefits system (Figure 10.1). Both were combined in 2006 to make up the Fraud Investigation Service (FIS).

Cases of potential fraud were referred for investigation on a risk assessment process conducted by the NIU and, at regional

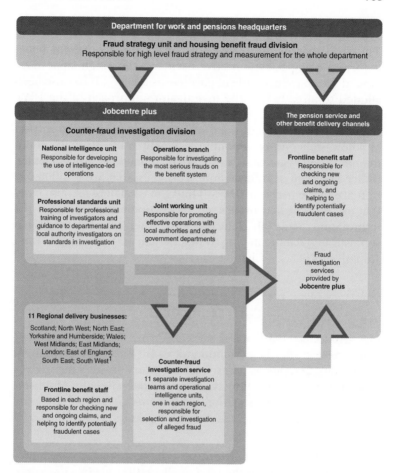

Figure 10.1 DWP organizational chart 1999–2005. DWP structure 2000–05. [adapted from NAO (2003)].

level, by OIUs. Both were to be responsible for the development of the use of intelligence-led operations in investigating fraud. The NIUs' main responsibilities were to provide the intelligence on trends in fraud for the FSU, and to transmit such strategies and policies to the area level via the OIUs. The OIUs were then responsible for evaluating the quality of the intelligence and allocating workloads to individual investigators (NAO, 2003).

DWP policy in practice

The DWP has made much of its campaigns to prevent benefits fraud using television advertisements, although some have
argued they have had little impact (Grover, 2005). It has also been
alluded to already that the investigatory approach of the DWP
is both reactive and proactive. The benefits telephone hotline
0800 854440 and a dedicated website enable people who suspect
or know someone of committing benefit fraud to make confi-
dential tip-offs (see Case Study 10.3). Indeed, statistics released
under Freedom of Information Act suggest that around 200,000
calls are made per year (Dizzy Thinks, n.d). There are also cases
that are investigated proactively based upon assessments of the
information made on claims against other sources, as well as
sophisticated data-matching strategies such as the National Fraud
Initiative (NFI) (see Chapter 7).

Case Study 10.3

A salsa dance teacher was sentenced to 200 hours' community service after being found guilty of fraudulently claiming
disability benefits as a result of an injury in his knees. He
was caught after an anonymous tip-off to the Benefits Hotline
which led to an investigation (BBC News, 2007c).

When the DWP staff do investigate a claimant, the approach they
use varies according to the type of alleged fraud. In some cases,
claimants might be visited and questioned regarding the information they had supplied. If this leads to evidence of fraud, a formal
interview under The Police and Criminal Evidence (PACE) Act
1984 might be conducted. There are situations where it is necessary to conduct surveillance and the DWP has a capacity to
do this, though it is strictly regulated under the Regulation of
Investigatory Powers Act (RIPA) 2000. The surveillance used by
the DWP is covert and usually involves cameras hidden on the
person or in cars/vans directed at the suspect. Most frequently, it
is used to determine if two people are living together (see Case
Study 10.4), when they claim they are not; if they are working, when they say they are not; or to determine their physical

condition, if they are claiming benefits for disabilities. The DWP may also work with other investigative bodies, most commonly local authorities, for cases involving HB, and with the police, where there is an organized criminal element. Investigators may also seek the support of police to make use of their powers of arrest and search where that is required in an investigation when a suspect is not co-operating.

Case Study 10.4

In a joint investigation between the DWP and a District Council, a man was found guilty of fraudulently claiming over £4000 of IS and HB in February 2007. When his claim was assessed, questions were raised over whether his wife was living with him, to which he claimed no. Surveillance by the investigators ascertained she was living with him, which meant he was not entitled to the benefits (EHDC, 2007).

Once the investigation is complete, the DWP has its own prosecution service, the Solicitors Branch, which pursues the case in the courts (see Table 10.1 for workload). Joint investigations with local authorities or the police may mean the case is prosecuted by the local authority or the Crown Prosecution Service (CPS). This was explored further in Chapter 8.

Table 10.1   Fraud cases of the DWP between 1999 and 2004

Fiscal year	Cases investigated	Effective outcomes[*]	Prosecutions	Admin penalties and cautions
1999–2000	562,235	198,467	9,272	11,029
2000–01	442,100	182,569	11,584	15,555
2001–02	397,035	160,974	11,355	13,551
2002–03	337,221	145,232	9,396	14,273
2003–04	326,599	135,710	9,204	16,159

[*] Effective outcomes are cases which have resulted in a benefit adjustment.
Source: Adapted from DWP (2006: 136).

Evaluating the strategy: Did it work?

The new intelligence-led approach proved to be controversial, with the DWP being charged with reducing the number of investigations undertaken as a result of referrals. For example, NAO Report (2003) noted that between 1999 and 2001, the number of referrals fell from 888,000 in 1999–2000 to 667,000 cases in 2001–02, a fall of 25 per cent. However, while the number of cases referred for investigation fell by nearly 42 per cent between 1999 and 2004, the number of successful outcomes of such investigations increased from 32 per cent to over 41 per cent in the same period. Most tellingly, the number of cases producing evidence strong enough to warrant prosecution remained approximately the same in absolute numbers, while the numbers of non-prosecutorial sanctions such as administrative penalties and sanctions increased both absolutely and as a proportion of the number of cases accepted.

This implies that the risk management approach has been effective. Additionally, the amount of fraud has fallen steadily since 1999, again both absolutely and as a proportion of all claims. Thus, the 2003 NAO Report, *Tackling Benefit Fraud*, estimated that working from a 1997–98 baseline figure, the DWP had reduced loss from error and fraud by 24 per cent by 2002. Even given the likelihood of a diminishing rate of loss, they still concluded that annual losses would be reduced by £640 million by March 2006. By 2005 the DWP could state that the department had reduced fraud in JSA and IS by two-thirds (DWP, 2005a: 3). By 2006 the department could claim that they had indeed exceeded expectations laid out in 1998 and refined in 2002 (White, 2006).

Table 10.2 illustrates this point in terms of the estimated losses for JSA, IS and Pension Credit benefits.

However, the new approach, with its emphasis on assessing allegations on evidence and probability, led to a situation where, while fraud was being steadily reduced, the amount of loss through official and customer error increased. This led to a change in the strategy in 2006 away from investigating claimants as potential fraudsters, towards getting them to comply with their obligations as claimants: the compliance strategy.

Table 10.2 Estimated losses for JSA, IS and Pension Credit benefits

Year	Fraud £ (million)	Customer error (million)	Official error (million)	Total (million)
1999–2000	830	170	310	1320
2000–01	780	160	310	1200
2001–02	700	190	260	1150
2002–03	620	180	290	1090
2003–04	420	250	390	1110
2004–05	360	230	380	960

Source: Adapted from DWP (2006).

The compliance strategy 2006–

The problematic nature of benefit fraud led to a situation where, while the DWP could claim that utilizing risk management techniques within the strategic framework had been effective in reducing fraud in the system, losses from official and customer error were either static or, in the case of customer error, increasing. Thus, by 2005 both official and customer error accounted for 60 per cent of the overpayment figure (Bourn, 2007). The effect of targeting resources on the cases where evidence was strongest for fraud, or 'Putting it right', was to discard those cases where evidence for investigation was considered insufficient. Consequently, the area of 'Keeping it right', by ensuring that changes in a claimant's circumstances were reflected in changes to benefit, was neglected. As the following comment suggested,

> Currently a large percentage of fraud referrals are overloaded or classified for no further action. These cases do not have specific allegations or evidence of incorrect benefit, but analysis has shown they are categories where it is highly likely that the customer has not declared a change.

> (DWP, 2006: 7)

The realization that such overpayments represented an increasing loss to the DWP led to the introduction of a system of 'compliance' and away from the principles of a risk and intelligence-led approach in assessing cases for intervention. From 2006, any cases where the evidence was not considered strong enough to merit investigation, but still had characteristics of fraud, were to be referred to a compliance process. Claimants would be interviewed to remind them that any change in their circumstances should be reported promptly. They would then be asked to sign a statement acknowledging their responsibility and the consequences of their alleged actions, the threat being that if any such suspicious behaviour continued, they would be investigated. As the DWP put it:

> The key issue for 2005/06 is to transform the way in which we tackle fraud and error. There are three key elements to our *new* approach: Process Compliance to get claims right and keep them right; Customer Compliance to ensure that customers tell us on time about changes that affect their benefit; and Criminal Investigation to sanction more complex cases of serious abuse.
>
> (DWP, 2006)

The change in direction hinted at the problems that the DWP has continued to face in assessing how successfully they have been in countering fraud. These have arisen for two main reasons:

- The way the DWP has continuously refined its methodology for measuring fraud and error.
- The problematic nature of what constitutes welfare fraud.

Measuring fraud: 'Catching the wind'

The degree of fraud committed against the DWP has continued to be problematic, with the DWP itself continuing to qualify its own statistics. Problems over the accuracy of figures arise for a number of reasons. Firstly, the DWP does not measure potential fraud across all of the benefits it administers. Thus, Sainsbury (2000) points out that organized fraud against the system is not mentioned; neither is Instrument of Payment (IOP), nor Instrument by Payment fraud. Also, until comparatively recently, detailed measurement was still confined to IS and JSA, the other benefits being subject to one-off national reviews such as those in the late 1990s. As the PAC commented,

The Department needs to supplement their estimates of fraud and error on Income Support and Jobseeker's Allowance, and their work to develop robust estimates for Housing Benefit, with a planned programme of reviews of other benefits. This will allow targets to be set for reducing fraud and error in all benefits and their performance to be measured.

(2002, para. 1)

This has now been addressed, but the lack of sufficient data before 2003–04 on, for example, HB means that it is difficult, if not impossible, to assess the effectiveness of the new structures and procedures over the period that the strategy has operated. Secondly, the continued refinements in the measurement, while making for an improving accuracy of the extent of fraud, nonetheless have made comparisons over time difficult, if not meaningless, as the DWP themselves conceded in 2005 when commenting on the 2003–04 reductions in fraud for fraud and error in JSA/IS:

The figures for Apr 2003–March 2004 have been adjusted for data quality problems found. Previous figures have not been adjusted in this way, as there is not enough information available to do so. They therefore are not all suitable for making reliable comparisons over time but give a reference of our best estimate of these overpayment figures in each year.

(DWP, 2006)

Besides methodological issues, there is the problematic nature of fraud itself and the continuing problems the DWP has in accurately defining what constitutes fraud. As the Permanent Secretary at DWP, in evidence to the Public Accounts Committee in 2002, admitted when assessing IS, 'Part of the trouble with income support is that it depends on self-declaration of means. The areas that are most difficult to police are income, savings and living together as man and wife' (Lomax, 2002: para. 4).

This is evident in the Department's concentration on 'overpayment' and 'incorrectness', as well as just fraudulent activity. Such 'incorrectness' has been categorized as Departmental/Official Error; Claimant/Customer Error; Suspicion of fraud and confirmed fraud. Departmental error includes mistakes in benefit calculation, or failure to process information fully or correctly. Claimant error was defined as errors committed by claimants that were accidental, or without intent to defraud. But suspicion of fraud can range from 'mild' to 'high' yet not be counted in the figures because they fail the evidential test for prosecution (Sainsbury, 2000, 2003). Instead, while those cases that attracted a high level of suspicion were investigated, until 2006, the rest were disregarded (White, 2006).

Conclusion

Social security fraud is one of the most publicized frauds in contemporary Britain, with, for example, far more attention paid to it by the media and politicians than, for example, frauds against the revenue. It has examined the nature and extent of social security fraud and outlined the development of strategies to counter it. In doing so, the chapter has highlighted the difficulty that can be involved when organizations try to gauge and detect the amount of fraud committed against them. In this case one of the DWP's greatest problems is in detecting frauds committed against them, due in part to the inherent nature of fraud. Associated with such difficulty, the DWP also has problems distinguishing between whether any overpayments made are the result of error or of fraudulent behaviour.

The chapter also highlighted the fact that the department has one of the largest number of dedicated staff in the UK and that they have pioneered a strategic management approach to countering fraud; by the increasing use of I.T. to assess the degree of risk attached to individual claims, in order to assist in more focused investigations. Following the introduction of the new policy, there has been a dramatic reduction in the levels of fraud committed against the department, a vindication of the 'putting it right' approach. However, its precise effect cannot as yet be certain due to methodological difficulties and the nature of fraud itself. What is known is that the new system led to a neglect of the 'Keeping it right' element of the strategy. To rectify this, there has been a change in emphasis in how cases of suspected fraud are handled, towards customer compliance.

Further reading

- DWP (1998b) *Beating Fraud Is Everyone's Business: Securing the Future* (Cm. 4012). London: The Stationery Office.
- DWP (2005) *Testing the Customer Compliance Operating Model.* Final Evaluation Report, Version no. 1 [Internal report]. June.
- DWP (2005a) *Reducing Fraud in the Benefit System: and Achievements and Ambitions.* London: HMSO.
- DWP (2008) *Fraud and Error in the Benefits System: April 2007 to March 2008.* London: DWP. Available from http://www.dwp.gov.uk/newsroom/press-releases/2009/november-2009/nsfr-041109.shtml.
- NAO (2008) *Department for Work and Pensions Progress in Tackling Benefit Fraud.* London: The Stationary Office.

CHAPTER 11

Transnational Fraud

Overview

The aims of this chapter are to provide

- an introduction to the legal and social context of transnational fraud
- an overview of the scope and character of transnational fraud
- an examination of the links between transnational fraud and organized crime and terrorism
- a review of the strategies to counter transnational fraud

Introduction

This chapter explores the problem of transnational fraud. The chapter is divided into five sections. The first discusses the process of globalization and defines the concept of 'transnational' crime. The second provides an outline of the general scope and character of transnational fraud. The third section focuses on the specific character of particular transnational frauds by looking at three examples: computer fraud, bribery and corruption and the so-called 'carousel' fraud. The last two sections look, respectively, at the links between transnational fraud, terrorism and organized crime and at means for countering transnational fraud.

Globalization and the transnational dimension

Modern capitalism developed through the nation-state, a body defined by its monopoly of the legitimate use of physical force within a given territory (Weber, 1946). While the nation-state remains a key component of capitalism, global forces now cut across national state boundaries, integrating and connecting state and non-state organizations in complex ways (Hall, 1992). Globalization gives rise to a number of effects. First, supersonic travel and instantaneous forms of electronic communication 'shrink' time and space, thereby facilitating novel forms of licit and illicit activity. Second, the emergence of global markets creates new economic opportunities, both criminal and non-criminal. Global crime is hardly new – a point confirmed by the activities of historical figures as varied as the Barbary pirates or the Italian Mafiosi. Yet, globalization changes the speed, extent and diversity of those involved in it (Shelley, 2005). Third, globalization spawns a host of supranational initiatives aimed at resolving the governance problems exposed by global processes. Thus, for example, EUROPOL has emerged as one of several governmental responses to the problem of cross-border crime in Europe.

The Rome Statute, which established the International Criminal Court, defines international crimes as those which threaten the peace, security and well-being of the world and are of concern to the international community. As Natarajan (2005) indicates, this covers three categories of 'core' crimes: genocide, war crimes and crimes against humanity. International crimes are defined as such by international agreements which, after ratification by large numbers of states and acceptance by others, come to be regarded as crimes under international law. Transnational crimes, by contrast, are those which span national borders, thereby violating the laws of more than one country. According to McDonald (1997, cited in Natarajan, 2005: xvi), an offence is transnational if it is committed.

- in more than one state;
- in one state but where a substantial part of its preparation, planning, direction or control occurs in another state;
- in one state but where an organized criminal group engaging in criminal activities in more than one state is involved;
- in one state but where such commission has substantial effects in another state.

When laws have been broken, transnational crimes demand action by the specific countries. However, when individual countries cannot respond effectively, action by a supranational body is called for.

The scope and character of transnational fraud

While it is impossible, for reasons that will become clear, to calculate the overall costs of either national or transnational fraud, available figures from developed countries suggest that the problem is severe. For example, in the USA securities regulators have estimated that securities and commodities fraud totals about $40 billion a year, while US cheque fraud costs about $10 billion a year. It has also been claimed that fraud accounts for up to 10 per cent of the $500 billion business in telemarketing occurring each year in the USA and Canada. Closer to home, in Europe during 2003, 570,000 counterfeit notes valued at €30 million were seized by the authorities (United Nations, 2005a: 4).

Fraud may be defined as 'the obtaining of goods and/or money by deception' (Levi, 2005: 361). Accordingly, transnational fraud may be defined as fraud which transcends national boundaries in one or more of the ways described by McDonald (1997) above. However, defining fraud is one thing. Measuring it – not least at the transnational level – is another. In 2006 the Fraud Review tried to make some international comparisons regarding the nature and character of fraud. One immediate problem the researchers faced was that different government departments in different countries use a variety of statistical methods for defining and measuring fraud. In addition to that, private sector companies engaged in combating fraud do not have standardized methods of date collection. For that reason, reliable international comparison of fraud incidents proved to be impossible. As an alternative, the researchers tried to estimate the cost of fraud in a number of countries.

Even here, however, as Table 11.1 illustrates, variations in national methodologies produced, what appear to be, extravagant results. The idea that Germany's fraud problem is 50 per cent greater than the UK's, or that Canada's is one-third that of its US neighbour, suggests that we treat such estimates with caution. Moreover, in the absence of reliable data for national jurisdictions, there is no real prospect of accurate measures being

Table 11.1 Estimated cost of fraud in each of seven countries

Country	Estimated cost of fraud	Cost of fraud as a percentage of GDP
United States	£378 billion	6
Germany	£137.1 billion	9
United Kingdom	£14 billion	2
Canada	£10 billion	2.1
Ireland	£4.35 billion	4
Australia	£2.3 billion	1.3
France	Impossible to obtain a satisfactory estimate	–

Source: Adapted from Fraud Review Team (2006b: 274).

available regarding the size and scope of transnational fraud, something which has implications for counter-fraud strategies. As the Fraud Review states,

> During our research into the estimates of the costs of fraud in each country, it has become evident that there is a distinct lack of robust methodologies for recording or even estimating the cost of fraud...Therefore, it is hard to arrive at any accurate conclusions regarding the level of resources required to counter fraud.
>
> (Fraud Review Team, 2006b: 275)

Though unambiguous information regarding the total quantifiable costs of transnational fraud is difficult to obtain, alternative sources of information do exist. One useful source is provided by the periodic global surveys undertaken by risk consultancies such as PricewaterhouseCoopers (2007), Kroll (2007) and Ernst and Young (2007).

Over 43 per cent of the 5400 companies interviewed by PricewaterhouseCoopers (2007) reported suffering one or more significant economic crimes, the average loss from fraud per company having increased almost 40 per cent in 2 years, from $1.7 million in 2005 to 2.4 million in 2007. Added to that – and further complicating the question of what constitutes the 'total quantifiable cost' of fraud – 80 per cent of those suffering fraud reported that this had caused either 'damage' or 'significant damage' to their businesses. Analysis of fraud in emerging markets also revealed serious problems here. For example, no less than 44 per cent of intellectual property infringements occurring worldwide and involving an overseas perpetrator were linked to a perpetrator from China.

Research undertaken by the Economist Intelligence Unit on behalf of Kroll (2007) surveyed around 900 senior executives worldwide, 80 per cent of whom reported having experienced some form of corporate fraud in the previous 3 years. Over the same period the average damage from corporate fraud among large companies – defined as those with an average turnover of over $5 billion – was more than $20 million with about 1 in 10 losing more than $100 million.

The problem of quantifying the size of the fraud problem is reaffirmed in Ernst and Young's (2007) analysis of fraud in emerging markets. Though in this study managers admit to experiencing greater unease about fraud exposure in emerging markets than in developed ones, the analysis suggests that companies from developed countries with links to emerging markets experience fraud more in their home market than elsewhere. The report's authors ask

> Is there more fraud in developed markets or does this apparent 'gap' between perception and experience suggest effective anti-fraud policies implemented in developed countries have not yet been properly introduced to overseas operations? It could be argued the implementation of more robust policies in these markets would have led to more fraud being detected, and a consequent narrowing of the 'gap'.
>
> (Ernst and Young, 2007: 18)

This comment suggests that the conceptual and methodological obstacles to quantifying fraud noted by Doig (2006) are, in fact, only part of the issue. Crucially, as this example indicates, counter-fraud strategies may, themselves, affect how the size of the transnational fraud problem is estimated.

An alternative source of information about transnational fraud comes from the examination of particular types of fraudulent activity. Three such examples are considered in the following section.

Examples of transnational fraud

Transnational computer fraud

Various different types of fraud may be perpetrated online including selling fraudulent items through electronic auctions, artificially inflating stock prices or obtaining individuals' identities by fraudulent means. Grabosky (2000) lists the following varieties of computer-related crime, emphasizing that neither the list is exhaustive nor the items are mutually exclusive.

- Theft of telecommunication services. In one case, computer hackers in the USA illegally obtained access to Scotland Yard's telephone network and made £620,000 worth of international calls for which Scotland Yard was responsible
- Communication in furtherance of criminal conspiracies (e.g. drug trafficking, gambling, prostitution, child pornography, etc.)
- Telecommunications piracy (e.g. pirating of unreleased feature films)
- Dissemination of offensive materials (e.g. pornography, racist propaganda)
- Electronic money laundering and tax evasion (e.g. using electronic funds transfers to conceal or move the proceeds of crime)
- Electronic vandalism and terrorism. In November 2007 a huge campaign to poison web searches and trick people into visiting malicious web sites was exposed. The criminals poisoned search results using thousands of domains – mostly Chinese-registered, US-hosted and only a few days old – in order to dupe search index software used by MSN, Google and Yahoo (Ward, 2007)
- Sales and investment fraud (e.g. 'pyramid schemes')
- Illegal interception of communications. In 1995, hackers employed by a criminal organization attacked the communications system of the Amsterdam Police. The hackers succeeded in gaining police operational intelligence, and in disrupting police communications
- Electronic funds transfer fraud (e.g. the interception of credit card numbers)

One costly form of Internet fraud involves 'advanced fee e-mail schemes': these are often referred to as 'Nigerian scams' because the e-mails often come from individuals claiming to live in a foreign country such as Nigeria. In such frauds the sender claims to need assistance in transferring large sums of money out of his or her country. In return, the sender promises to share a portion of the sum with the individual in receipt of the e-mail. Huge quantities of 'advanced fee' e-mails are transmitted worldwide on a daily basis, and while most recipients ignore them, a small percentage of them become victims of financial loss and/or identity theft. In 2006 the median loss among US victims of 'advanced fee' ('Nigerian letter') scams was $5100 (National White Collar Crime Center and Federal Bureau of Investigation, 2006: 3). More generally, it has been estimated that fraudulent e-mails have cost individuals and businesses throughout the world around $1 billion in the last decade.

In a recent paper, Holt and Graves (2007) undertook a qualitative analysis of 412 fraudulent e-mail messages received in two e-mail accounts at two medium-sized state universities. The messages appeared to have been generated from 121 different public and private e-mail providers throughout the world including domains in Italy, the UK, China, Zaire and Russia. However, the fact that the originating e-mail addresses in messages can be falsified made it impossible to verify the sources of the message sample. It was also the case that spam-filtering software used by the universities would have filtered out most fraudulent messages so, again, the sample might not have been representative. A more important point for our purposes, however, is the criminal potential offered by global electronic technologies: in this case massive financial losses accrue from victims' exposure to only minute proportions of the messages transmitted (due to filtering), and then from a tiny proportion of victims falling for the scam. The best analogy would be if industrial trawlers threw away all the fish they caught bar 1 in every 100,000. This analogy may not be far from the truth. As Holt and Graves' (2007) qualitative analysis of the message texts shows, fraudsters use common syntax and phrases – in effect, using standardized scripts or templates on an 'industrial' basis. This enables multiple messages to be transmitted with little effort on the part of the sender.

As Grabosky points out, there is a danger that premature or over-zealous regulation of the Internet may not only be counter-productive but may also have a negative impact on the development of technology for common benefit. Ultimately, 'the challenge for those who would minimise computer-related crime is to seek a balance which would allow a tolerable degree of illegality in return for creative exploitation of the technology' (2000).

Bribery and corruption

In 2006 Control Risks and Simmons and Simmons jointly commissioned telephone interviews with 350 international companies across seven jurisdictions (the UK, the USA, Germany, France, the Netherlands, Brazil and Hong Kong) in order to examine international business attitudes towards corruption. This was the fourth time such a survey has been undertaken. In three of the five jurisdictions first surveyed in 2002 (Hong Kong, the Netherlands and the USA) there was a noticeable increase in the proportion of companies believing they had lost business to bribery in the previous 5 years. For example, in Hong Kong, the site recording the highest perception of loss, 76 per cent of companies believed they had 'failed to win a contract or gain new business because competitors paid bribes' in 2006, compared to 69 per cent in 2002 (Control Risks and Simmons and Simmons, 2006: 5).

The same survey asked respondents to predict the maximum cost that corruption could add to an international project. Though around a quarter of respondents estimated maximum cost to be no higher than 5 per cent, more than one-fifth predicted costs of 'between 6 per cent and 10 per cent', and a further 17.4 per cent estimated likely cost to be 'between 11 per cent and 25 per cent' – very significant for what are often multi-billion-pound contracts. Companies estimating maximum corruption at more than a quarter of the total project cost were most likely to come from construction, defence and finance (Control Risks and Simmons and Simmons, 2006: 9).

Significantly, few companies thought they could take effective action in circumstances where a competitor had paid a bribe. By far the largest number of respondents (41.7 per cent) said that they would 'avoid working again with the same customer and simply look elsewhere in the future'. Only 6.5 per cent said that they would notify the law enforcement authorities. A German respondent commented that there was little purpose in reporting bribery to the authorities in high-risk environments when those authorities are themselves likely to be corrupt; a Hong Kong respondent summarized the view of many others by saying that bribery by competitors was just 'part of the business' (Control Risks and Simmons and Simmons, 2006: 6).

A final problem noted in the report is that, because of particular countries having a reputation for corruption, emerging economies 'lose out'. One Brazilian company summarized the position as follows:

> We tried to get finance from a non-Brazilian bank for the project last year. It proved impossible because no one would trust us...In the end, we had to go through the normal process of using a Brazilian bank and they wanted the 'usual consideration' to process the finance.
>
> (Control Risks and Simmons and Simmons, 2006: 9)

Most Western companies have codes forbidding bribes to secure business. By contrast, companies in the two emerging market countries surveyed (Hong Kong and Brazil) were much less likely to have such codes. Yet, even when present, the extent to which codes were backed by effective management practices was found to be patchy. To complicate matters further, there is ambivalence regarding the distinction between 'bribes to secure business' and 'facilitation payments' (defined by the US Foreign Corrupt Practices Act (FCPA) 1977 as payments to 'expedite routine governmental actions'). The FCPA excludes facilitation payments from its definition of bribery but many other countries (e.g. the UK and Germany) make no such distinction. Overall many adopted a pragmatic attitude. As one Dutch respondent said, 'In an ideal situation we would not want any of our executives to pay to speed up customs. However, when the customer is putting pressure on us to complete the project on time, then we have to do this' (Control Risks and Simmons and Simmons, 2006: 14).

Carousel fraud

Carousel fraud (or missing trader fraud) is a type of tax fraud which exploits the way Value Added Tax (VAT) is treated in multi-jurisdictional trading. The fraud exploits the fact that the movement of goods between EU member states is VAT free. It is particularly well-suited to small, high-value items, such as microchips and mobile phones.

Carousel fraud involves the following cycle of activity (Oliver, 2006):

- Small high-value goods, such as mobile phones, are imported free of VAT from EU countries and sold with 17.5 per cent tax added in the UK.
- Instead of handing the VAT to the Government, the importing company, run by criminals, is shut down and the cash is kept by the importers.
- This loss of tax is often compounded when the new owners of the goods export them again and can legally reclaim the VAT they paid.
- Goods go round in a 'carousel' via bogus supply chains within and beyond the EU as they are repeatedly imported and exported.
- By exporting the goods to Dubai, the fraudsters break the evidential chain making the fraud harder to detect.

Herman (2006) illustrates how carousel fraud works in practice. In a simple version, a fraudster (say, from the UK) might import some goods (say, mobile phones) from a trader in another EU country. Under EU law no VAT has to be paid. The trader sells the phones then, instead of paying the Government, absconds with the VAT and closes down the company. This situation, where the goods are made available for consumers in the importer's home market, is often known as 'acquisition fraud'.

A more complex version occurs when the trader sells the phones to a criminal accomplice, again not declaring the VAT, and the accomplice sells the goods on to a third party – often a legitimate business person – who, in turn, exports them. The legitimate trader pays VAT on the transaction, which the criminal, who is second in the chain, keeps, and then sells the goods on to a fourth (legitimate) trader in another European country. Because the legitimate UK trader has bought the phones for export, a claim for the repayment of any VAT incurred can be made to Revenue and Customs – despite the fact that no VAT was paid in the first place. Up to this point in the carousel, two fraudulent traders will have made money by stealing VAT while Revenue and Customs will have reimbursed a legitimate trader from the public purse. To make matters worse, the original fraudulent trader might then buy the phones back from the last purchaser, thus enabling the process to occur again. Since British regulations do not require the fraudulent trader to send the VAT charged on UK sales to the Revenue and Customs until 4 months have elapsed, chains of criminals have an opportunity to buy, sell, import and export goods repeatedly. Tax experts estimate that the same batches of goods may be sold up to 40 times during this period. Once the 4-month period has expired, the fraudulent trader will close the business and either disappears or starts up a new one, leaving the Revenue and Customs to pick up the bill.

In November 2007 a lay preacher and law lecturer from Nottinghamshire was jailed for 10 years for offences, including setting up a carousel fraud, that cheated the government out of £51 million in VAT on non-existent mobile phones, computer chips and 'Sat-Nav' equipment. One of fraudster's paper companies claimed to have imported £28 million worth of mobile phones in only 4 weeks, a transaction involving £4.7 million of VAT. The judge in the case said that 'comprehensive failures' by the prosecution meant that eight other defendants accused of taking part in the fraud walked free because they could not receive a fair trial. The judge added that the fraudster, who had received just £200,000 out of the millions stolen, was by no means the ringleader of the gang involved (Brooke, 2007; Wainwright, 2007; BBC News, 2007d).

A Panorama programme broadcast in July 2006 (Oliver, 2006) quoted a report from Eurocanet, an EU-sponsored project that draws on data from police and other sources. The Report claimed that the UK lost five times more money (£8.4 billion) to VAT fraud than any other EU member during 2005–06. According to *Eurocanet*, almost three-quarters of the tax stolen by fraudsters in the UK between June 2005 and June 2006 involved carousel frauds using the 'Dubai Connection'. The UK Government (which reported VAT fraud losses of £1.9 billion for the previous year) contested these figures. Following this, the Treasury pledged to tackle the problem through a 'reverse charge' scheme, whereby the last company to sell on goods is liable for the tax. That scheme came into effect on 1 June 2007.

By late 2006 *The Economist* had begun to link unexpected trade gap figures with missing-trader mobile phone fraud. Soon

after, the then Home Secretary John Reid stated to a G6 meeting of Interior Ministers that there was an explicit link between
carousel fraud and terrorism. According to one report, losses
from carousel fraud cost the EU the same as total Common Agricultural Policy spending and five times more than expenditure
on employment and social affairs (Anon, 2007).

Links between transnational fraud, terrorism and organized crime

An increasingly important issue concerns the linkages between
fraud, organized crime and terrorism. Significantly, the United
Nations connects these linkages to the globalization process:

> While the motivation for terrorists to use organised crime methods
> has increased since the end of the cold war, new opportunities have
> also become widely available as a result of globalization of trade,
> finance and communications.
>
> (2005b: 9)

As the same report notes, in some cases organized crime is part of
the fund-raising strategy of terrorist groups (e.g. the use of credit
card fraud and forgery). In other cases organized crime provides
'logistical support' by facilitating easy and undetectable movement of personnel or money across borders (e.g. the engagement
of terrorist groups in money-laundering or document fraud).
A third category involves criminal activities designed to protect
terrorist groups from law enforcement and intelligence agencies (e.g. the cultivation by terrorist organizations of corrupt
government officials in order to gain protection).

Increasingly, one of the most lucrative fraudulent activities
engaged in by terrorist groups is intellectual property crime. This
is a classic case of transnational fraud where counterfeit goods are
transported across national boundaries. According to Interpol,
this has become the preferred method of funding for some terrorist groups – partly because it is not given high priority by
enforcement bodies. Moreover, when pirated or counterfeited
goods are tracked down, the emphasis tends to be on seizure
rather than on tracking the onward flows of money to the ulti-
mate beneficiaries. Other types of fraudulent activity contributing
to terrorism include the use and sale of fraudulent and stolen

credit cards and various forms of cyber crime, including online fraud and extortion (United Nations, 2005b).

The United Nations (2005a) notes three things about global economic and financial crimes. First, while many of these offences can be, and are, perpetrated by legitimate companies, the propensity for transnational criminal organizations to engage in them has increased for two reasons: on the one hand, the blurring between legitimate and illegitimate activity in some sectors; on the other hand, the greater use by criminal groups of both formal legal businesses to 'launder' money or to invest profits and of 'front companies' in order to mask illegal activities. Second, the global integration of financial markets means that the knock-on effects of economic and financial crime cannot be confined to a single country. Thus, the implications of substantial fraud in the banking system in recent years were global, particular damage being inflicted on the banking systems of some developing economies. Finally, related to this is the fact that fraud has damaging implications for developing economies. Economic harm comes not just from the crime but from the perception that it is endemic to some economies – and from the subsequent loss of trust in the system. The United Nations (2005a) contends that economic crimes pose a serious long-term threat to peaceful and democratic socio-economic development in some countries. It also impacts most seriously on the poorest people. For example, the 2002 International Crime Victims Survey reported considerably higher proportions of victims of consumer fraud in developing economies than in developed ones. In addition to that, states which experience humanitarian emergencies may be doubly victimized when donor funds are exploited by criminals and corrupt officials. Moreover, donors may be deterred from supporting charitable requests if they perceive some systems to be inherently corrupt.

Countering transnational fraud

The Fraud Review Team (2006b) noted that the UK did not yet have a national strategy for fighting fraud and, as in many other jurisdictions, public and private sector bodies in the UK had developed their own counter-fraud strategies. Under the proposals arising from the Review, a UK fraud strategic authority and a new fraud reporting centre will be established (Canada has Reporting Economic Crime Online (RECOL) (http://www.recol.ca/intro.aspx) for reporting economic crime online and the USA has similar means for reporting Internet crime). The government has allocated £29 million (to be spent up to 2010) to put these recommendations into place.

Current arrangements for investigation in the UK are varied. The Review suggested the possibility of the increased use of specialist investigators and also examined the Garda Bureau of Fraud Investigation in Ireland which works on a cross-border basis with the Police Service of Northern Ireland. One product of this collaboration was the Cross Border Organised Crime Assessment which the Review cites as an exemplar of cross-border co-operation between law enforcement agencies in dealing with organized crime.

Legislation, detection and enforcement are, of course, key strategies in countering transnational fraud. Seager and Cobain (2007) have recently reported on government progress in respect of carousel fraud which, according to official data, has reduced significantly. Their report describes a joint operation between Revenue and Customs and the Dutch authorities which closed the First Curacao International Bank (FCIB) in the Caribbean. The FCIB had been at the centre of the carousel operations, computer programmes having been developed which created 'virtual carousels' (where no goods actually needed to be traded). Under new laws the government now has powers to force financial institutions to reveal details of suspect transactions. Sentences for those convicted have also risen substantially. In January 2007, a mobile phone trader with dual Belgian-French nationality was gaoled for 15 years for masterminding a £54 million fraud. His gang of eight accomplices received a total of 38.5 years in prison.

Nevertheless, the efficacy of enforcement arrangements remains controversial. Despite the government allocating £28 million to implement the Fraud Review's recommendations, some organizations still question the extent of its commitment to tackling fraud. Members of the Corporate IT Forum have been particularly concerned that the Home Office's promise to establish a dedicated police unit for dealing with high-tech criminal gangs – the previous National High Tech Crime Unit having been scrapped in 2006 – should be honoured. At present, they argue, crimes have to be reported to local police who simply lack the expertise to deal with them. There is also concern that having responsibility for e-crime split between local police forces, MI5 and the Serious Organised Crime Agency (SOCA) may be problematic when those same agencies are more and more called upon to deal with anti-terrorism issues (Cellan-Jones, 2007).

There are also more general obstacles to enforcement and to the multi-agency cooperation on which effective enforcement increasingly depends. Grabosky (2000) identifies various 'extra-territorial' issues which impact on the policing of cyber crime – though they apply to other types of transnational fraud. Cyber crime is challenging because the global nature of cyberspace enhances the ability of offenders to commit crimes in one country which affect individuals in other countries. This poses unique challenges for the detection, investigation and prosecution of offenders. Two particular problems arise: first, the issue of determining where the offence occurred in order to decide which law to apply, and the second, the issue of obtaining evidence and ensuring that the offender can be located and tried before a court. Both these questions raise complex legal problems of jurisdiction and extradition. And, even if it is possible to decide which law is relevant, applying it may be impossible:

> A resident of Chicago who falls victim to a telemarketing scam originating in Albania ... can expect little assistance from law enforcement agencies in either jurisdiction. As a result, regulation by territorially-based rules may prove to be inappropriate for these types of offences.
>
> (Grabosky, 2000: n.p.).

As Grabosky (2000) points out, however, jurisdictional issues are not the only obstacle to effective enforcement. First, extra-territorial law enforcement costs are often prohibitive. Second, co-operation across international boundaries in furtherance of enforcement usually requires a congruence of values and priorities which rarely exists. Third, the sheer volume of material and the fact that it may be encrypted can make accessing evidence difficult, impossible or uneconomic. Fourth, international co-operation in respect of enforcement is unlikely to be forthcoming except in those cases where there is widespread international consensus about the activity in question (such as child pornography or fraud on a scale likely to destabilize financial markets).

Fifth, even this much assumes a seamless world system of stable sovereign states which no longer exists. Law enforcement and regulatory vacuums exist in some parts of the world, certainly in those settings where the state has effectively collapsed. Even where state power does exist in full force, the corruption of individual regimes can impede international co-operation.

Given these inevitable limitations, countering transnational fraud will, increasingly, demand a multiplicity of reactive and proactive measures (see Schneider et al. (2000) for a similar argument in respect of alternative approaches to combating transnational organized crime). It will also demand a clearer understanding of the contributions different agencies can make to the task. In a recent paper, Dyck et al. (2006) asked 'what external control mechanisms are most effective in detecting corporate fraud?' In order to address this issue they examined all reported cases of fraud in US companies with more than $750 million in assets between 1996 and 2004. They concluded that fraud detection does not rely on any single mechanism, but on a wide range of, often improbable, actors. In their study, only 6 per cent of frauds were revealed by the Securities Exchange Commission and 14 per cent by the auditors. More important monitors turned out to be the media (14 per cent), industry regulators (16 per cent) and employees (19 per cent). Before the Sarbanes Oxley Act 2002 (the Public Company Accounting Reform and Investor Protection Act, enacted in the wake of the corporate accounting scandals at Enron, Tyco International and elsewhere) only 35 per cent of the cases were discovered by actors with an explicit reporting mandate. After the Act, the performance of mandated actors improved, but still accounted for only a little more than 50 per cent of the cases. The authors conclude that non-mandated actors have an important role in exposing fraud and corruption, and that the provision of monetary incentives for detecting frauds may influence detection without increasing frivolous suits.

The fact that multiple measures, including reactive, preventive and risk-oriented ones, will be required is evidenced in the work of several international organizations. The World Bank (2004) investigates allegations of fraud and corruption in Bank operations through its Department of Institutional Integrity. Based on these investigations, the Bank's Sanctions Committee decides whether evidence exists that firms have acted fraudulently or corruptly in connection with Bank-financed contracts. If such evidence is found, the Committee identifies an appropriate sanction, such as debarment, for a specified period. The Bank also encourages firms to come forward voluntarily with information about fraud and corruption in Bank-financed projects. This risk management approach is reflected in the annual integrity report (World Bank, 2006: vi). The Voluntary Disclosure Program gives firms identified the opportunity to cease corrupt practices; to voluntarily disclose information about misconduct; to adopt a compliance programme for 3 years – overseen by a Compliance monitor; and to avoid disbarment for disclosed past debarment. The firm enjoys confidentiality in return for full and proactive co-operation.

Transparency International (TI), founded in Germany in 1993, is an international non-governmental organization dedicated to fighting corruption which TI defines as 'the abuse of entrusted power for private gain'. Rather than seeking to expose or investigate individual incidents of corruption, TI's objective is to develop techniques for addressing the problem and for working within anti-corruption coalitions. TI is a global network operating across more than 90 locally established national chapters. These bodies fight corruption by bringing together government, business, civil society and the media to promote transparency in elections, public administration, procurement and business. TI's *Anti-Corruption Handbook* (Transparency International, n.d.) aims to provide a holistic approach to countering corruption. This involves much more than legislative intervention with strong focus being placed on preventive, proactive, educative, political and other work at various levels.

> The ACH is based on TI's National Integrity System approach to countering corruption, which offers a framework for assessing the adequacy and effectiveness of national anti-corruption efforts. The ACH seeks to build on this approach, addressing the key elements of anti-corruption reform in a useful and practical way.
>
> (Transparency International, n.d.)

Finally, it is also important to note that, in addition to organizations such as TI and the World Bank, the commercial security sector has a long-established role in both risk management and fraud investigation. Major risk and security consultancies such as Kroll, Control Risks and Global Risk Groups minimize the risks of fraud to businesses by providing services such as employment screening, due diligence checks and local market analyses. Latterly, these organizations have a much enhanced role in the provision of these and other services to the state sector (Johnston, 2006; O'Reilly, 2006).

Conclusion

This chapter has explored the phenomenon of transnational fraud. This is becoming an increasing problem as globalization continues and has been demonstrated to be responsible for funding other aspects of organized crime and even terrorism. Transnational fraud presents familiar problems to national governments as well as posing new ones. Thus it has proved almost impossible to measure accurately its impact on the global economy: not only because of the inherent difficulties fraud poses, as outlined in Chapters 2 and 3, but also because of its transnational nature – committed across national borders and boundaries. This characteristic also poses challenges to those national agencies such as the Serious Fraud Office (SFO), charged with investigating and prosecuting fraud, and international agencies such as EUROPOL and Office Européen De Lutte Anti-Fraude (OLAF), as they face legal and cultural definitions of fraud and corruption.

This chapter has explored the growing problem of transnational fraud. It began by discussing its legal and social context before examining its general scope and character. Having looked at fraud generically, the chapter went on to examine three specific forms of transnational fraud: computer fraud, bribery and corruption and carousel fraud. The last two sections of the chapter looked, respectively, at the links between transnational fraud, terrorism and organized crime and at various means for countering transnational fraud.

Further reading

- Grabosky, P. (2000) Computer Crime in a World without Borders, *Platypus Magazine: The Journal of the Australian Federal Police.*
- Levi, M. (2005) International Fraud, in Natarajan, M. (Ed.). *Introduction to International Criminal Justice* (pp. 361–369). Boston: McGraw Hill.

- Schneider, S., Beare, M. and Hill, J. (2000) *Alternative Approaches to Combating Transnational Crime*, Ottawa: Solicitor General Canada. Available from http://ww2.ps-sp.gc.ca/Publications/Policing/TransCrime_e.pdf.

Organizations with information on transnational fraud:

- Consumer Sentinel Network: http://www.ftc.gov/sentinel/reports.shtml.
- RECOL: http://www.recol.ca/intro.aspx.

CHAPTER 12

Final Reflections

Since our argument has been reviewed at the end of each chapter there is little point in summarizing it again. Instead, we close by reflecting upon some recent and ongoing events in the light of our previous discussion. As this book was nearing completion, there was widespread public disquiet about the economic and social consequences of the global financial crisis. Though this crisis had been brewing for some time, its first public manifestation occurred with a 'run' on the Northern Rock Bank in late 2007. In the following 18 months a number of UK banks were bailed out by the state and the economy became enmeshed in a global recession. What is significant about these events is that they provoked public debate about fraud: a debate that touched on some of the key issues discussed previously regarding how authorities define and regulate fraudulent practice.

The financial crisis

Background

Early signs of the financial crisis that was eventually to culminate in global recession had appeared in 2004 (see Figure 12.1). By 2007–08 a number of events were unfolding that were particularly noteworthy. The first occurred in September 2007 when there was a 'run' on the Northern Rock Bank, its beleaguered branches being overrun by queues of customers desperate to reclaim their deposits. The second occurred in September 2008 when Lehman Brothers, the huge American investment bank, filed for bankruptcy. News broadcasts showed images of Lehman's London employees being escorted from the building, carrying their belongings in cardboard boxes.

2004–06

- Early signs of trouble. Rising US interest rates cause high levels of 'sub-prime' mortgage defaulting.

2007

- 9 August. French investment bank BNP Paribas tells investors they cannot take money from two of its funds because of 'complete evaporation of liquidity' in the market.
- 13–14 September. Northern Rock granted emergency financial support by British Government. Depositors withdraw £1 billion in a single day.

2008

- 21 January. Huge falls in global stock markets
- 17 January. Nationalization of Northern Rock announced.
- 28 August. Bradford and Bingley posts half-year losses of £26.7 million.
- 7 September. US Government bails out Fannie Mae and Freddie Mac, the two largest providers of home loans.
- 15 September. Lehman Brothers files for bankruptcy.
- 16 September. US Federal Reserve announces $85 billion rescue package for AIG Insurance.
- 29 September. Bradford and Bingley nationalized.
- 30 September. Irish Government guarantees bank deposits for 2 years.
- 3 October. US House of Representatives passes $700 billion plan to rescue financial sector.
- 8 October. British Government announces £50 billion bank rescue package.
- 13 October. British Government announced £37 billion nationalization programme for RBS, Lloyds TSB and HBOS.
- 6 November. IMF loans $16.4 billion to Ukraine to prop up its economy.
- 9 November. China announces 2-year $586 billion stimulus package to boost its economy.
- 14 November. Euro zone officially enters recession.
- 20 November. IMF approves $2.1 billion loan for Iceland after collapse of its banking system.
- 25 November. Federal Reserve injects a further $800 billion into US economy.
- 1 December. USA officially enters recession.

2009

- 23 January. UK officially enters recession.
- 2 March. AIG announces the biggest corporate loss in US history ($61.7 billion).
- 2 April. G20 summit announces measures worth £681 billion to tackle global economic crisis.

Figure 12.1 Timeline: The financial crisis [adapted from BBC News (2009f)].

The roots of the crisis lay in the practice of 'securitization' – the process by which banks turn mortgage loans into paper securities so as to generate cash. Under the traditional system banks kept mortgages on their books for 25–30 years, relied on them for revenue and, eventually, would get paid back the principal sum. Under securitization, that situation changed. Banks, like Northern Rock, would first borrow money, short-term, from other banks. Next, it would lend that money out as mortgages. Finally, it would sell off the mortgages as securities. The result was 'a conveyer belt of funding', according to Bob Bennett, former Finance Director, Northern Rock (BBC, 2009a). Securitization transformed banking, enabling banks to borrow and lend more, and then sell off the loans to pay off some of the debts, *ad infinitum*. It gave the banks the benefits of maximum lending without the associated risks because, if loans 'went bad', they had already become 'somebody else's problem'. Investment banks, like Lehman Brothers, took this process a stage further by 'manufacturing' securities, that is, by buying mortgages in order to sell them at a profit. In order to facilitate this process, the investment banks 'sliced up' mortgages to suit the needs of different investors (e.g. as to whether they wanted their investment to be 'safe' or whether they wanted to take risks).

At this point, 'the tail started to wag the dog'. As the BBC's former Economic Editor, Evan Davies, put it, 'Instead of banks producing securities to fund more lending, they [did] more lending to give them an excuse to produce more securities' (BBC, 2009b). However, in an environment where conventional demand for credit was already exhausted, new demand had to be generated. The solution was to tap the so-called 'sub-prime' market of people who, previously, would have been considered too high a risk for receiving loans. After all, it was reasoned, if these loans 'went bad' in a buoyant property market, the property could simply be repossessed and the bank reimbursed. Accordingly, banks and building societies granted loans to 'sub-prime' customers and the loans, together with the associated risks, were sold to companies like Lehman Bothers.

In order to make money out of this practice, banks would put the mortgages they owned into packages – so-called 'Collateralized Debt Obligations' (CDOs) – for selling on to investors. These CDOs contained a bewildering mixture of products ranging from good quality to sub-prime loans, so in order to reassure investors about their stability, investment banks employed rating agencies to grade them. The fact that those doing the grading were employed by the company selling the product being graded created obvious opportunities for questionable business practices and, at the very least, presented a serious conflict of interest. Added to that, there was concern that the complexity of CDO packages rendered them immune from the application of any rational risk assessment methodology. Growing fears among banks, the largest investors in securities, regarding the 'sub-prime' market – not knowing which debt was toxic, who owned it and in what quantities – exacerbated by signs of a house-price crash in 2007, led to the drying up of the inter-bank market (the so-called 'credit-crunch'). In the case of Northern Rock, two-thirds of the bank's funding supply disappeared overnight. Globally, the result was bank bail-outs, restrictions on lending and, eventually, worldwide recession.

Blurred boundaries

The financial crisis was accompanied by a 'blurring' of conventional boundaries. One example concerned shifting organizational boundaries in the banking sector, with 'high-street' banks, such as Northern Rock, behaving more and more like investment banks. Financial crisis also precipitated the blurring of 'fraud' and 'business'. Levi captures one aspect of that process:

> We can expect a lot more fraud over the next couple of years because a lot of companies who were trading honestly turn to fraud when things get tight, if only to keep going. They may not think of themselves as fraudsters but are in fact trading when they don't have a chance of repaying their creditors... Some of them could be committing fraud to keep going and can rationalise it as helping the people they employ as well as themselves.
>
> (cited in McIntosh, 2008)

There were also more complex forms of blurring. The financial crisis arose out of risky business practices associated with sub-prime mortgages and CDOs. These practices became, progressively, more and more reckless, bordering on and sometimes crossing over into criminality. Research by Ericson and Doyle (2006) on deceptive sales practices in the insurance industry captures, precisely, how in market economies, 'the distinctions between risky, shady, unfair and illegal practices are blurred' (Karstedt et al., 2006: 972). Because of this, researchers studying market misconduct encounter definitional problems 'due to the blurring boundaries of what constitutes a crime or violation in marketing practices' (Ericson and Doyle, 2006: 995). For that reason, rather than focussing exclusively on 'fraud', their study addressed issues of 'moral risk': 'the ways in which an insurance relationship fosters behaviour by any party in the relationship that immorally increases risk to the others' (2006: 994). Moral risk, Ericson and Doyle suggest, is institutionalized in the structure and culture of the life insurance industry. As they put it, life insurance 'is socially organized in ways that paradoxically encourage its salespeople frequently to put their clients at risk, ironically by selling a product that is purported to minimize risk' (2006: 994).

The concept of 'moral risk' is precisely applicable to aspects of the financial crisis discussed previously. Thus, for example, the deployment of rating agencies, by investment banks, to reassure investors about the stability of CDOs amounted to a classic case of 'morally risky' behaviour.

The problem of regulation

Two issues are worthy of comment in respect of regulation. The first concerns variations in jurisdictional responses to fraud and financial mismanagement. In this regard, Hirsch (2009) compares the response of the British authorities to the disastrous management of the Royal Bank of Scotland (£28 billion losses in investments and purchases in a single year) with regulatory regimes in the USA. In Sir Fred Goodwin's case, the sanction was retirement on an £8.4 million pension. In the USA four executives from Bear Stearns and Credit Suisse were charged with fraud for misleading investors, and major financial institutions – Freddie Mac, Fannie Mae and AIG – are under investigation. By contrast, the Financial Services Authority (FSA) at this point had only prosecuted market abuse once, although there has been an increase recently as discussed in Chapter 8 (SFO, 2009).

A second issue concerns our understanding of what regulation actually implies. A prominent response to the financial crisis has been to bemoan the inadequacy of neoliberal regulatory structures. While that view is undoubtedly justified, it is important to understand why, in the light of what we have said previously, regulatory structures are inadequate. One critical factor concerns the nature of the object to be regulated. Both the financial crisis and, to some degree, the row over MPs' expenses suggest that the arena we describe as 'fraud' (a legal-criminal category) is undercut by a variety of 'moral risks' and 'blurred boundaries'. In other words, the object to be regulated is both more complex and more nuanced than the mere legal category would suggest. Spalek (2007: 8) notes that conventional regulatory theory and practice are driven by the simplistic assumption that 'individuals have some degree of choice over the risks that they are exposed to, and that they can act to avoid becoming the victims of financial crime and abuses.' Yet, as she points out, 'free choice' implies a capacity on the part of potential victims to discriminate between 'good' and 'bad' financial decisions. This, in turn, presupposes their possession of the necessary knowledge to make such discriminations. However, as our previous account of the sale of CDOs demonstrates, it was precisely that capacity which the 'morally risky' behaviours engaged in by rogue bankers and their rating agents undermined. Investors could not make informed judgements precisely because they were deprived of the information that would have enabled them to do so.

Final comments

We began this book by suggesting that criminology, and particularly white collar crime, 'forms the spine of counter-fraud studies'. We close it by reflecting, briefly, on that statement in the context of the case just discussed. A common theme throughout this case and throughout the book concerns the difficulties of defining fraud and the complex relationship between fraud, acts which border on fraud and acts which, while being substantively similar to fraud, are not 'fraudulent' in the strict, criminal–legal sense. Of course, that problem is by no means peculiar to fraudulent behaviour. It applies to all forms of crime, criminology having grappled with the question of how its subject matter is constituted since its very inception. This enduring problem is illustrated in the events leading up to the financial crisis discussed here. This demonstrates two points: the fragile boundary between fraudulent acts and similar acts that, while not criminal, may be deemed 'morally risky' and the fact that 'morally risky' acts may have harmful consequences for victims that are at least as significant as those inflicted by criminal ones.

This begs the question of whether criminology's exclusive focus on issues of crime, law and criminal justice is sufficient to the task. Some writers (e.g. Hillyard and Tombs, 2005) argue that this focus on crime needs to be supplemented by – and eventually supplanted by – a focus on social harms ('zemiology'). Among other things, it is argued, such an approach would enable a more cogent analysis of harms inflicted by the state (e.g. where loss of life in natural disasters has been exacerbated by the 'morally risky' planning decisions of politicians and officials) and by business corporations (e.g. where, as in mortgage or pension mis-selling, 'morally risky' behaviour has victimized large numbers of individual investors). This argument would suggest that, in the future, counter-fraud studies might want to pay more attention than it has done previously to the relationship between behaviours that are clearly fraudulent and those 'morally risky' actions that impose comparable economic, social and psychological harms on victims.

Bibliography

ABI (n.d.). *Tackling Fraud*. Retrieved 27 November 2007, from http://www.abi.org.uk/Display/default.asp?Menu_ID=1140andMenu_All=1,946,1140andChild_ID=458.

———. (2001). *Fraud – It Honestly Does Not Pay: Association of British Insurers Briefing Note on Insurance Fraud*. Retrieved 27 November 2007 from http://www.abi.org.uk/Display/File/Child/458/Anti_Fraud_Committee.pdf.

———. (2003). *What is Dishonest?* Retrieved 26 November 2007 from http://www.abi.org.uk/Media/Releases/2003/02/ABI_Research_shows_insurance_fraud_part_of_public_uncertainty_on_dishonesty1.aspx.

———. (2006). *Submission to the Fraud Review*. Retrieved 28 November 2007 from http://www.google.co.uk/url?sa=t&source=web&ct=res&cd=1&ved=0CAcQFjAA&url=http%3A%2F%2Fwww.abi.org.uk%2Fcontent%2Fcontentfilemanager.aspx%3Fcontentid%3D24901&rct=j&q=ABI+TACKLING+FRAUD&ei=Ua9hS6fYEpa6jAeH8rm4DA&usg=AFQjCNHCulIow3kx4Kl9w51M1SmLH8X5lQ.

———. (2007a). *General Insurance Claims Fraud*. London: Association of British Insurers.

———. (2009a). *UK Insurance – Key Facts*. London: Association of British Insurers.

———. (2009b). *Association of British Insurers Research Brief*. Retrieved 15 February 2010, from http://www.abi.org.uk/Media/Releases/2009/07/40569.pdf.

ACFE (2004). *Report to the Nation on Occupational Fraud and Abuse*. Retrieved 27 January 2008 from http://acfe.com/documents/2004RttN.pdf.

———. (2007a). *2006 ACFE Report to the Nation*. Retrieved 28 January 2008 from http://www.acfe.com/documents/2006-rttn.pdf.

———. (2007b). *About the ACFE*. Retrieved 28 January 2008 from http://www.acfe.com/about/about.asp.

———. (2009). *2008 Report to the Nation*. Retrieved 23 January 2010 from http://www.acfe.com/documents/2008-rttn.pdf.

Accountancy Age (2007). *SEC to Fine Nortel for Accounting Fraud.* Retrieved 5 March 2008 from http://www.accountancyage.com/accountancyage/news/2191784/sec-fine-nortel-accounting.

AGO (n.d.). *The Work of the Office.* Retrieved 13 December 2007 from http://www.attorneygeneral.gov.uk/AboutUs/Pages/default.aspx.

Albrecht, W.S., Albrecht, C.C. & Albrecht, C.O. (2006). *Fraud Examination* (2nd Edition). Mason, OH: Thomson South-Western.

Albrecht, S.W., Howe, K.R. & Rommey, M. (1984). *Deterring Fraud: The Internal Auditor's Perspective.* Altamonte Springs, FL: Institute of Internal Auditors Research Foundation.

Allen, S. (1998). *The Fraud Report.* Brighton: Business Defence Europe Ltd.

Anon (2007). Value Added Fraud, *G4S International*, March, 34–35.

APACS (2009). *Fraud the Facts 2009.* Retrieved 23 January 2010 from http://www.theukcardsassociation.org.uk/files/fraud_the_facts_2009.pdf.

Arlidge, A., Parry, J. & Gatt, I. (1996). *Arlidge and Parry on Fraud.* London: Sweet and Maxwell.

Artis, M., Ayuso, M. & Guillen, M. (1999). Modelling Different Types of Automobile Insurance Fraud Behaviour in the Spanish Market. *Insurance: Mathematics and Economics*, 24(1), 67–81.

———. (2002). Detection of Automobile Insurance Fraud with Discrete Models and Misclassified Claims. *The Journal of Risk and Insurance*, 69(3), 325–340.

Audit Commission (n.d.). *Fraud FAQs.* Retrieved 13 December 2009 from http://www.audit-commission.gov.uk/aboutus/Pages/faqs.aspx#q1.

Auld Report (2002). Retrieved 30 June 2008 from http://www.justice.org.uk/images/pdfs/Auld.pdf.

Bamfield, J. (1998). A Breach of Trust: Employee Collusion and Theft from Major Retailers. In M. Gill (Ed.), *Crime at Work* (pp. 123–143). Leicester: Perpetuity Press.

Barnes, P. & Allen, S. (1998). *The Fraud Report.* Brighton: Business Defence Europe Ltd.

Barr, R. & Pease, K. (1990). Crime Placement, Displacement and Deflection. In M. Tonry, & N. Morris (Eds), *Crime and Justice: A Review of Research* (pp. 277–318). Chicago, IL: University of Chicago Press.

Barrett, D. (17 May 2009). MPs Expenses: How Additional Costs Allowance Works, *The Daily Telegraph.* Retrieved 26 May 2009, from http://www.telegraph.co.uk/news/newstopics/mps-expenses/5335097/MPs-expenses-how-Additional-Costs-Allowance-works.html.

Bayley, D.H. & Shearing, C.D. (1996). The Future of Policing. *Law and Society Review* 30, 585–606.

BBC (2009a). *The Birth of the Credit Slump.* Retrieved 27 May 2009 from http://www.youtube.com/watch?v=Ms7xtehCacQandfeature=related.

————. (2009b). *The Today Programme*, 22 May. Retrieved 22 May 2009 from http://news.bbc.co.uk/today/hi/listen_again/default.stm.

BBC News (1999). Record Fine for Maxwell Accountants. *BBC News Online*. Retrieved 1 April 2008 from http://news.bbc.co.uk/1/low/business/the_company_file/270359.stm.

————. (2001a). *One in Three 'Lie on CVs'*. Retrieved 18 October 2007 from http://news.bbc.co.uk/1/hi/business/1475221.stm.

————. (2001b). *Italy Insurance Scam's Chainsaw Horror*. Retrieved 26 November 2007 from http://news.bbc.co.uk/1/hi/world/monitoring/media_reports/1683738.stm.

————. (2002). *Postie Dumped his Deliveries*. Retrieved 18 February 2008 from http://news.bbc.co.uk/1/hi/scotland/1953258.stm.

————. (2003a). *Jailed Head Protests Innocence*. Retrieved 18 October 2007 from http://news.bbc.co.uk/1/hi/england/london/3131406.stm.

————. (2003b). *Two Face Fraud Charges*. Retrieved 18 February 2008 from http://news.bbc.co.uk/1/hi/northern_ireland/3184897.stm.

————. (2003c). *'Millionaire' Major Guilty of Fraud*. Retrieved 26 November 2007 from http://news.bbc.co.uk/1/hi/england/wiltshire/3220135.stm.

————. (2003d). *Victims to Sign Declaration of Truth*. Retrieved 26 November 2007 from http://news.bbc.co.uk/1/hi/england/berkshire/3092087.stm.

————. (2006a). *Dentist Struck Off for NHS Fraud*. Retrieved 18 October 2007 from http://news.bbc.co.uk/1/hi/england/london/5181706.stm.

————. (2006b). *Skipper Admits Boat Sinking Fraud*. Retrieved 26 November 2007 from http://news.bbc.co.uk/1/hi/scotland/north_east/5406056.stm.

————. (2006c). *Fraud Body Warns of Crash Scams*. Retrieved 15 January 2007 from http://news.bbc.co.uk/1/hi/programmes/moneybox/6186027.stm.

————. (2006d). *Wheelchair claim fraud man jailed*. Retrieved 26 November 2007 from http://news.bbc.co.uk/1/hi/england/somerset/5275450.stm.

————. (2006e). *Skipper Admits Boat Sinking Fraud*. Retrieved 26 November 2007 from http://news.bbc.co.uk/1/hi/scotland/north_east/5406056.stm.

————. (2007a). *Malaria Drugs Recalled in Kenya*. Retrieved 5 March 2008 from http://news.bbc.co.uk/1/hi/world/africa/6951586.stm.

————. (2007b). *'Crackdown on "Holiday Club" Scam'*. Retrieved 20 May 2009 from http://news.bbc.co.uk/1/hi/business/6730691.stm.

————. (2007c). *Salsa Teacher in Benefits Fraud*. Retrieved 25 April 2008 from http://news.bbc.co.uk/1/hi/wales/mid/6680813.stm.

————. (2007d). *Preacher Jailed Over £51 Million Fraud*. Retrieved 20 December 2009 from http://news.bbc.co.uk/1/hi/england/nottinghamshire/7118579.stm.

————. (2008). *Tory MP Conway says 'I'm sorry'*. Retrieved 30 January 2008 from http://news.bbc.co.uk/1/hi/uk_politics/7212990.stm.

————. (2009a). *Fraudster Madoff Gets 150 Years*. Retrieved 15 December 2009 from http://news.bbc.co.uk/1/hi/business/8124838.stm.

————. (2009b). *MPs and Peers Cases Referred to Prosecutors*. Retrieved 15 December 2009 from http://news.bbc.co.uk/1/hi/uk_politics/8374994.stm.

————. (2009c). *'German Robin Hood Banker gets Suspended Sentence'*. Retrieved 24 November 2009, from: http://news.bbc.co.uk/1/hi/world/europe/8376532.stm.

————. (2009d). *Disability Cheat was Club Bouncer*. Retrieved 15 December 2009, from http://news.bbc.co.uk/1/hi/england/south_yorkshire/8295414.stm.

————. (2009e). *Q and A: MP Expenses Row Explained*. Retrieved 25 May 2009 from http://news.bbc.co.uk/1/hi/uk_politics/7840678.stm.

————. (2009f). *Timeline: Credit Crunch to Downturn*. Retrieved 27 May 2009 from http://news.bbc.co.uk/1/hi/business/7521250.stm.

BBC News Wales (1999). *'UK: Wales Councillors Sentenced for Expenses Fraud'*. Retrieved 26 May 2009 from http://news.bbc.co.uk/1/hi/wales/440837.stm.

BDO Stoy Hayward (2008). *Fraud a Global Challenge*. United Kingdom: BDO Stoy Hayward.

————. (2005). *White Collar Crime Doubles in a Year*. United Kingdom: BDO Stoy Hayward.

Benedictus, L. (26 November 2009). 'The Robin Hood Banker: Does "Helper Syndrome" Exist?' *The Guardian*. Retrieved 26 November, from http://www.guardian.co.uk/science/2009/nov/26/robin-hood-banker-helper-syndrome.

Benson, M.L. & Cullen, T.F (1998). *Combating Corporate Crime: Local Prosecutors at Work*. Boston, MA: Northeastern University Press.

————. & Moore, E. (1992). Are White Collar and Common Offenders the Same? *Journal of Research in Crime and Delinquency*, 29(3), 251–272.

Blythe, C. (1995). You Little Fiddler. *News of the World*.

Boisjoly, R.M. et al. (1995). Commentary on 'Technology and Civil Disobedience': Why Engineers Have a Special Duty to Obey the Law. *Science and Engineering Ethics*, 1(2), 169–171.

Borodzicz, E. (2005). *Risk, Crisis and Security Management*. Chichester: Wiley.

Bourn, J. (2007). *DWP Resource Accounts 2006–07*. NAO, London: National Audit Office.

Bournemouth Online (2007). *Spirit Swap Fraud – £1000 Fine*. Retrieved 5 March 2008 from http://www.bournemouth.gov.uk/News/press_office/Press_Archive/PR_2007/sept2007/1000fine.asp.

Bowers, S. & Wintour, P. (23 February 2007). Move to Close Down Serious Fraud Office. *The Guardian*. Retrieved 27 February 2008 from http://www.guardian.co.uk/business/2007/feb/23/politics.arms.

Box, S. (1983). *Power, Crime and Mystification*. London: Tavistock.

———. (1987). *Recession, Crime and Punishment*. Basingstoke: Macmillian.

Braithwaite, J. (1985). White Collar Crime. *Annual Review of Sociology*, 11, 1–25.

British Standards Institution (2006). *BS 7858 Security Screening for Persons Employed in a Security Environment*. BSI: UK.

Brooke, C. (30 November 2007). Fraudster Who "Bought Lordship" in £51 million VAT Scam Jailed for Ten Years, *Mail Online*. Retrieved 2 December 2009 from http://www.mailonsunday.co.uk/pages/live/articles/news/news.html?in_article_id=497471andin_page_id=1770.

Bulmer, M. (1977). *Sociological Research Methods: An Introduction*. Basingstoke: Macmillan.

———. (1984). *Sociological Research Methods: An Introduction* (2nd Edition). Basingstoke: Macmillan.

Button, M., Johnston, L. & Frimpong, K. (2008). The Fraud Review and the Policing of Fraud: Laying the Foundations for a Centralised Fraud Police or Counter Fraud Executive. *Policing*, 2(2), 241–250.

———. & Smith, G. (2007). New Directions in Policing Fraud: The Emergence of the Counter Fraud Specialist in the United Kingdom. *International Journal of the Sociology of Law*, 35(4), 192–208.

Button, M., Lewis, C. & Tapley, J. (2009). *Fraud Typologies and the Victims of Fraud Literature Review*. London: National Fraud Authority.

Cabinet Office (2002). *Identity Fraud a Study*. Retrieved 16 October 2007 from http://www.identitycards.gov.uk/downloads/id_fraud-report.pdf.

Cadbury Report (1992). Committee on the Financial Aspects of Corporate Governance. *Report of the Committee on the Financial Aspects of Corporate Governance*. London: Professional Publishing Ltd.

Camenson, B. (2001). *Opportunities in Forensic Science Careers*. Lincolnwood, IL: N T C/Contemporary Publishing Company.

Carratu (n.d.). *Employee Screening Services*. Retrieved 16 October 2007 from http://www.eurocomci.co.uk/Services-Business.html.

Carcach, C. (1997). *Reporting Crime to the Police: Trends and Issues. No. 68*. Australian Institute of Criminology.

Cellan-Jones, R. (5 December 2007). Government "Failing on E-crime". *BBC News 24*. Retrieved 8 January 2007 from http://news.bbc.co.uk/1/hi/technology/7128491.stm.

Chakraborti, N. & Garland, J. (2009). *Hate Crime*. London: Sage.

CILA (2007). *Membership Information*. Retrieved 28 November 2007 from http://www.cila.co.uk/members/membership-information.

CIFAS (n.d.) *What is CIFAS?* Retrieved 18 October 2007 from http://www.cifas.org.uk/default.asp?edit_id=564-73.

Clark, D. (2007). Covert Surveillance and Informer Handling. In T. Newburn, T. Williamson & A. Wright (Eds), *Handbook of Criminal Investigation* (pp. 426–449). Devon: Willan.

Clarke, M. (1989). Insurance Fraud. *British Journal of Criminology*, 29(1), 1–20.

———. (1990). The Control of Insurance Fraud A Comparative View. *British Journal of Criminology*, 30(1), 1–23.

Clarke, R.V.G. (2005). Seven Misconceptions of Situational Crime Prevention. In N. Tilley (Ed.), *Handbook of Crime Prevention and Community Safety*. Cullompton: Willan.

Clarke, R.V. & Mayhew, P. (1988). The British Gas Suicide Story and its Implications for Prevention. In M. Tonry & N. Morris (Eds), *Crime and Justice: A Review of Research*, Vol. 10. Chicago: University of Chicago Press.

Coalition Against Insurance Fraud (n.d.). *By the Numbers: Fraud Stats*. Retrieved 20 November 2007 from http://www.insurancefraud.org/stats.htm.

Cohen, L. & Felson, M. (1979). Social Change and Crime Rate Trends: A Routine Activity Approach. *American Sociological Review*, 44, 588–605.

Cole, M. (2009). The FSA's Agenda for Fighting Financial Crime. Speech by Margaret Cole, Director, Enforcement and Financial Crime Division, FSA to the British Bankers Association.

Coleman, J.W. (1999). Motivation and Opportunity: Understanding the Causes of White-Collar Crime. In M. Levi (Ed.), *Fraud: Organization, Motivation and Control (Vol. 1: The Extent and Causes of White-Collar Crime)*. Aldershot: Ashgate.

Comer, M. (1985). *Corporate Fraud* (2nd Edition). Aldershot: Gower.

———. (2003). *Investigating Corporate Fraud*. Aldershot: Gower.

Control Risks and Simmons and Simmons (2006). *International Business Attitudes to Corruption – Survey*. Retrieved 29 January 2007 from http://www.crg.com/pdf/corruption_survey_2006_V3.pdf.

Cook, D. (1989). *Rich Law, Poor Law: Differential Responses to Tax and Supplementary Benefit Fraud*. London: McGraw-Hill.

———. (2006). *Criminal and Social Justice*. London: Sage.

CPS (2007). *Annual Report and Resource Account 2007–2008*. London: CPS.

———. (2010). *Statement from Keir Starmer QC, Director of Public Prosecutions, on Parliamentary Expenses Charging Decisions*. Retrieved 2 March 2010 from http://www.cps.gov.uk/news/press_statements/parliamentary_expenses_charging_decisions/.

Cressey, D. (1973). *Other People's Money*. Montclair, NJ: Patterson Smith.

Criminal Justice System Press Release (2005). *Government Announces Review to Tackle Fraud*. Retrieved 30 January 2008 from http://

webarchive.nationalarchives.gov.uk/20081212184214/http://www.
attorneygeneral.gov.uk/attachments/fraud_review_and_s43.doc.

Croall, H. (1992). *White Collar Crime*. Buckingham: Open University
Press.

———. (2001). *Understanding White Collar Crime*. Buckingham: Open
University Press.

Daily Telegraph (2003). *Insurers Crack Down on Fraudsters*. Retrieved
1 March 2010 from http://www.telegraph.co.uk/finance/personal
finance/insurance/2867958/Insurers-crack-down-on-the-fraudsters.
html.

———. (2008). *Canoe Man John Darwin Timeline*. Retrieved 10 March
2008 from http://www.telegraph.co.uk/news/main.jhtml?xml=/news/
2007/12/11/ncanoe111.xml.

———. (2009a). *IMF Puts Total Cost of Crisis at £7.1 Trillion*. Retrieved
15 December 2009 from http://www.telegraph.co.uk/finance/
newsbysector/banksandfinance/5995810/IMF-puts-total-cost-of-
crisis-at-7.1-trillion.html.

———. (2009b). *Dentist and Son Jailed for Three Years for Insider Trading*.
Retrieved 15 January 2010 from http://www.telegraph.co.uk/news/
uknews/crime/6780821/Dentist-and-son-jailed-for-three-years-for-
insider-trading.html.

Dale, P. (5 April 2005). Labour Councillors Sacked for Vote Fraud. *Birmingham Post*. Retrieved 5 March 2008, from http://www.birmingham
post.net/news/west-midlands-news/tm_objectid=15367971&method=
full&siteid=50002&headline=labour-councillors-sacked-for-vote-
fraud-name_page.html.

Davies, D. (2000). *Fraudwatch*. London: KMPG.

De Grazia, J. (2008). *Review of the Serious Fraud Office Final Report*.
London: SFO.

Dean, H. (1998). Benefit Fraud and Citizenship. In P. Taylor-
Gooby (Ed.), *Choice and Public Policy*. Hemel Hempstead: Harvester
Wheatsheaf.

———. & Melrose, M. (1996). Unravelling Citizenship: The Significance
of Social Security Fraud. *Critical Social Policy*, 16(3), 3–31.

———. (1997). Manageable Discord: Fraud and Resistance in the Social
Security System. *Social Policy and Administration*, 31(2), 103–118.

Deem, D.L. (2000). Notes From the Field: Observations in Working with
the Forgotten Victims of Financial Crimes. *Journal of Elder Abuse and
Neglect*, 12, 33–48.

Department of Justice (2008). *Father and Daughter Charged with International Investment Fraud and Money Laundering Scheme*. Retrieved 1
March 2010 from http://www.cityoflondon.police.uk/NR/rdonlyres/
116D0AD7-DB3F-4164-AD65-99147480E3ED/0/March1315000
Britishvictimsofboilerroomfraud.pdf.

Department of Justice (2009). *Sentencing Transcript Dated June 29, 2009*. Retrieved 1 March 2010 from http://www.justice.gov/usao/nys/madoff/20090629sentencingtranscriptcorrected.pdf.

Dittenhofer, M.A. (1995). The Behavioural Aspects of Fraud and Embezzlement. *Public Money and Management*, January–March 1995.

Ditton, J. (1977). Alibis and Aliases: Some Notes on the 'Motives' of Fiddling Bread Salesmen, *Sociology*, 11(2), 233–255.

Dizzy Thinks (n.d.). *Fraudulent Benefit Fraud Figures?* Retrieved 25 April 2008 from http://dizzythinks.net/2007/03/fraudulent-benefit-fraud-figures.html.

Doherty, M. (1997). *Criminology*. London: Old Bailey Press.

Doig, A. (2006). *Fraud*. Cullompton: Willan.

———, Jones, B. & Wait, B. (1999). The Insurance Industry Response to Fraud. *Security Journal*, 12(3), 19–30.

DWP (1998a). *New Ambitions for Our Country: A New Contract for Welfare* (Cm. 3805). London: The Stationery Office.

———. (1998b). *Beating Fraud is Everyone's Business: Securing the Future* (Cm. 4012). London: The Stationery Office.

———. (2005a). *Reducing Fraud in the Benefit System: Achievements and Ambitions*. London: DWP, p. 136.

———. (2006). *Fraud and Error in Income Support: Jobseeker's Allowance and Pension Credits April 2004–March 2005*. London: DWP.

———. (2009). *Fraud and Error in the Benefit System: April 2008 to March 2009*. Retrieved 4 November 2009 from http://research.dwp.gov.uk/asd/asd2/fem/fem_apr08_mar09.pdf.

Dyck, I.J., Morse, A. & Zingales, L. (2006). *Who Blows the Whistle on Corporate Fraud?* AFA 2007 Chicago Meeting Paper. Retrieved 29 April 2007 from http://papers.ssrn.com/sol3/papers.cfm?abstract_id=891482.

Edwards, R. (2007). *£2m Thief 'Lived Like a Footballer's Wife'*. Retrieved 15 January 2008 from *Daily Telegraph* website http://www.telegraph.co.uk/news/main.jhtml?xml=/news/2007/10/27/nthief127.xml.

EHDC (2007). *Press Release*. Retrieved 26 April 2008 from http://www.easthants.gov.uk/ehdc/newsandvacancies.nsf/0/F0CF6048D84E10F2802573990055E884?OpenDocument.

Equifax (2006). *Equifax Launches SIRAN, The Most Advanced Application Fraud Detection System Available Today*. Retrieved 27 January 2008 from Equifax website http://www.equifax.co.uk/our_company/press_room/2006/Siran_Launch.html.

Ericson, R.V. & Doyle, A. (2006). 'The Institutionalization of Deceptive Sales in Life Insurance: Five Sources of Moral Risk', *British Journal of Criminology*, 46(6), 993–1010.

Ernst and Young (2006). *Fraud Risk in Emerging Markets*. Retrieved 18 April 2008 from http://66.102.9.132/search?q=cache:LEPihL8ek-cJ:www.ey.com/Publication/vwLUAssets/9th_Global_Fraud_Survey_

(Report)/%24FILE/EY_9th_Global_Fraud_Survey_2006.pdf+Ernst+
and+Young+(2006).+Fraud+Risk+in+Emerging+Markets.&cd=2
&hl=en&ct=clnk&gl=uk.

————. (2007). *9th Global Fraud Survey: Fraud in Emerging Markets.*
Retrieved 27 January 2010, from http://www.financialexecutives.
org/eweb/upload/FEI/FINAL%209TH%20GLOBAL%20FRAUD%20
SURVEY%20ELECTRONIC%20PDF.pdf.

Farrell, G. & Pease, K (2006). Criminology and Security. In G. Martin
(Ed.), *Handbook of Security* (pp. 179–196). Basingstoke: Palgrave
Macmillan.

Farrell, S., Yeo, N. & Ladenburg, G. (2007). *Blackstone's Guide to the Fraud
Act 2006.* Oxford: Oxford University Press.

Financial Ombudsman (2002a). *Insurance Fraud.* Retrieved 26 November
2007   from   http://www.financial-ombudsman.org.uk/publications/
ombudsman-news/21/insurance-fraud.htm.

————. (2002b). *Critical Illness.* Retrieved 26 November 2007 from
http://www.financial-ombudsman.org.uk/publications/ombudsman-
news/13/jan-critical-illness.htm.

FSA (2009). *Enforcement Annual Performance Account 2008/09.* Retrieved
14 December 2009 from http://www.fsa.gov.uk/pubs/annual/ar08_09/
enforcement_report.pdf.

Findlaw (2009). *Plea Allocution of Bernard Madoff (U.S. v. Bernard Madoff).*
Retrieved 12 March 2009 from http://news.findlaw.com/hdocs/docs/
madoff/bernard-guilty-plea31209statement.html.

Flood-Page, C. & Mackie, A. (1998). *Sentencing Practice: An Examination
of Decisions in Magistrates' Courts and the Crown Court in the Mid–1990's*
(HORS Paper 180). London: Home Office.

Fox, J.D., Munch, W. & Othman, K.I. (2000). *Strengthening the Investigative Function in United Nations Systems Organisations.* Retrieved 18
January 2008 from the United Nations website http://www.unjiu.org/
data/reports/2000/en2000_9.pdf.

Fraud Advisory Panel (FAP) (n.d.). *Our Role.* Retrieved 13 December
2007 from http://www.fraudadvisorypanel.org/newsite/About/About_
ourrole.htm.

————. (2006). *Improving the Investigation and Prosecution of Serious
Fraud.* Retrieved 15 May 2009 from http://www.fraudadvisorypanel.
org/newsite/publications_search.php?search=prosecution.

Fraud Review Team (2006a). *Interim Report.* Retrieved 22 June
2006   from   http://www2.northumberland.gov.uk/fraud/Documents/
General/Interim_Fraud_Report_03_06.pdf.

————. (2006b). *Final Report.* Retrieved 28 July 2006 from http://www.
aasdni.gov.uk/pubs/FCI/fraudreview_finalreport.pdf.

FSA (2001). *FSA Uses Its Enforcement Powers to Protect Consumers.*
Retrieved 10 March 2008 from http://www.fsa.gov.uk/Pages/Library/
Communication/PR/2001/075.shtml.

Garland, D. (2002). Of Crimes and Criminals: The Development of Criminology in Britain. In M. Maguire, R. Morgan, & R. Reiner (Eds), *The Oxford Handbook of Criminology*. Oxford: Oxford University Press.

Gee, J. (2007). Measuring Fraud Accurately. *Fighting Fraud*, Issue 22. Special edition: *The Impact of the UK Fraud Review and Fraud Act 2006*. London: KPMG.

———. (2009). *Fraud, Economics and the Credit Crisis* (Presentation to Inaugural Centre for Counter Fraud Studies Conference at the House of Commons, London 8th June 2009). Unpublished Internal Document: Fraud Economics Ltd.

———, Button, M. & Brooks, G. (2009). *The Financial Cost of Fraud*. London: MacIntyre Hudson/CCFS.

Geis, G. (1992). White Collar Crime: What Is It? In K. Scheregal & D. Weisburd (Eds), *White Collar Crime Revisited* (pp. 31–52). Boston, MA: Northeastern University Press.

George, B. & Button, M. (2000). *Private Security*. Leicester: Perpetuity.

Gill, M. (2005). *Learning from Fraudsters*. Leicester: Perpetuity Research and Consultancy International.

———. & Hart, J. (1997). Exploring Investigative Policing. *British Journal of Criminology*, 37(3), 549–567.

Gill, K.M., Woolley, A., & Gill, M.L. (1994). Insurance Fraud: The Business as a Victim? In M. Gill (Ed.), *Crime at Work: Studies in Security and Crime Prevention*. Leicester: Perpetuity Press.

Government Information (2002). *Leicester Pair Found Guilty of £241,000 VAT Fraud*. Retrieved 5 March 2008 from http://www.ginfo.pl/more/283472,leicester,pair,found,guilty,of,241,000,vat,fraud.html.

Grabosky, P. (2000). Computer Crime in a World without Borders. *Platypus Magazine: The Journal of the Australian Federal Police*, June.

Gray, S. (14 March 2008). Britain's Tricked Out of £35 Million in 'Boiler Room' Phone Scam [Electronic Version] *The Independent*. Retrieved 1 April 2008 from http://www.independent.co.uk/news/world/americas/britons-tricked-out-of-16335m-in-boiler-room-phone-scam-795817.html.

Greek, D. (11 March 2009). Consumer Direct Warns of Pyramid Selling Scams. *Computeractive*. Retrieved 20 May 2009 from http://www.computeractive.co.uk/computeractive/news/2238332/consumer-direct-warns-public.

Griew, E. (1986). *The Theft Acts 1968 and 1978*. London: Sweet and Maxwell.

Grover, C. (2005). Advertising Social Security Fraud. *Benefits* 44(3), 199–207.

Guardian (2004). *Tories Privatisation Advisor Struck Off*. Retrieved 25 February 2008 from http://guardian.co.uk/business/2004/nov/18/4.

———. (2007). *£47,000 Benefits Claimant Also Ran Company*. Retrieved 23 April 2008 from http://www.guardian.co.uk/uk/2007/nov/24/ukcri.jamesmeikle.

———. (2008a). *Broadcasters Face Spot Checks on Phone Lines*. Retrieved 3 March 2008 from http://www.guardian.co.uk/media/2008/feb/20/ofcom.television.

———. (2008b). *Immigrant Jailed for Funding £4 Million Property Empire with Benefits*. Retrieved 23 April 2008 from http://www.guardian.co.uk/uk/2008/jan/19/immigration.ukcrime.

Hall, N. (2005). *Hate Crime*. Cullompton: Willan.

Hall, S. (1992). The Question of Cultural Identity. In S. Hall, D. Held & T. McGrew (Eds), *Modernity and Its Futures*. Cambridge: Polity.

Hansard (2008). *Parliamentary Business News: Statements and Debates*. Retrieved 31 January 2008 from http://www.commonsleader.gov.uk/output/page2278.asp.

Hartlepool Mail (2008). *Anne Darwin Guilty*. Retrieved 1 March 2010 from http://www.hartlepoolmail.co.uk/anne-darwin-trial/Anne-Darwin-guilty.4316889.jp.

HBMS (2007). *HBMS Newsletter, June 2007 Edition*. Retrieved 3 December 2007, from DWP website http://www.dwp.gov.uk/docs/jun07.pdf.

Health and Safety Executive (n.d.). *Drug Misuse at Work A Guide for Employers*. Retrieved 18 October 2007 from http://www.hse.gov.uk/alcoholdrugs/.

Henry, S. & Mars, G. (2001). Crime at Work: The Social Construction of Amateur Property Theft. In G. Mars (Ed.), *Occupational Crime*. Dartmouth: Ashgate.

Herman, M. (26 October 2006). How Does Carousel Fraud Work? *Times Online*. Retrieved 4 December 2007 from http://business.timesonline.co.uk/tol/business/law/public_law/article614417.ece.

Hessing, D.J., Elffers, H., Robben, H.S.J. & Webley, P. (1993). Needy or greedy? The Social Psychology of Individuals who Fraudulently Claim Unemployment Benefits. *Journal of Applied Social Psychology*, 23(3), 226–243.

Higson, A. (1999). *The Fraud Advisory Panel Working Party Paper: Why is Management Reticent to Report Fraud?* Retrieved 30 March 2008 from: http://www.fraudadvisorypanel.org/newsite/PDFs/research/Why%20is%20Mgt%20Reticent%20to%20Report%20Fraud.pdf.

Hillyard, P. & Tombs, S. (2005). Beyond Criminology? In D. Dorling, D. Gordon, D., P. Hillyard, C., Pantazis, S. Pemberton, & S., Tombs (Eds), *Criminal Obsessions: Why Harm Matters More than Crime* (pp. 6–23). Kings College London: Centre for Crime and Justice Studies.

Hirsch, F. (20 January 2009). Should Sir Fred Get Away Scot-Free? *The Guardian*. Retrieved 27 May 2009 from http://www.guardian.co.uk/commentisfree/2009/jan/20/banking-banks.

HMIC (2004). *Modernising the Police Service: A Thematic Inspection of Workforce Modernisation – The Role, Management and Deployment of Police Staff in the Police Service of England and Wales.* London: HMIC.

HM Treasury (1994). *Government Accounting.* London: HMSO.

———. (1997). *Managing the Risk of Fraud: A Guide for Managers.* London: HM Treasury.

———. (1998). *Public Services for the Future.* London: HMSO.

———. (2002). *Fraud Report: An Analysis of Reported Fraud in Government Departments and Best Practice Guidelines.* London: HMSO.

———. (2004). *Fraud Report: An Analysis of Reported Fraud in Government Departments.* London: HMSO.

———. (2008). *Fraud Report 2007–2008: An Analysis of Reported Fraud in Government Departments.* Retrieved 4 September 2008 from http://www.hm-treasury.gov.uk/d/govt_fraudreport031008.pdf.

Hollinger, R. & Clark, J.P. (1983). *Theft by Employees.* Lexington, KY: Lexington Books.

Hollinger, R.C. & Davis, J.L. (2006). Employee Theft and Staff Dishonesty. In M. Gill (Ed.), *The Handbook of Security* (pp. 203–228). Basingstoke: Palgrave.

Holt, T.J. & Graves, D.C. (2007). A qualitative Analysis of Advance Fee Fraud Email Schemes. *International Journal of Cyber Crimes and Criminology*, 1(1), 137–154. Retrieved 26 April 2007 from http://www.cybercrimejournal.co.nr/.

Home Office (2000). *A Guide to the Criminal Justice System in England and Wales. London: Home Office.* Retrieved 21 October 2008 from http://rds.homeoffice.gov.uk/rds/pdfs/cjs2000.pdf.

———. (2009). *Crime in England and Wales 2008/09.* Retrieved 23 January 2010 from http://www.homeoffice.gov.uk/rds/pdfs09/hosb1109vol1.pdf.

Hope, C. (19 May 2009a). MP's Expenses: Ian Davidson Paid Friend £5,500 to Renovate Flat then Took him Shooting. *The Daily Telegraph.* Retrieved 25 May 2009 from http://www.telegraph.co.uk/news/newstopics/mps-expenses/5351148/MPs-expenses-Ian-Davidson-paid-friend-5500-to-renovate-flat-then-took-him-shooting.html.

———. (14 May 2009b). 'Don Touhig', An MP who "Flipped", to Decide if it Should be Banned: MP's Expenses. *The Daily Telegraph.* Retrieved 25 May 2009 from http://www.telegraph.co.uk/news/newstopics/mps-expenses/5320191/Don-Touhig-an-MP-who-flipped-to-decide-if-it-should-be-banned-MPs-expenses.html.

Horning, D. (1970). Blue Collar Theft: Conceptions of Property, Attitudes towards Pilfering and Work Group Norms in a Modern Industrial Plant. In E.D. Smigel & H.L. Ross (Eds), *Crimes Against Bureaucracy.* New York: Van Nostrand Reinhold Company.

House of Commons (1997). *The Code of Conduct Together with the Guide Relating to the Conduct of Members*, London: House of Commons.

————. (2009). *The Green Book: A Guide to Members' Allowances*. London: House of Commons.

House of Commons Written Answers (31 January 2006). *Work and Pensions*. Retrieved 2 March 2010 from http://www.publications. parliament.uk/pa/cm200506/cmhansrd/vo060131/text/60131w40.htm #60131w40.html_sbhd6.

Hutter, B.M. (1988). *The Reasonable Arm of the Law?: The Law Enforcement Procedures of Environmental Health Officers*. Oxford: Clarendon Press.

————. (1997). *Compliance: Regulation and Environment*. Oxford: Clarendon Press.

Independent (2003). *'Near-Bankrupt' Ingram Walks Free in Fraud Case*. Retrieved 1 March 2010 from http://www.independent.co.uk/news/ uk/crime/nearbankrupt-ingram-walks-free-in-fraud-case-736576. html.

Inman, P. (2006). *Critical Points About Sickness Cover*. Retrieved 26 November 2007 from http://www.guardian.co.uk/money/2006/jun/10/ moneysupplement.healthinsurance.

IFB (2007). *Insurance Fraud Bureau First Year Anniversary – 26th July 2007*. Retrieved 27 November 2007 from http://www.insurancefraud bureau.org/files/press_release_pdfs/media_pack_insurance_fraud_ bureau_year_book_26-7-07.pdf.

IFIG (n.d.). *The History of IFIG*. Retrieved 27 November 2007 from http://www.ifig.org/about-ifig/.

Johnston, L. (2000). *Policing Britain: Risk, Security and Governance*. Harlow: Longman,

————. (2006), Transnational Security Governance. In J. Wood & B. Dupont (Eds), *Democracy, Society and the Governance of Security* (pp. 33–51). Cambridge: Cambridge University Press.

Jones, P. (2004). *Fraud and Corruption in Public Services*. Aldershot: Gower.

Jupp, V. (1989). *Methods of Criminological Research*. London: Routledge.

Kanellis, P., Kiountouzis, E., Kolokotronis, N. & Martakos, D. (Eds) (2006). *Digital Crime and Forensic Science in Cyberspace*. Hershey, PA: Idea Group.

Kapardis, A. & Krambia-Kapardis, M. (2004). Enhancing Fraud Prevention and Detection by Profiling Fraud Offenders. *Journal of Criminal Behaviour and Mental Health*, 14(3), 189–201.

Karstedt, S., Levi, M. & Godfrey, B. (2006). 'Introduction' to Special Issue on 'Market, Risk and "White-Collar" Crimes: Moral Economies from Victorian Times to Enron'. *British Journal of Criminology*, 46(6), 971–975.

Katungi, D., Neal, E. & Barbour, A. (2006). *People in Low-Paid Informal Work: 'Need not Greed'*. London: The Rowntree Foundation.

Kempson, E. & Bryson, A. (1994). *Hard Times? How Poor Families Make Ends Meet*. London: Policy Studies Institute.

KPMG (2004a). *KPMG Forensic Fraud Survey 2004*. Retrieved 15 March 2008 from http://www.kpmg.com.au/aci/docs/Fraud-Survey-2004.pdf.

———. (2004b). *KPMG Forensic Fraud Survey 2003*. Retrieved 28 January 2008 from http://www.kpmg.com/aci/docs/surveys/Fraud%20Survey_040855_R5.pdf.

———. (2004c). *KPMG Forensic Fraud Survey 2004*. Retrieved 28 January 2008 from http://www.kpmg.com.au/aci/docs/Fraud-Survey-2004.pdf.

———. (2006). *KPMG Forensic Fraud Survey 2006*. Retrieved 28 January 2008 from http://www.kpmg.com.au/Portals/0/FraudSurvey%2006%20WP(web).pdf.

———. (2007a). *Profile of a Fraudster 2007 Survey*. Retrieved 15 August 2008 from http://www.kpmg.co.uk/pubs/ProfileofaFraudster Survey(web).pdf.

———. (2007b). *Fraud Services*. Retrieved 18 October 2007 from http://www.kpmg.co.uk/services/f/fs/index.cfm.

———. (2008a). *Fraud Hits 12 Year High in 2007*. Retrieved 23 January 2010 from http://www.kpmg.co.uk/news/detail.cfm?pr=3028.

———. (2008b). *Credit Crunch Increases Fraud Fears*. Retrieved 18 January 2008, from KPMG website http://www.kpmg.co.uk/news/detail.cfm?pr=3019.

———. (2009). *KPMG Forensic Fraud Barometer, February 2009*. Retrieved 23 January 2010 from http://www.yhff.co.uk/Fraud%20 Barometer%20-%20Feb%202009%20_2_.pdf.

Kroll (2007). *Global Fraud Report*. Retrieved 30 November 2007 from http://www.kroll.com/about/library/fraud/

Law Commission (2002). *Fraud: Report on a Reference Under Section 3(1)(e) of the Law Commissions Act 1965* (LAW COM No 276). London: HMSO.

Leeson, N. (1996). *Rogue Trader*. London: Little Brown.

Levi, M (1981). *The Phantom Capitalists: The Organisation and Control of Long-Firm Fraud*. London: Heinemann.

———. (1987). *Regulating Fraud*. New York: Tavistock Publications.

———. (1988). Prevention of Fraud, CPU Paper 17. London: HMSO.

———. (1993). *The Investigation, Prosecution and the Trial of Serious Fraud: The Royal Commission on Criminal Justice*. London: HMSO.

———. (1994). Masculinities and White Collar Crime. In T. Newburn & E. Stanko (Eds), *Just Boys Doing Business? Men, Masculinity and Crime*. London: Routledge.

———. (1995). Serious Fraud in Britain. In F. Pearce & L. Snider (Eds), *Corporate Crime: Contemporary debates*. Toronto, ON: Toronto University Press.

———. (1998). *The Prevention of Plastic and Credit Card Fraud Revisited*. HORS Paper 182. London: HMSO.

————. (2000). *The Economic Cost of Fraud Report for the Home Office*. London: NERA.

————. (2003). The Roskill Fraud Commission Revisited: An Assessment. *Journal of Financial Crime*, 11(1), 38–44.

————. (2005). International Fraud. In M. Natarajan (Ed.), *Introduction to International Criminal Justice* (pp. 361–369), Boston, MA: McGraw Hill.

————. (2006). *Sentencing Frauds: A Review*. Retrieved 28 May 2009 from http://www.cf.ac.uk/socsi/resources/Levi_GFR_Sentencing_Fraud.pdf.

————. (2008). *The Phantom Capitalists*. Basingstoke: Ashgate.

Levi, M., Burrows, J., Fleming, H. & Hopkins, M. (2007). *The Nature, Extent and Economic Impact of Fraud in the UK*. London: ACPO.

Lidstone, K.W., Hogg, R. & Sutcliffe, F. (1980). *Prosecutions by Private Individuals and Non-Police AGENCIES* (Research Study No.10). London: HMSO.

Lomax, R. (2002). *Evidence before Public Accounts Committee 55th Report: Fraud and Error in Income Support*. London: HMSO.

London Borough of Hammersmith and Fulham (2005). *Fraud Investigation Plan – Section IV*. Retrieved 23 January 2008 from London Borough of Hammersmith and Fulham website http://www.lbhf.gov.uk/Images/AFCS_FraudInvestigationPlan_tcm21-24793.pdf.

Mars, G. (1973). Hotel Pilferage: A Case Study in Occupational Theft. In M. Warner (Ed.), *The Sociology of the Workplace*. London: Allen and Unwin.

————. (1982). *Cheats at Work: Anthropology of Workplace Crime*. London: Allen and Unwin.

————. (1984). *Cheats at Work: An Anthropology of Workplace Crime* (2nd Edition). London: Allen and Unwin.

————. (2001). *Occupational Crime*. Dartmouth: Ashgate.

Mason, R. (14 July 2009). Under Tough New Regime, the SFO is on the Case. *The Daily Telegraph*, p. 4.

Maslow, A.H. (1943). A Theory of Human Motivation. *Psychological Review*, 50, July 1943, pp. 370–396.

Mayhew, P., Clarke, R., Sturman, A. & Hough, M. (1976). *Crime as Opportunity*. London: HMS.

McDonald, W. (1997). *Crime and Law Enforcement in the Global Village*. Cincinnati, OH: Anderson Publishing.

McIntosh, L. (28 July 2008). Boom in Fraud … and There's Worse to Come as Credit Crunch Bites. *The Scotsman*. Retrieved 26 May 2009 from http://news.scotsman.com/uk/Boom-in–fraud-.4332734.jp.

Mennell, J. & Shaw, I. (2006). The Future of Forensic and Crime Scene Science. *Forensic Science International*, 157: S7–S12.

Messerschmidt, J.W. (1986). *Capitalism, Patriarchy and Crime: Towards a Socialist Feminist Criminology*. Totowa, NJ: Rowan and Littlefield.

Mitton, L. (2009). *Factors Affecting Compliance with Rules: Understanding the Behaviour and Motivations behind Customer Fraud* (DWP Working Paper No. 67). London. The Stationary Office.

Morley, N.J., Ball, L.J. & Ormerod, T.C. (2006). How the Detection of Insurance Fraud Succeeds and Fails. *Psychology, Crime and Law,* 12(2), 163–180.

Morton, J. & Bateson, H. (2007). *Conned, Scams, Frauds and Swindles.* London: Portrait.

Mullins, L.J. (1992). *Management and Organisational Behaviour* (2nd Edition). London: Pitman Publishing.

Murray, G. (1996). *The Business Security Handbook.* London: Simon Schuster.

NAO (1997). *National Audit Office Measures to Combat Housing Benefit Fraud.* London: HMSO.

———. (2003). *Tackling Benefit Fraud HC 393 2002–2003.* London: HMSO.

———. (2006). *Audit Commission National Fraud Initiative: Code of data matching practice 2006.* London: Audit Commission.

Natarajan, M. (2005). International Crime and Justice: An Introduction. In M. Natarajan (Ed.), *Introduction to International Criminal Justice* (pp. xv–xxiii). Boston, MA: McGraw Hill.

National Fraud Authority (2010). *Annual Fraud Indicator.* London: National Fraud Authority.

National White Collar Crime Center and Federal Bureau of Investigation (2006). *Internet Crime Report January 1, 2006–December 31, 2006.* Retrieved 3 December 2007 from http://www.ic3.gov/media/annualreport/2006_IC3Report.pdf.

Naughton, P. (22 March 2005). Massive Jubilee Line Fraud Trial Collapses. *Times Online.* Retrieved 5 January 2010 from http://www.timesonline.co.uk/tol/news/uk/article434657.ece.

NERA (2000). *The Economic Cost of Fraud.* London: NERA Associates.

Newburn, T. (2007). *Criminology.* Cullompton: Willan.

———, Williamson, T. & Wright, A. (2007). *Handbook of Criminal Investigation.* Cullompton: Willan.

NFI (2009). NFI Matters: An Update on the Audit Commission's National Fraud Initiative. *NFI Matters,* Issue 6. Retrieved 20 January 2010 from http://www.audit-commission.gov.uk/SiteCollectionDocuments/Downloads/NFIMattersFeb2009.pdf.

NHS BSA Press Release (2009). *Midwife Supervisor Sentenced for £63,000 Timesheet Fraud.* Retrieved 14 January 2009 from http://www.nhsbsa.nhs.uk/2743.aspx.

NHS CFSMS (2007a). *NHS CFS Performance Report 2006–07.* Retrieved 22 January 2008 from http://www.wales.nhs.uk/sites3/Documents/501/Annual%20Report%20%28England%29%2006%2007%20Performance_Report.pdf.

————. (2007b). *Creating an Anti-Fraud Culture: Discovering the Public's Perception of Fraud in the NHS*. Retrieved 31 January 2008 from http:// www.nhsbsa.nhs.uk/CounterFraud/Documents/Fifth_fraud_public_ opinion_poll.pdf.

NHS CFS (2003). *Countering Fraud in the NHS: Applying Appropriate Sanctions Consistently*. London: Department of Health.

North East Fraud Forum (n.d.). *North East Fraud Forum*. Retrieved 30 January 2008 from http://www.northeastfraudforum.co.uk/.

O' Brien, M. (2006). *Reported in Non-Jury Fraud Trial Bill Introduced*. Retrieved 20 January 2008, from http://www.legalday.com/ commentaries/Home_Office/Non-jury_fraud_trial_bill.html.

OFT (2006). *Research on Impact of Mass Marketed Scams*. Retrieved 25 January 2010 from http://www.oft.gov.uk/shared_oft/reports/ consumer_protection/oft883.pdf.

OFWAT (2008). *OFWAT Fines Southern Water £20.3 million*. PN 02/08. Retrieved 1 March 2010 from http://www.ofwat.gov.uk/legacy/aptrix/ ofwat/publish.nsf/Content/pn0208.html.

Oliver, J. (22 September 2006). VAT Scams Hit UK Taxpayers Hard. *BBC News*. Retrieved 28 April 2007 from http://news.bbc.co.uk/1/hi/ business/5369776.stm.

O'Reilly, C. (2006). *Towards State/Corporate Symbiosis: The Role of the Security Consultancy Industry in Transnational Policing*, unpublished PhD., Faculty of Arts, Humanities and Social Sciences, Queen's University Belfast.

Ormerod, D. (2007). Criminalising Lying. *Criminal Law Review*, March Edition, 193–219.

Pearce, F. (1976). *Crimes of the Powerful: Marxism, Crime and Deviance*. London: Pluto Press.

Perry, B. (2001). *In the Name of Hate: Understanding Hate Crime*. London: Routledge.

————. (2003). *Hate and Bias Crime*. London: Routledge.

Picard, P. (1996). Auditing Claims in the Insurance Market with Fraud: The Credibility Issue. *Journal of Public Economics*, 63(1), 27–56.

Pomeranz (1995). Fraud: The Root Causes. *Public Money and Management*, 15–18 January–March.

PR Newswire (2003). *Esure to Use Voice Risk Analysis to Cut Fraud and Speed Genuine Claims*. Retrieved 28 November 2007 from http://www. prnewswire.co.uk/cgi/news/release?id=112808.

PriceWaterhouseCoopers (2007). *Economic Crime, People, Culture and Controls*. Retrieved 30 November 2007 from http://www.pwc.com/en_GX/ gx/economic-crime-survey/pdf/gecs_transportation_and_logistics_ supplement.pdf.

Public Accounts committee (2002). *55th Report: Fraud and Error in Income Support*. London: Parliament.

Public Concern at Work (n.d.) *Making Whistle-Blowing Work*. Retrieved 13 December 2007 from http://www.pcaw.co.uk.

Pykett, E. (9 February 2008). Relief as 'Missing' Millions Written Off. *The News*. Retrieved 5 March 2008 from http://www.portsmouth.co. uk/news/Relief-as-39missing39-millions-written.3761825.jp.

Rainbow, L. (2007). The Role of Behavioural Science in Criminal Investigations. *Forensic Update* Issue 88. Retrieved 15 May 2009 from www.bps.org.uk/downloadfile.cfm?file_uuid=27E792C9-1143-DFD0-7E4C-8578CB2194A3andext=pdf.

Renooy, P.H. (1990). *The Informal Economy: Meaning Measurement and Social Significance*. Amsterdam: Regioplan.

Reppetto, T. (1976). Crime Prevention and the Displacement Phenomenon. *Crime and Delinquency*, 22, 166–177.

Report of the Committee on Abuse of Social Security Benefits (1973). London: HMSO.

Reporting Economic Crime Online (RECOL). Retrieved 30 April 2007 from https://www.recol.ca/intro.aspx.

Robins, J. (25 February 2007). 'Clairvoyant' Conmen Reap Millions by Preying on Weak and Vulnerable. *The Observer*. Retrieved 20 May 2009 from http://www.guardian.co.uk/money/2007/feb/25/ scamsandfraud.observercashsection.

Rogerson, S. (1997). *Data Matching*. Retrieved 2 December 2007 from the Centre for Computing and Social Responsibility Website http:// www.ccsr.cse.dmu.ac.uk/resources/general/ethicol/Ecv7no1.html.

Roque, J. (2000). *The Collection of Excise Duties by HM Custom and Excise*. CMP 5239. London: HMSO.

Roskill, Lord (1986). *Fraud Trials Committee Report*. London: HMSO.

Rowlingson, K., Whyley, C., Newburn, T. & Berthoud, R. (Eds) (1997). *Social Security Fraud: The Role of Penalties*, DSS Research Report No. 64, London: The Stationery Office.

Russell, N. (1998). *Dealing with Fraud: A Survey of UK Companies*. London: Neville Russell.

Sainsbury, R. (2000). Getting the Measure of Fraud. *Poverty*, 108, 9–13.

———. (2003). Understanding Social Security Fraud. In J. Millar (Ed.), *Understanding Social Security: Issues for Policy and Practice* (pp. 277–295), Bristol: Policy Press.

Sawer, A. (24 May 2009). MP's Expenses: Tory Claimed £10,000 for Website. *The Daily Telegraph*. Retrieved 26 May 2009 from http:// www.telegraph.co.uk/news/newstopics/mps-expenses/5375300/MPs-expenses-Tory-claimed-10000-for-website.html.

Scampion, J. (2000). *Organised Benefit Fraud: A Report by John Scampion*. London: Department of Social Security.

Schneider, S., Beare, M. & Hill, J. (2000). *Alternative Approaches to Combating Transnational Crime*. Ottawa, ON: Solicitor General Canada. Retrieved 29 April 2007 from http://ww2.ps-sp.gc.ca/Publications/ Policing/TransCrime_e.pdf.

Seager, A. & Cobain, I. (7 February 2007). Ten Held After VAT Fraud
    Raids in Britain and Europe. *The Guardian.* Retrieved 15 December
    2008 from http://www.guardian.co.uk/business/2007/feb/07/5.
Sentencing Guidelines Council (2007). *Consultation Paper on Sentenc-
    ing for Fraud Offences.* Retrieved 1 June 2009 from http://www.
    sentencing-guidelines.gov.uk/docs/Fraud%20Consultation%20Paper
    %20-%20version%20for%20printing%202007-08-07.DB.pdf.
Shichor, D., Sechrest, D. & Doocy, J. (2001). Victims of Investment Fraud.
    In H.N. Pontell. & J. Doocy (Eds), *Contemporary Issues in Crime and
    Criminal Justice* (pp. 81–96). Upper Saddle River, NJ: Prentice Hall.
SFO (2007a). *Annual Report from April 2006–April 2007.* Retrieved 5
    March 2008 from http://www.sfo.gov.uk/media/91852/sfo%20annual
    %20report%202006-2007.pdf; http://www.sfo.gov.uk/publications/
    2007-2008/factsandfigures.asp#results.
———. (2007b). *SFO Criteria for Cases.* Retrieved 20 January 2010 from
    http://www.sfo.gov.uk/fraud/report-it-in-confidenceanonymously/
    serious-fraud-office-(sfo)-criteria.aspx.
———. (2008). *Accountants Guilty in $200 Million Investment Fraud and
    Attempt to Bribe US Official.* Retrieved 5 March 2008 from http://
    www.sfo.gov.uk/press-room/latest-press-releases/press-releases-2008/
    accountants-jailed-for-$200m-investment-fraud-and-conspiracy-to-
    corrupt-a-us-official.aspx.
———. (2009). *Annual Report 2008–09.* Retrieved 23 January
    2010 from http://www.official-documents.gov.uk/document/other/
    9780108508431/9780108508431.pdf.
Shawyer, A. & Walsh, D. (2007). Fraud and PEACE: Investigative Inter-
    viewing and Fraud Investigation. *Crime Prevention and Community
    Safety,* 9, 102–117.
Shelley, L. (2005). The Globalization of Crime. In M. Natarajan (Ed.),
    Introduction to International Criminal Justice (pp. 3–10). Boston, MA:
    McGraw Hill.
Shury, J., Speed, M., Vivian, D., Kuechel, A. & Nicholas, S. (2005).
    *Crime Against Retail and Manufacturing Premises: Findings from the 2002
    Commercial Victimisation Survey* (Home Office Research Online Report
    37/05). Retrieved 23 January 2008 from the UK Home Office http://
    www.homeoffice.gov.uk/rds/pdfs05/rdsolr3705.pdf.
Skogan, W.G. (1984). Reporting Crimes to the Police: The Status of
    World Research. *Journal of Research in Crime and Delinquency,* 21,
    113–137.
Slapper, G. & Tombs, S. (1999). *Corporate Crime.* London: Longman.
Slovin, D. (2006). Blowing the whistle: A Well-Designed, Accessible
    Whistleblower Hotline can be a Powerful Tool in the Fight Against
    Fraud. *Internal Auditor,* 63(3), 45–55.
Smegal, E.O. & Ross, H.L. (1970). *Crimes Against Bureaucracy.* New York:
    Van Nostrand Reinhold Company.

Smith, G. (2007). Countering Fraud against the Department of Work and Pensions: A Case Study in Risk Management. *Crime Prevention and Community Safety: An International Journal*, 9(2), 74–92.

Smith, G.R. (2005). *Public Sector Fraud and Corruption*. Retrieved 10 September 2008 from http://192.190.66.44/en/about_aic/research_programs/staff/~/media/conferences/other/smith_russell/2005-07-iir.ashx.

Smith, J. (1995). *Fraud and the Criminal Law*. Society of Public Teachers of Law Seminar.

Smith, R.G. (1997). *Measuring the Extent of Fraud in Australia*. Retrieved 15 February 2007 from The Australian Institute of Criminology website: http://www.aic.gov.au/publications/tandi/ti74.pdf.

SOCA (2006). *Serious and Organised Crime Agency Aims*. Retrieved 13 December 2007 from http://www.soca.gov.uk/aboutUs/aims.html.

Spalek, B. (2007). Knowledgeable Consumers? Corporate Fraud and its Devastating Impacts. *Briefing 4*. Kings College, London: Centre for Crime and Justice Studies. Retrieved 3 June 2009 from http://www.crimeandjustice.org.uk/publications.html.

Spence (8 December 2009). Two-Year Jail Sentence Underpins FSA's Crackdown on Insider Trading. *The Times*, p. 65.

Stephen, J.F. (1973). *A History of the Criminal Law of England*. New York: Burt Franklin.

Sutherland, E. (1949). *White Collar Crime*. New York: Holt.

Summers, B. (2008). *The Fraud Act 2006: Has it Had Any Impact?* Retrieved 18 December 2009 from http://www.petersandpeters.com/news/documents/FraudAct2006-HasItHadAnyImpact.pdf.

SWTimes (2008). *District Audit: $1 Million Embezzled*. Retrieved 5 March 2008 from http://www.swtimes.com/articles/2008/03/04/week_in_review/news/sunday/news03.txt.

Tapsfield, J. (21 March 2008). 'Lack of Systems' Halts Police Investigation into MPs Expenses. *The Independent*. Retrieved 26 May 2009 from http://www.independent.co.uk/news/uk/politics/lack-of-systems-halts-police-investigation-into-mps-expenses-799175.html.

Taylor, I. (1999). *Crime in Context: A Critical Criminology of Market Societies*. Oxford: Polity.

The Fraud Act 2006. Retrieved 20 January 2007 from http://www.opsi.gov.uk/Acts/acts2006/pdf/ukpga_20060035_en.pdf.

Thelwell, E. (15 November 2007). Southern Water Fined Record £20 Million by OFWAT [Electronic Version]. *Daily Telegraph*. Retrieved 30 January 2008 from http://www.telegraph.co.uk/money/main.jhtml;jsessionid=FCOGC13V0HIQDQFIQMGCFFWAVCBQUIV0?xml=/money/2007/11/14/bcnsouthern114.xml.

Timesonline (2005). *Q and A: Abolishing Juries in Fraud Trials*. Retrieved 13 December 2007 from http://www.timesonline.co.uk/tol/news/uk/article535751.ece.

———. (2007). *Norwich Union Fined Record £1.26 Million Over Fraud Risk*. Retrieved 5 March 2008 from http://business.timesonline.co.uk/tol/business/industry_sectors/banking_and_finance/article3062076.ece.

———. (2008). *John and Anne Darwin Sentenced to Total of More Than 12 Years in Jail*. Retrieved 1 March 2009 from http://www.timesonline.co.uk/tol/news/uk/crime/article4384627.ece.

———. (2009). *MP Nadine Dorries Censured by Tories over Expenses Suicide Remark*. Retrieved 25 January 2010 from http://www.timesonline.co.uk/tol/news/politics/article6346254.ece.

Tombs, S. & Whyte, D. (2007). *Safety Crimes*. Cullompton: Willan.

Transparency International (n.d.) *The Anti-Corruption Handbook*. Retrieved 29 April 2007 from http://www.transparency.org/news_room.

Tucker (1989). Employee Theft as Social Control. *Deviant Behaviour*, 10, 319–334.

Tunbridge Wells Borough Council (2006). *Benefit fraud: Interview Under Caution, What it Means*. Retrieved 22 January 2008 from http://www.tunbridgewells.gov.uk/section.asp?catid=555.

United Nations (2005a). '*Economic and Financial Crime: Challenges to Sustainable Development*'. Working Paper prepared by the Secretariat. 11th United Nations Congress on Crime Prevention and Criminal Justice, Bangkok 18th–25th April.

United Nations (2005b). '*International Cooperation Against Terrorism and Links between Terrorism and Other Criminal Activities in the Context of the Work of the United Nations Office on Drugs and Crime*'. Working Paper prepared by the Secretariat.11th United Nations Congress on Crime Prevention and Criminal Justice, Bangkok, 18th–25th April.

U.S. Securities and Exchange Commission (2001). *Insider Trading*. Retrieved 5 March 2008 from http://www.sec.gov/answers/insider.htm.

US Senate (2002). *The Role of the Board of Directors: Senate Report Prepared by the Committee on Government Affairs*, 8 July 2002. Retrieved 14 May 2008 from http://bodurtha.georgetown.edu/enron/The%20Role%20of%20the%20Board%20of%20Directors%20in%20Enron's%20Collapse_070702_main.htm.

Vaughan, D. & Carlo, G. (1975). The Appliance Repairman: A Study of Victim-Responsiveness and Fraud. *Journal of Research in Crime and Delinquency*, 12, 153–161.

Verkaik, R. (6 June 2009). Four MPs Face Police Probe on Expenses. *The Independent*. Retrieved 8 June 2009 from http://www.independent.co.uk/news/uk/politics/four-mps-face-police-probe-on-expenses-1698143.html.

Vrij, A. (2008). *Detecting Lies and Deceit: Pitfalls and Opportunities*. Chichester: Wiley.

Wainwright, M. (30 November 2007). Lay Preacher Gets Ten Years After Admitting £51 Million VAT fraud. *The Guardian Unlimited*. Retrieved 2 December 2007 from http://www.guardian.co.uk/crime/article/0,2219488,00.html.

Walker, J. (1997). *Estimates of the Costs of Crime in Australia in 1996* (Trends and Issues in Crime and Criminal Justice, No 72). Retrieved 15 February 2007 from the Australian Institute of Criminology website: http://www.aic.gov.au/documents/8/0/2/%7B802105A2-3DE8-4C42-A08B-0EC47AAF93D0%7Dti72.pdf.

Ward, M. (27 November 2007). Hackers Hijack Web Search Results. *BBC News*. Retrieved 3 December 2007 from http://news.bbc.co.uk/1/hi/technology/7118452.stm.

Wardle, R. (15 May 2009). Expenses Scandal: Proving MPs Committed Fraud would be Difficult. *The Times*. Retrieved 26 May 2009 from http://www.timesonline.co.uk/tol/news/politics/article6289751.ece.

Weber, M. (1946). *From Max Weber: Essays in Sociology*. New York: Galaxy.

Weisburd, D., Waring, E. & Chayet, E.F. (2001). *White Collar Criminal Careers*. Yale: University Press.

———, Wheeler, S., Waring, E. & Bode, N. (1991). *Crimes of the Middle Classes*. Yale: University Press.

Wells, J.T. (1997). *Occupational Fraud and Abuse*. Dexter, MI: Obsidian.

Westphal, C. & Blaxton, T. (1998). *Data Mining Solutions: Methods and Tools for Solving Real-World Problems*. New York: Wiley.

Wheeler, S. (1999). The Problem of White Collar Motivation. In M. Levi (Ed.), *Fraud: Organization, Motivation, and Control* (Vol. 1). Aldershot: Ashgate.

White, D. (2006). *Interview with head of Fraud Investigation Service, DWP*. 13 September 2006.

Widlake, B. (1995). *Serious Fraud Office*. London: Warner Books.

Winters, R. (2007). *What is Hate Crime?* Chicago, IL: Greenhaven Press.

World Bank (2004). *Annual Report 2004*. Retrieved 29 April 2007 from http://www.worldbank.org/html/extpb/2004/legal_systems.html.

———. (2006). *Department of Institutional Integrity: Annual Integrity Report. Fiscal Year 2005–6*. Retrieved 29 April 2007 from http://siteresources.worldbank.org/INTDOII/Resources/complete.pdf.

Wright, R. (2003). Fraud After Roskill: A View from the Serious Fraud Office. *Journal of Financial Crime*, 11(1), 10–16.

Wright, R. (2006). Why (some) Fraud Prosecutions Fail. *Journal of Financial Crime*, 13(2), 177–182.

Zeiltin, L.R. (2001). A Little Larceny Can Do a Lot for Employee Morale. *Psychology Today*, 5(1), 22–24.

Zietz, D. (1981). *Women Who Embezzle or Defraud: A Study of Convicted Felons*. New York: Praegar.

192.com Business Services (n.d.) *192 Fraud-ID*.

Index